Virtual Reality: Theory and Practice

Virtual Reality: Theory and Practice

Maxwell Oliver

STATES
ACADEMIC PRESS
www.statesacademicpress.com

Published by States Academic Press,
109 South 5th Street,
Brooklyn, NY 11249, USA

ISBN: 978-1-63989-560-1

Cataloging-in-Publication Data

Virtual reality : theory and practice / Maxwell Oliver.
   p. cm.
Includes bibliographical references and index.
ISBN 978-1-63989-560-1
1. Virtual reality. 2. Computer simulation. I. Oliver, Maxwell.
QA76.9.C65 V57 2022
006.8--dc23

For information on all States Academic Press publications
visit our website at www.statesacademicpress.com

Table of Contents

Preface

It is with great pleasure that I present this book. It has been carefully written after numerous discussions with my peers and other practitioners of the field. I would like to take this opportunity to thank my family and friends who have been extremely supporting at every step in my life.

Virtual reality refers to a simulated experience that can be same or different as compared to the actual world. It uses multi-projected environments that generate realistic sounds, images and other sensations that simulate a person's physical presence in the virtual world. A user can move and look around the virtual world with the help of virtual reality equipments. Virtual reality headsets and head-mounted displays are the tools used to generate this artificial world. There are various methods used by this discipline to create the artificial world. Some of these are avatar image-based virtual reality, desktop-based virtual reality and simulation-based virtual reality. This field finds its applications in areas such as entertainment, psychology and social sciences, and medicine. This book provides comprehensive insights into the field of virtual reality. It is a valuable compilation of topics, ranging from the basic to the most complex theories and principles related to this discipline. As this field is emerging at a rapid pace, the contents of this book will help the readers understand the modern concepts and applications of the subject.

The chapters below are organized to facilitate a comprehensive understanding of the subject:

Chapter – Introduction

Virtual reality is defined as the three-dimensional, computer generated experience which can be similar or completely different from the real world. Unity3D, lumberyard, blender, cryengine, etc. are a few tools used for VR development. This is an introductory chapter which will briefly introduce about virtual reality and its tools.

Chapter – Types of Virtual Reality

There are three major types of virtual reality that are used to transform the world. It includes non-immersive, semi-immersive and fully-immersive simulations. This chapter has been carefully written to provide an easy understanding of these types of virtual reality.

Chapter – Hardware and Software

Different kinds of software and hardware are used for the working and operations of the virtual reality systems. Some of them are head mounted display, EyeTap, contact lens, virtual retinal display, etc. The topics elaborated in this chapter will help in gaining a better perspective of various VR hardware and software.

Chapter – 3D Graphics

3D graphics refers to the use of three-dimensional geometric data and algorithms for rendering 2D images, etc. It makes use of wire-frame model, Schlick's approximation, depth map, false radiosity and smoothing group. All the concepts related to 3D graphics have been carefully analyzed in this chapter.

Chapter – Applications

There are a wide-range of applications of virtual reality in different fields such as gaming, defence, sports, medical sciences, mining, education, robotics, etc. This chapter sheds light on the varied applications of virtual reality for a thorough understanding of the subject.

Chapter – Issues Related to Virtual Reality

There are many issues that persist with the use of virtual reality including health related issues like headaches, eyestrain, dizziness, and nausea, cyber sickness and other security risks. This chapter closely examines these issues related to virtual reality.

Maxwell Oliver

1

Introduction

Virtual reality is defined as the three-dimensional, computer generated experience which can be similar or completely different from the real world. Unity3D, lumberyard, blender, cryengine, etc. are a few tools used for VR development. This is an introductory chapter which will briefly introduce about virtual reality and its tools.

Virtual Reality

Virtual reality (VR) is a brand new user interface unlike the conventional one, immersing a person in a digital 3D environment, instead of watching on a display. Computer-generated imagery and content aim at simulating a real presence through senses (sight, hearing, touch).

Virtual reality simulation requires two main components: a source of content and a user device. Software and hardware, in other words. Currently, such systems include headsets, all-directions treadmills, special gloves, goggles. VR tools should be providing realistic, natural, high-quality images and interaction possibilities. For this, devices rely on measurements like:

- Image resolution.
- Field of view.
- Refresh rate.
- Motion delay.
- Pixel persistence.
- Audio/video synchronization.

The main challenge of VR is tricking the human brain into perceiving digital content as real. That is not easy, and this "immersion" issue is what still holds virtual reality experiences back from being enjoyable. For example, the human visual field doesn't work as a video frame, and besides about 180 degrees of vision, we also have a peripheral vision.

Yet, the VR visionaries are confident of overcoming such issues sooner or later, campaigning for the concept and collecting investments in millions. The virtual experience like 360-degree videos and pictures, VR apps and games, are already available. There's a good enough choice of headsets as well.

For more basics of VR, and how you can explore it, watch this dope and simple explanation with fun facts along.

Working of VR

VR requires several devices such as a headset, a computer/smartphone or another machine to create a digital environment, and a motion-tracking device in some cases. Typically, a headset displays content before a user's eyes, while a cable (HDMI) transfers images to the screen from a PC. The alternative option is headsets working with smartphones, like Google Cardboard and GearVR – a phone that acts both as a display and a source of VR content.

Some vendors apply lenses to change flat images into three-dimensional. Usually, a 100/110-degree field of sight is achieved with VR devices. The next key feature is the frame rate per second, which should be 60 fps at a minimum to make virtual simulations look realistically enough. For user interaction there are several options:

Head Tracking

The head tracking system in VR headsets follows the movements of your head to sides and angles. It assigns X, Y, Z axis to directions and movements, and involves tools like accelerometer, gyroscope, a circle of LEDs (around the headset to enable the outside camera). Head tracking requires low latency, i.e. 50 milliseconds or less, otherwise, users will notice the lag between head movements and a simulation.

Eye-tracking

Some headsets contain an infrared controller that tracks the direction of your eyes inside a virtual environment. The major benefit of this technology is to get a more realistic and deeper field of view.

Motion Tracking

Though not engineered and implemented well enough yet, motion tracking would raise VR to a totally new level. The thing is, that without motion tracking you'd be limited in VR – unable to look around and move around. Through concepts of the 6DoF (six degrees of freedom) and 3D space, options to support motion tracking fall into 2 groups, optical and non-optical tracking. Optical tracking is typically a camera on a headset to follow the movements, while non-optical means the use of other sensors on a device or a body. Most of the existing devices actually combine both options.

Types of VR

Virtual reality app development has been of major concern these recent times as we have had various people setting up or establishing a VR app development company. There are different types of virtual reality technology and they include:

Non-immersive Reality

This type can be seen in the virtual reality flight simulator. It has a widescreen PC with a surround system and comes with other accessories like headphones, joysticks etc. It is non–immersive reality because the viewer does not get fully immersed in the reality this device produces. It won't give a viewer the experience of being back in time or even ignite the person's senses but one would still get a virtual reality experience.

Fully Immersive Reality

One would experience full virtual experience because this type of virtual reality comes with a very powerful computer. This powerful computer must be able to detect sounds, sight, and even the slightest movement. It should be able to adjust the person's experience. The viewer would have a head-mounted display (HMD) and would also put on sensory gloves. To achieve the fully immersed virtual reality, the device will make use of two monitors and a sound system.

Augmented Reality

Here one is experiencing a real world in such a way that it feels like a virtual reality experience. One can't define it as an unreal experience but an experience of the reality around us. For instance, when a person visits an historical site on the internet, there are 3D mappings that would show the person landmarks, buildings, historical locations and other relevant information. One can move around areas in the computer to see fascinating historical sites using a smartphone.

Collaborative

Collaborative reality is usually in the form of virtual reality games and they are not fully immersive. This virtual reality gives the viewer an interactive experience and so one can even share their experience with other people in the virtual world.

Web-based

Some Scientists have discovered ways to use virtual reality over the internet using the Virtual Reality Markup Language (VRML). This gives people an opportunity to discover new and interesting things the internet can offer. Also, people get to interact and have real experiences with their friends on social media.

Benefits of VR

Training

In some sectors, VR is used to train employees, especially in dangerous environments. For example, pilots use simulators in case they make a mistake, and aspiring doctors take advantage of virtual reality to avoid medical accidents. Pilots landing a plane, fire fighters prepping before their first fire – this is immersive learning at its most powerful. Immersive learning will lessen the difference between rookies and veterans in many professions. These practices will only expand to other sectors in the future, and in the event of traumatic on-the-job experiences, VR can provide a means of therapy.

Conferencing

Think Skype for Business on steroids. VR has the potential to bring digital workers together in digital meetings and conferences. There will be real-time event coverage, something like Facebook Live with VR. Rather than merely seeing the other person on a screen, you'll be able to feel as if you are in the same room with them, despite being miles away. With the rise of the freelancer economy, virtual meetings may become the norm rather than the exception.

Convenience

VR can save organizations time and money and make work more convenient. Workers won't have to travel in order to make decisions and complete projects. For example, architects from across the globe can use virtual reality to evaluate designs. This alone is a monetary godsend. VR also opens the door for a virtual marketplace, where shoppers can try on garments, and you can see what that Arabian rug will look like in your den.

Guidelines for GUI Design

Generally, it is recommended to always design GUIs following usability guidelines so users in an easy and satisfying way can reach their pragmatic goals. At the same time, the design of the GUI should also allow the user to fulfil the users' hedonic goals as soon as possible. This includes keeping the pragmatic goals of the users achievable within a few selections as possible and also easy to find. For a VoD application in VR according to the research, this could be to keep previously watched videos on the start view of the application and a search functionality, following the users' needs and preferences, where they can easily find the video they are looking for. However, these recommendations are specific for the application of VoD services and are not the main focus of this thesis. The following guidelines are developed for the application of VoD services but are believed to be more generally applicable for other applications and contexts and therefore, serve towards answering the research question in a broader sense.

Place the Graphical User Interface so it is Comfortable to Explore and Interact With

In VR the GUI has unlimited possible placements in three dimensions. When compared to designing for digital 2D screens where the user usually is able to see the whole screen at once and easily get an overview, the user can not usually see the entire virtual environment at the same time.

The maximum field of view (FOV) of the human visual system, is approximately 200 degrees. However in head-mounted displays (HMDs), the FOV is about 94 degrees. Users can change the orientation of their heads to explore more of the virtual world. According to Chu, users' can turn their heads comfortably 30 degrees to the left and right side, 12 degrees down and 20 degrees up. Moreover, the depth perception is also important in virtual environments. Objects should be placed at a distance between 75 centimetres and 20 meters away from the user. Following an older recommendation for the minimum distance, Mike Alger suggests a main content zone that is displayed within 155 degrees horizontally and at a distance between 0,5 meters to 20 meters away from the user. However, there is a difference between content and a GUI, and therefore, these distance suggestions are replaced.

The recommendation of placement to make the UI comfortable to explore follows the degrees suggested by Alger, the minimum distance suggested by Oculus VR and the maximum distance suggested by Oculus VR. This leads to a recommended placement within 155 degrees horizontally, at least 75 centimetres away from the user but not further than three metres away in the virtual environment.

More importantly is that the elements of the GUI that the user should interact with or needs to place the gaze cursor over should be kept within the comfortable interaction zone. The suggested 52 comfortable interaction zone is based on the ideas of Chu about how people can comfortably turn their heads. The centre of the zone, here referred to as the centre point, is where the user's head gaze is naturally positioned when the user looks straight forward with the head in the most comfortable natural orientation. Surrounding the centre point, the zone is based on 60 degrees horizontally, evenly distributed to the left and right side from the centre point and 32 degrees vertically, where 12 of the degrees are down from the centre point and 20 degrees are up. Furthermore, the comfortable interaction zone follows the same distance recommendations for the comfortable exploring placement.

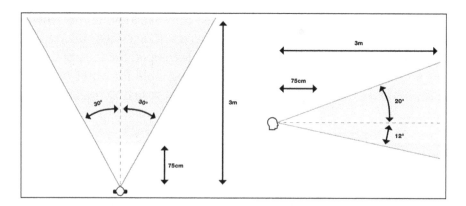

The suggested comfortable interaction zone visualised. The zone illustrates where user interface elements that can be selected or interacted with in a virtual reality graphical user interface controlled by head orientation input and head gaze should be placed.

While the recommended comfortable view and comfortable interaction zone is based on literature from the background study of the thesis, the guideline is a result of the research in this thesis. Although the guideline's name focuses on comfortable exploration and interaction, the reasons to follow it exceeds solely ergonomic and visual comfort. Several of the user experience, UX, problems discovered during the research that lead to users' shortage of information and control, relate to Nielsen's usability heuristics about visibility of system status, user control and freedom, recognition rather than recall, and flexibility and efficiency of use. Examples included that users did not find all parts of the VRGUI since they tended to turn their heads far enough in order for the VRGUI to open up and become visible to them. Since the whole VRGUI was not visible at the same time, the cognitive load was heavy and this while the users had to change the orientation of their heads in non-ergonomic ways to interact with the VRGUI.

If the guideline is followed, it helps users to easily find, explore, and interact with the VRGUI in an ergonomically, visually, and cognitively comfortable way while supporting the user to reach both the pragmatic and hedonic goals. Furthermore, it will help users to use the HMDs in contexts were they want to limit the movements required. For example, when travelling, they might sit next to another person, who should not be bothered when they are interacting with the VRGUI and also the user should not hesitate to use the HMD of fear of looking 'dumb' while turning his or her head.

Place Visual Feedback to Selections within the Immediate Interaction Area

The interaction method that uses head orientation input to project an approximated gaze cursor in the centre of the user's FOV, has in this thesis been referred to as head gaze. Even though head gaze is controlled by how the user turns his or her head, the user experiences it as if the cursor is controlled by the direction of the eye gaze. One illustrating example is that the user could turn his or her head in a certain direction and then explore the area in the virtual environment with the head orientation fixated while relocating the eye gaze only. This would leave the cursor fixated while the user explores the surroundings but since the user experiences that s/he is controlling the cursor with his or her eye gaze direction, this might not be considered as an option by the user. Therefore, the user tends to focus with the eye gaze at the same location where the head gaze is currently located to make sure that the selection of the desired functionality is completed. The eye gaze is also necessary to keep nearby the head gaze cursor for the user to make sure the head gaze controlled cursor stays located over the UI element the user want to interact with. Since the user is focusing and concentrating on the object s/he wants to interact with, the surrounding area in the VRGUI becomes out of focus and turns nearly invisible to the user during the interaction.

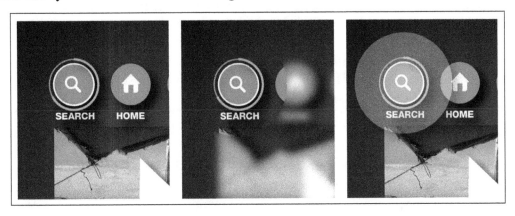

The approximated area, double the size of the head gaze cursor, where the visual feedback from a selection should be placed in order for the user to see it. The first image from the left show the circular progress bar of the head gaze cursor during a selection and the second image show the estimation of how the small cone of focus make the surroundings blurry while the third image has marked the area where the visual feedback should be placed in order for the user to see and discover it.

Therefore, it is necessary to place visual feedback to a selection within the immediate interaction area where the user is currently focusing. The approximated area where the feedback should be placed is within the double diameter of the cursor being used.

This guideline is developed based on research result and analysis in this thesis. During the research, several participants did not understand the functionality of on and off buttons in the VRGUI since they were not able to see the change that occurred when they interacted with the buttons. Furthermore, several were not able to reach their pragmatic goals since they did not know where to continue the interaction with the GUI after they selected a certain button in a menu. This lead to a shortage of information and control previously described. Furthermore, it relates to Nielsen's usability heuristics about visibility of system status, match between the system and the real world, user control and freedom, error prevention, recognition rather than recall, flexibility and efficiency of use.

If the guideline is followed, it helps the user to easily see the result of their actions and where to continue the interaction to reach their pragmatic goals.

Keep Information Dense Areas Interaction-free

With the head gaze interaction method, the interaction with and selection of a UI element starts as soon as the user places the gaze cursor over the element. After the gaze cursor is placed, the user has a limited time to decide if the selection is a wanted action or not since a predetermined gaze time will trigger the selection of the element. In the research, this caused several UX problems such as the users making accidental selections since they were not finished with interpreting and understanding the functionality a selection of the UI element would lead to. Furthermore, this caused a stressful situation where users turned their heads from element to element since they were afraid of staying with the head gaze for too long and performing an unwanted selection. This limited their curiosity, made them feel stressed and several times they were not finished with the exploring of the objects and element before a selection had occurred. This is an example of the Midas touch problem.

This UX problem also relates to the user not realising they can move their eye gaze while keeping the head gaze cursor at one spot in the VRGUI. Therefore, the developed guideline suggests that information dense areas should be kept interaction-free. If the parts of the VRGUI that contain extensive information and content is kept interaction-free, the user will have the opportunity to explore the information in a relaxing way, one of the hedonic goals with the use, and then be able to interact and select a certain content when s/he is ready.

The suggested guideline is therefore to maintain information dense areas interaction-free. If this is not possible, an interaction-free area should be placed in the immediate area surrounding the element. Specifically for information dense areas or areas that are harder for the user to understand, they need more time to interpret and explore the information. To minimize the cognitive load of the user trying to interpret and read information while keeping track of a moving progress bar for the selection at the same time, the area should be interaction-free. This relates to Nielsen's usability heuristics about user control and freedom, error prevention, and flexibility and efficiency of use.

Use Dwell Times of Various Lengths

With head gaze interaction, a dwell time is used to trigger selections in the VRGUI. In the prototype used for part of the research, the dwell time used for selections was constant across different parts of the VRGUI. The user sometimes need more time to interpret or explore the information before s/he interacts with it and was to keep information dense areas interaction-free but an additional recommendation could be to consider using dwell times of varying lengths.

By allowing the dwell time for different selections in the VRGUI to differ, it could work towards improving the usability, related to Nielsen's usability heuristics of user control and freedom, error prevention, and flexibility and efficiency of use. Parts of the UI that require more time to be read or interpreted by the user should have a longer dwell time for selections. Furthermore, the dwell time could be adjusted depending on the user's knowledge and experience of the VRGUI. An experienced user might want shorter dwell times while a novice user needs longer dwell times.

Avoid using Time-limited Information

In the tested prototype, the VRGUI was kept minimalistic and near to text free. If the user did not understand the icon of a button s/he was required to place the gaze cursor over the button in order to see the explanatory text for it. However, the hovering information was only available for the limited time before the selection was triggered. If the user was unable to understand the icon from the beginning, and then moved the head gaze over it and was not able to finish reading the hovering explanatory text while keeping track of the selection progress bar, s/he ended up selecting the button. Some users tried to prevent the unwanted selection by moving their head gaze quickly over and away from the button to extend the reading time they were offered. This caused the users to feel stressed, confused when they performed a selection and was not even sure what they had selected. Furthermore, the quick rotations for moving the head gaze was observed as non-ergonomic and the users were notably concentrated since they were required to try to read the text while keeping track of the selection progress bar.

The developed guideline is therefore to avoid time limited hovering information. If the users are presented with the information without having a time limitation to interpreting it, this is believed to reduce the stress, the cognitive load and furthermore, the non-ergonomic head rotations.

The UX problems are related to Nielsen's usability heuristics of user control and freedom, error prevention, and flexibility and efficiency of use. If the guideline is followed, it will reduce the cognitive load of the user and allow a stress-free interaction where undesired selections are prevented.

Never Force Users to Interpret Information in Movement

When users are forced to interpret information that is currently moving in front of their eyes, it leads to a high cognitive load where they need to be highly concentrated and focused on the task. Furthermore, this can cause simulator sickness. In the research, only one out of the six participants experienced simulator sickness. Even though it was not ranked as a common problem, it is still extremely negative for the UX and therefore, considered important to reduce.

This relates to the previously described guideline to 'Avoid rapid movements, do not drop frames or lose head tracking'. However, this developed guideline extends the guideline to avoid forcing the user to interpret information in movement. The UX problems closely relate to Nielsen's usability heuristic of the visibility of system status.

Use Standards and Affordances to Minimize the Cognitive Load

Minimalistic GUI design is a trend limiting the amount of information displayed to the user. Visual clutter should be avoided to minimize the cognitive load but when too much information is removed, hidden or icons are too simplified, the cognitive load of the user will increase. In GUIs for screens, this is often easily solved by the user hovering to see an explanatory text or by the user clicking on the element to explore what the functionality of it means. However, since an undo or back action is not as easily performed in a VRGUI controlled by head gaze and since the hovering over a UI element that the user can interact with is time limited to the dwell time for the selection, the VRGUI is not as easy and quick for the user to explore if the they do not understand the functionality of a UI element from the beginning. Therefore, the suggestion is to use explanatory information of the UI element functionality that is as clear as possible to the user, requiring a minimal cognitive effort for the user to interpret. This usually includes clear icons and short but descriptive titles for the functionality.

Virtual Reality and Computational Design

Virtual reality (VR) has been used for diverse purposes, including medical surgery training, visualizing metabolic pathways, socio psychological experiments, flight and driving simulation, as well as industrial and architectural design. In these applications the role of VR is to represent objects for visual experience by a human expert. In engineering and design applications the purpose is to verify the performance of a design object with respect to the criteria involved in the task during a search for superior solutions. In computational design, where this verification and search process are performed by means of computation, the instantiation of objects in virtual reality may become a necessary feature. The necessity occurs when the verification process requires the presence of 'physical' object attributes beyond the parameters that are subject to identification through search. For example, in an architectural design the goal may be to determine the most suitable position of an object, while the suitability is verified based on visual perception characteristics of the object. That is, the verification requires the presence of object features beyond the object's location in order to exercise the evaluation of the object's performance regarding the perception-based requirements. These features are provided when the object is instantiated in VR. This way a measurement process driving the evaluation, such as a virtual perception process in the form of a stochastic sampling process, can be executed to assess the perceptual properties of the object concerned.

Computational Design System Implemented in Virtual Reality

In several instances during a design process VR enables decision makers to better comprehend the implications of design decisions. Two aspects can be distinguished in this process.

First, a design's implication in terms of the degree that it satisfies the objectives pursued is subject to assessment. This process may be termed as verification, as it entails the verification of the requirements' satisfaction during a search to maximize the satisfaction degree. It is noted that the concept of Pareto optimality plays an important role in the search for optimality. Namely in general it is problematic for a decision maker to commit himself for a specific relative importance among the major goals for the design at hand prior to knowing the implications of such a commitment. This is due to the generally abstract nature of the goals in design. For example the aims to have high functionality or low cost, clearly are difficult to put in perspective prior to knowing what solutions may be attained when maximizing the satisfaction of these goals in the present task. Pareto optimality addresses this issue by permitting to postpone the commitment on relative importance until a set of equivalent solutions is obtained that cannot be improved further. This is achieved by establishing those solutions where no others exist that outperform them in all goals at the same time.

A second process concerns validation of the objectives. That is, the question if the right objectives are pursued during verification is addressed. The latter process requires insights beyond knowing how to reach optimality for the given goals at hand. Namely contingent requirements that have not been put into the play during verification are to be pin-pointed. It is clear that the latter process requires verification to occur before it, since otherwise there is no rationale to modify the objectives. That is, based on the Pareto optimal solutions found, a designer is to compare these solutions against his/ her preferences, yielding clues on the modification of criteria. The relation between the verification and validation process in design are shown in figure.

The reason why VR facilitates validation is that it allows considering the solution in the physical domain beyond an abstract description of the targeted performance features, so that a decision maker may become aware of directions for modifying the objectives. The validation process is especially soft, since it is highly contingent to circumstances so that potentially a vast amount of desirable objectives may be subject to inclusion in a design task, and it is generally problematic to have a hint about which ones to include as well as their relative importance. Therefore it is a challenging issue to provide computational support for the validation process.

In order to investigate the role of VR in the search for optimality during verification, we take a closer look at verification and its associated search process. A computational system accomplishing this task is shown in figure. It aims to establish set of Pareto optimal solutions for a number of requirements, where the requirements are allowed to be soft in character, i.e. they may contain imprecision and uncertainty.

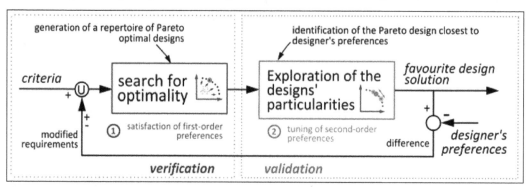

Verification and validation in design.

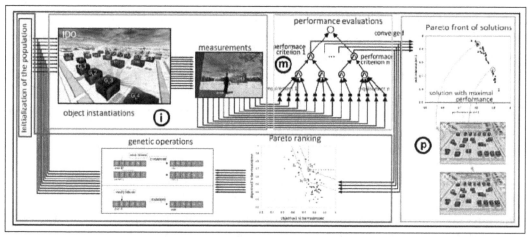

Computational design system implemented in virtual reality.

From the figure it is noted that the system consists of four components: a multi-objective genetic algorithm; a neuro-fuzzy model; object instantiation in VR; and instantiation of Pareto optimal solutions in VR. The genetic algorithm is marked by the red box, the fuzzy model is marked by the green box. The two components involving VR are shown in the blue boxes. In order to pin-point the role VR plays in the system, first it is necessary to explain the evolutionary and the fuzzy system components.

Evolutionary Search for Multi-objective Optimality

The task of the multi-objective search algorithm in the design system above is to gear the process towards desirable solutions. Multi-objective optimization deals with optimization where several objectives are involved. In design generally multiple objectives are subject to simultaneous satisfaction. Such objectives e.g. are high functionality and low cost. These objectives are conflicting or in competition among themselves. For a single objective case there are traditionally many algorithms in continuous search space, where gradient-based algorithms are most suitable in many instances. In discrete search spaces, in the last decade evolutionary algorithms are ubiquitously used for optimization, where genetic algorithms (GA) are predominantly applied. However, in many real engineering or design problems, more than two objectives need to be optimized simultaneously. To deal with multiobjectivity, evolutionary algorithms with genetic operators are effective in defining the search direction for rapid and effective convergence. Basically, in a multi-objective case the search direction is not one but may be many, so that during the search a single preferred direction cannot be identified and even this is not desirable.

To deal with multi-objectivity evolutionary algorithms are effective in defining the search direction, since they are based on a population of solutions. Basically, in a multi-objective case the search direction is not one but may be many, so that during the search a single preferred direction cannot be identified. In this case a population of candidate solutions can easily hint about the desired directions of the search and let the candidate solutions during the search process be more probable for the ultimate goal. Essential machinery of evolutionary algorithms is the principles of GA optimization, which are the genetic operations. Genetic operations entail the probabilistic combination among favourable solutions in order to provoke the emergence of more suitable solutions. Use of these principles is inspired from the phenomenon of biological evolution. It proves to be effective for multi-modal objective functions, i.e. problems involving many local optima. Therefore the evolutionary approach is robust and suitable for real-world problems.

Next to the evolutionary principles, in multi-objective (MO) algorithms, in many cases the use of Pareto ranking is a fundamental selection method. Its effectiveness is clearly demonstrated for a moderate number of objectives, which are subject to optimization simultaneously. Pareto ranking refers to a solution surface in a multidimensional solution space formed by multiple criteria representing the objectives. On this surface, the solutions are diverse but they are assumed to be equivalently valid. The driving mechanism of the Pareto ranking based algorithms is the conflicting nature of criteria, i.e. increased satisfaction of one criterion implies loss with respect to satisfaction of another criterion. Therefore the formation of Pareto front is based on objective functions of the weighted N objectives $f_1, f_2, ..., f_N$ which are of the form:

$$F_i(\mathbf{x}) = f_i(\mathbf{x}) + \sum_{j=1, j \neq i}^{j=N} a_{ji} f_i(\mathbf{x}), \quad i = 1, 2, ..., N$$

where $F_i(x)$ are the new objective functions; a_{ji} is the designated amount of gain in the j-th objective function for a loss of one unit in the i-th objective function. Therefore the sign of a_{ji} is always negative. The above set of equations requires fixing the matrix a. This matrix has all ones in its diagonal elements. To find the Pareto front of a maximization problem we assume that a solution parameter vector x_1 dominates another solution x_2 if $F(x_1) \geq F(x_2)$ for all objectives. At the same time a contingent equality is not valid for at least one objective.

In solving multi-objective optimization, the effectiveness of Pareto-ranking based evolutionary algorithms has been well established. For this purpose there are quite a few algorithms which are running quite well especially with low dimensionality of the multidimensional objective space. However, with the increase of the number of objective functions, i.e. with high dimensionality, the effectiveness of the evolutionary algorithms is hampered. Namely with many objectives most solutions of the population will be considered non-dominated, although the search process is still at a premature stage. This means the search has little information to distinguish among solutions, so that the selection pressure pushing the population into the desirable region is too low. This means the algorithm prematurely eliminates potential solutions from the population, exhausting the exploratory potential inherent to the population. As a result the search arrives at an inferior Pareto front, and with aggregation of solutions along this front. One measure of effectiveness is the expansion of Pareto front where the solution diversity is a desired property. For this purpose, the search space is exhaustively examined with some methods, e.g. niched Pareto ranking. However these algorithms are rather involved so that the search needs extensive computer time for a satisfactory solution in terms of a Pareto front. Because of this extensive time requirement, distributed computing of Pareto-optimal solutions is proposed, where multiple processors are needed.

The issue of solution diversity and effective solution for multi-objective optimization problem described above can be understood considering that the conventional Pareto ranking implies a kind of greedy algorithm which considers the solutions at the search area delimited by orthogonal axes of the multidimensional space, i.e. a_{ji} in equation

$$F_i(\mathbf{x}) = f_i(\mathbf{x}) + \sum_{j=1, j \neq i}^{j=N} a_{ji} f_i(\mathbf{x}), \, i = 1, 2, \dots, N$$ becomes zero. This is shown in figure by means

of the orthogonal lines delimiting the dominated region.

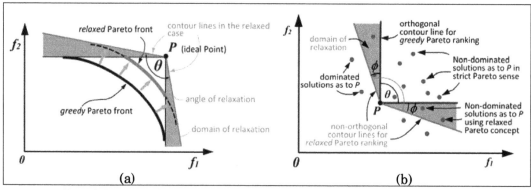

Contour lines defining the dominated region in relaxed versus greedy case (a); implementation of the relaxation concept during the evolutionary search process (b).

The point P in figure is ultimately subject to identification as an ideal solution. To increase the pressure pushing the Pareto surface towards to the maximally attainable solution point is the main problem, and relaxation of the orthogonality with a systematic approach is needed and applied. It is noted that by increasing the angle at P from the conventional orthogonal angle to a larger angle implies that the conventional dominated region is expanded by domains of relaxation. This also entails that theoretically a Pareto front is to be reached that is located closer towards the ideal Point P.

Such an increase of the angle delimiting the search domain implies a deviation from the conventional concept of Pareto dominance, namely the strict Pareto dominance criterion is relaxed in the sense that next to non-dominated solutions also some dominated solutions are considered at each generation. This is seen from figure, where the point P denotes one of the individuals among the population in the context of genetic algorithm (GA) based evolutionary search. In the greedy search many potential favourable solutions are prematurely excluded from the search process. This is because each solution in the population is represented by the point P and the dominance is measured in relation to the number of solutions falling into the search domain within the angle $\theta=\pi/2$. To avoid the premature elimination of the potential solutions, a relaxed dominance concept is implemented where the angle θ can be considered as the angle for tolerance provided $\theta>\pi/2$. The resulting Pareto front corresponds to a non-orthogonal search domain. The wider the angle beyond $\pi/2$ the more tolerant the search process and vice versa. For $\theta<\pi/2$, θ becomes the angle for greediness. Domains of relaxations are also indicated in figure. In the greedy case the solutions are expected to be more effective but to be aggregated. In the latter case, the solutions are expected to be more diversified but less effective. That is because such dominated solutions can be potentially favourable solutions in the present generation, so that they can give birth to non-dominated solutions in the following generation.

Although, some relaxation of the dominance is addressed in literature, in a multidimensional space, to identify the size of relaxation corresponding to a volume is not explicitly determined. In such a volume next to non-dominated solutions, dominated but potentially favourable solutions, as described above, lie. To determine this volume optimally as to the circumstantial conditions of the search process is a major and a challenging task. The solution for this task is essentially due to the mathematical treatment of the problem where the volume in question is identified adaptively during the search that it yields a measured pressure to the Pareto front toward to the desired direction, at each generation as follows.

The fitness of the solutions can be ranked by the fitness function:

$$\mathbf{R}_{\text{fit}} = \frac{1}{N(\theta)+n}$$

where n is the number of potential solutions falling into the search domain consisting of the conventional orthogonal quadrant, with the added areas of relaxation. To obtain n in above equation, for each solution point, say P in figure, the point is temporarily considered to be a reference point as origin, and all the other solution points in the orthogonal coordinate system are converted to the non-orthogonal system coordinates. This is accomplished by means of the matrix operation given by equation:

$$
F\begin{bmatrix} F_1 \\ F_2 \\ \cdots \\ F_n \end{bmatrix} = \begin{bmatrix} 1\,a_{21}\cdots a_{n1} \\ a_{12}1\cdots a_{1n} \\ \cdots\cdots\cdots \\ a_{1n}a_{2n}\cdots 1 \end{bmatrix}\begin{bmatrix} f_1 \\ f_2 \\ \cdots \\ f_n \end{bmatrix} = \begin{bmatrix} 1 & \tan(\phi_2) & \cdots\cdots\tan(\phi_n) \\ \tan(\phi_2) & 1\cdots\cdots & \tan(\phi_n) \\ \cdots\cdots\cdots \\ \tan(\theta_2)\tan(\theta_n)\cdots\cdots 1 \end{bmatrix}\begin{bmatrix} f_1 \\ f_2 \\ \cdots \\ f_n \end{bmatrix}
$$

where the angles φ, ϕ, ... θ represent the respective relaxation angles between one axis of the coordinate system and the other axes. After coordinate transformation using above equation, all points which have positive coordinates in the non-orthogonal system correspond to potential solutions contributing to the next generation in the evolutionary computation. If any point possesses a negative component in the new coordinate system, the respective solution does not dominate P and therefore is not counted. This is because otherwise such a solution may lead the search in a direction away from P. The importance of this coordinate transformation becomes dramatic especially with greater amounts of objective dimensions. In such cases the spatial distribution of domains of relaxation becomes complex and is therefore difficult to implement. Namely, in multidimensional space the volume of a relaxation domain is difficult to imagine, and more importantly it is difficult to identify the population in such domains. Therefore many different methods for effective Pareto front formation in the literature are reported. However the above equation provides a decisive and easy technique revealed in this work for the same goal. The approach through the coordinate transformation is a systematic and elegant approach, alleviating the bottleneck of conventional Pareto ranking dealing with many objectives to some extend, so that the evolutionary paradigm becomes more apt for applications in design usually containing a great many requirements.

In order to maximize the effectiveness of the relaxation, the determination of the suitable relaxation angle is a contingent issue, i.e. it depends on the particular conditions occurring during the stochastic search process. For instance, during a prematurely developed Pareto front, applying large relaxation angles may not permit effective distinction among the solutions regarding their suitability for the ultimate goal. Or during later stages of Pareto front development, a smaller angle will exhaust the diversity in the population and thus diminish the selection pressure towards the desirable regions. This means fixing the relaxation angle in advance may not be able to let the population arrive at a Pareto front as close to the ideal point compared to a strategy where the angle is adaptively changing during the search, taking the present conditionality of the Pareto front into account.

Adaptively changing the angle implies that the angle used to grade the individual solution's suitability is considered in perspective with the relaxation angles presently associated to the other solutions in the population. This is implemented by means of the equation below, where the ratio between the relaxation angle and average relaxation angle is used. $N(\theta)$ in the equation below can be considered as expressing the amount of virtual solutions that are accrued to the counted number of dominant solutions given by n in $\mathbf{R}_{fit} = \dfrac{1}{N(\theta)+n}$, reflecting the fact that when we take the greedy dominance concept solutions that are dominated by s more solutions may turn out to be favourable in the search process although they normally would be eliminated due to greediness of the algorithm.

$$N(\theta) = \frac{s}{1+\left(\theta/\overline{\theta}\right)}$$

Considering equation $\mathbf{R}_{fit} = \dfrac{1}{N(\theta)+n}$ and equation $N(\theta) = \dfrac{s}{1+\left(\theta/\overline{\theta}\right)}$ together it is clear that the purpose is to reward a chromosome for affording a wide relaxation angle θ, relative to the average angle of the population $\overline{\theta}$, and still having a low dominance count, denoted by n. The wide angle provides more diversity in the population for the next generation. However, when the relaxation angle would be excessively big, the population for the next generation can be crowded with trivial solutions. To prevent that, in

$\mathbf{R}_{fit} = \dfrac{1}{N(\theta)+n}$ the number of non-dominated solutions with respect to the particular

solution considered denoted by n, is summed up with the function of the angle $N(\theta)$. This means that between two solutions with the same amount of non-dominated solutions, the one with the wider angle is preferred. This is done for every solution in the population. This implies that the average angle $\overline{\theta}$ is changing for every generation adaptively. It is noted that the numbers appearing in equation $N(\theta) = \dfrac{s}{1+\left(\theta/\overline{\theta}\right)}$ is a constant

number, used to adjust the relative significance of relaxation angle versus count n. This means the value of s should be selected bearing in particular the population size in mind, so that for instance solutions using wide angles are adequately rewarded.

Fuzzy Model for Performance Evaluation

The fuzzy model marked by the letter m in figure enables the multi-objective search process to evaluate the solutions it generates and combines genetically, using some humanlike reasoning capabilities. That is, the solutions are evaluated with respect to complex, vague objectives having a linguistic character. Design tasks, in particular in the domain of built environment, involve goals with such properties, e.g. functionality, or sustainability. During the search for optimality in design the suitability of a solution for the goals needs to be estimated. This means beyond observing the direct physical features of a solution, they need to be interpreted with respect to the goals pursued. For example, designing a space it may be desirable that the space is large or it is nearby another space. Clearly these requirements have to do with the size of the space, and the distance among spaces respectively, which are physical properties of the design. However, it is clearly noted that largeness is a concept, i.e. it does not correspond immediately to a physical measurement, but it is an abstract feature of an object. It is also noted that there is generally no sharp boundary from on which one may attribute such a linguistic feature to an object. For instance there is generally no specific size of a room from on which it is to be considered large, and below which it is not large. Many design requirements have this character, i.e. they do not pin-point a single acceptable parameter value for a solution, but a range of values that are more or less satisfactory. This is essentially because design involves conflicting requirements, such as spaciousness versus low cost. Therefore many requirements are bound to be merely partially fulfilled. Such requirements characterized as soft, and they can be modelled using fuzzy sets and fuzzy logic from the soft computing paradigm. A fuzzy set is characterized via a function termed fuzzy membership function (mf), which is an expression of some domain knowledge. Through a fuzzy set an object is associated to the set by means of a membership degree μ. Two examples of fuzzy sets are shown in figure. By means of fuzzy membership functions a physical property of a design, such as size, can be interpreted as a degree of satisfaction of an elemental requirement. The degree of satisfaction is represented by the membership degree.

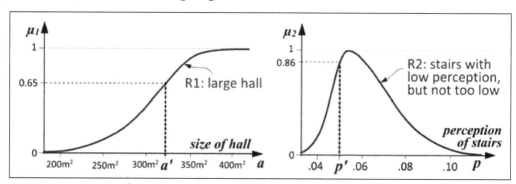

Two fuzzy sets expressing two elemental design requirements.

The requirements considered in figure are relatively simple, whereas the ultimate requirement for a design - namely a high design performance - is complex and abstract. Namely the latter one is determined by the simultaneous satisfaction of a number of elemental requirements.

The performance is computed using a fuzzy neural tree. It is particularly suitable to deal with the complex linguistic concepts like performance of a design. A neural tree is composed of one or several model output units, referred to as root nodes that are connected to input units termed terminal nodes, and the connections are via logic processors termed internal nodes. An example of a fuzzy neural tree for performance evaluation of a design is shown in figure. The neural tree is used for the evaluation by structuring the relations among the aspects of performance. The root node takes the meaning of high sustainability performance and the inner nodes one level below are the aspects of the performance. The meaning of each of these aspects may vary from design project to project and it is determined by experts. The model inputs are shown by means of squares in figures, and they are fuzzy sets, such as those given in figure.

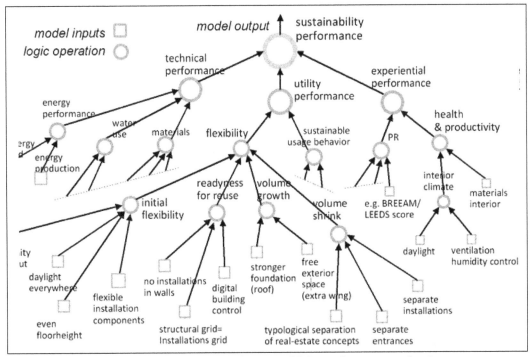

The structure of a fuzzy neural tree model for performance evaluation.

The detailed structure of the nodal connections with respect to the different connection types is shown in figure, where the output of i-th node is denoted μ_i and it is introduced to another node j. The weights w_{ij} are given by domain experts, expressing the relative significance of the node i as a component of node j.

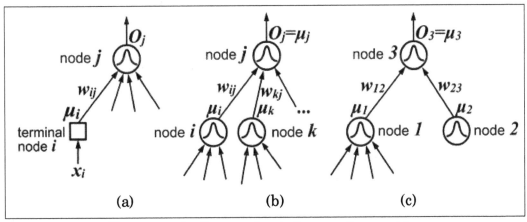

Different type of node connections in the neuro-fuzzy model.

The centres of the basis functions are set to be the same as the weights of the connections arriving at that node. Therefore, for a terminal node connected to an inner node, the inner node output denoted by O_j, is obtained by:

$$O_j = \exp(-\frac{1}{2}\sum_i^n \left[\frac{(\mu_i - 1)}{\sigma_j / w_{ij}} \right]^2)$$

where j is the number of the node; i denotes consecutive numbers associated to each input of the inner node; n denotes the highest number of the inputs arriving at node j; w_i denotes the degree of membership being the output of the i-th terminal node; w_{ij} is the weight associated with the connection between the i-th terminal node and the inner node j; and σ_j denotes the width of the Gaussian of node j.

It is noted that the inputs to an inner node are fuzzified before the AND operation takes place. This is shown in figure a. It is also noted that the model requires establishing the width parameter σ_j at every node. This is accomplished by means of imposing a consistency condition on the model. This is illustrated in figure b where the left part of the Gaussian is approximated by a straight line. In figure b, optimizing the σ_j parameter, we obtain:

$$O_j \cong \mu$$

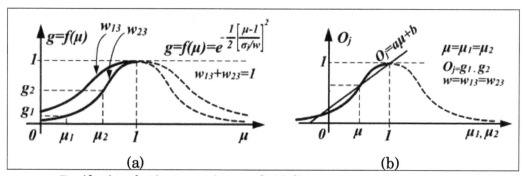

Fuzzification of an input at an inner node (a); linear approximation to Gaussian function at AND operation (b).

for the values μ and O_j can take between zero and one. In any case, for a node in the neural tree, equation $O_j \cong \mu$ is satisfied for $\mu = O_j = 0$ (approximately) and for $\mu = O_j = 1$ (exact) inherently, while g_1 and g_2 are increasing function of μ_1 and μ_2. Therefore a linear relationship between O_j and μ in the range between 0 and 1 is a first choice from the fuzzy logic viewpoint; namely, as to the AND operation at the respective node, if inputs are equal, that is $\mu = \mu_1 = \mu_2$ then the output of the node of μ_1 AND μ_2 is determined by the respective triangular membership functions in the antecedent space. Triangular fuzzy membership functions are the most prominent type of membership functions in fuzzy logic applications. For five inputs to a neural tree node, these membership functions are represented by the data sets given by tables.

Dataset at Neural Tree Node Input

.1	.2	.3	.4	.5	.6	.7	.8	.9
.1	.2	.3	.4	.5	.6	.7	.8	.9
.1	.2	.3	.4	.5	.6	.7	.8	.9
.1	.2	.3	.4	.5	.6	.7	.8	.9
.1	.2	.3	.4	.5	.6	.7	.8	.9

.1	.2	.3	.4	.5	.6	.7	.8	.9

In general, the data sets given in tables above are named in this work as 'consistency conditions'. They are used to calibrate the membership function parameter σ. This is accomplished through optimization. The consistency condition is to ensure that when all inputs take a certain value, then the model output yields this very same value, i.e. $\mu_1 = \mu_2 \approx O_j$ This is illustrated in figure b by means of linear approximation to the Gaussian. The consistency is ensured by means of gradient adaptive optimization, identifying optimal σ_j values for each node. It is emphasized that the fuzzy logic operation performed at each node is an AND operation among the input components μ_i coming to the node. This entails for instance that in case all elemental requirements are highly fulfilled, then the design performance is high as well. In the same way, for any other pattern of satisfaction on the elemental level, the performance is computed and obtained at the root node output. The fuzzy neural tree can be seen as a means to aggregate elemental requirements yielding fewer requirement items at higher levels of generalization compared to the lower level requirements. This is seen from figure.

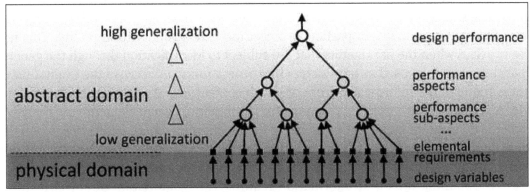

Degrees of generalization in the neuro-fuzzy performance evaluation.

At this point a few observations are due, as follows. If a weight w_{ij} is zero, this means the significance of the input is zero, consequently the associated input has no effect on the node output and thus also the system output. Conversely, if a w_{ij} is close to unity, this means the significance of the input is highest among the competitive weights directed to the same node. This means the value of the associated input is extremely important and a small change about this value has big impact on the node output O_j. If a weight w_{ij} is somewhere between zero and one, then the associated input value has some possible effect on the node output determined by the respective AND operation via equation

$O_j = \exp(-\dfrac{1}{2}\sum_i^n \left[\dfrac{(\mu_i - 1)}{\sigma_j / w_{ij}} \right]^2$). In this way, the domain knowledge is integrated into the

logic operations. The general properties of the present neural tree structure are as follows: If an input of a node is small (i.e., close to zero) and the weight w_{ij} is high, then, the output of the node is also small complying with the AND operation; If a weight w_{ij} is low the associated input cannot have significant effect on the node output. This means, quite naturally, such inputs can be ignored; If all input values coming to a node are high (i.e., close to unity), the output of the node is also high complying with the AND operation; If a weight w_{ij} is high the associated input x_i can have significant effect on the node output. It might be of value to point out that, the AND operation in a neural-tree node is executed in fuzzy logic terms and the associated connection weights play an important role on the effectiveness of this operation.

Role of VR in the System

It is clear that in order for the genetic algorithm to be effective, the suitability of the solutions it generates needs to evaluated using the fuzzy model. In conventional applications of multi-objective GA, for instance maximizing the strength of a structural component and minimizing its weight at the same time, this evaluation is rather simple. The simplicity is in the sense that the fitness function is crisp and the parameters of the function, such as geometric parameters of the beam's cross-section, are directly those parameters that are subject to evolutionary identification. In these cases there is no necessity for instantiation of the beam object during the search for optimality. However, in other search tasks, as they occur for instance in architectural design, the problem requires more elaborate treatment, in particular object instantiation in virtual reality. This necessity arises when the parameters that are subject to identification through the genetic algorithm cannot be used as parameters in a fitness function because the evaluation of fitness requires the information from other object features. As an example let us consider a problem, where optimal positions for a number of design elements are pursued, while the determination of the suitability of the positioning requires information on the perceptual properties of the objects. A virtual perception process is needed that obtains the required input information used in the human-like reasoning during the evaluation process. Obtaining the input information requires the instantiation of object features beyond the parameters that are subject to identification through the search.

Role of VR in the design system is to permit instantiation of the candidate solutions, as indicated by the letter i, so that measurements required for the fuzzy performance evaluation are executed for these solutions. The measurements deliver input information for the human-like reasoning about the suitability of a solution using the neuro-fuzzy model marked with the letter m. With this understanding the role of VR in the search process can be considered as the interface between the two components evolutionary algorithm and fuzzy performance evaluation. In particular, referring to figure, the instantiation of objects in VR permits the execution of measurement procedures that deliver input information from the parameter domain for the interpretations with respect to the abstract goals.

It is noted that for the effective multi-objective optimization in the application below the relaxation angle is computed adaptively for every chromosome, and at every generation. This is implemented by having the angle be a part of the chromosome of every solution. The fitness of a chromosome is obtained by considering two properties of the solution at the same time. One is the degree of dominance in terms of the amount of solutions dominating an individual, the second is the relaxation angle used to measure this amount. Based on equations $\mathbf{R}_{fit} = \dfrac{1}{N(\theta)+n}$ and $N(\theta) = \dfrac{s}{1+(\theta/\overline{\theta})}$ the fitness in the

applications is assessed with s=20, i.e. explicitly:

$$R_{fit} = \frac{1}{\dfrac{20}{1(\theta/\overline{\theta})}+n}$$

Next to the need for object instantiation in VR during the search for optimal solutions there is a second instance during a design process when virtual reality plays a significant role. This is indicated by the letter p in figure, and concerns the investigation of the Pareto optimal solutions previously obtained. It is noted that generally multi-objective optimization involves no information on the relative importance among the objectives. This is in particular due to the abstract nature of the major goals making such a-priori commitment problematic. It is emphasized that in the present work this is the reason why the optimization takes place for the nodes at the penultimate neural level and not for the root node. Due to the lacking information on the relative importance among the criteria, generally Pareto optimal solutions cannot be distinguished without bringing into play higher-order criteria. That is, once a Pareto front is established, the difference among the solutions is subject to analysis, in order to determine a preference vector grading the objectives w.r.t. each other. In order for this process to be informative, it is required that the solutions found through evolutionary search be located at diverse positions on the Pareto front. This is to avoid that potentially interesting regions in objective space remain unexplored during the analysis of the Pareto front. It is emphasized that this diversity is obtained through the relaxation of the Pareto angle in this work.

With a diversely populated Pareto front it is possible to explore the front in a way that allows a decision-maker to intuitively grasp the relation between parameters of the solutions and corresponding performance characteristics, and in this way a decision maker is able to approach his most preferred solution among the Pareto optimal ones. Namely, the very nature of Pareto front implies that the trade-off that is afforded when moving along the Pareto surface is the inevitable trade-off inherent in the problem. This means, in case one is moving along the Pareto surface in a certain direction, for example towards better cost performance, the reduction of performance in the other dimensions, say the loss of functionality, is as small as possible through the definition of Pareto front. This means when a decision maker is observing a solution instantiated in virtual reality, i.e. in the parameter domain, he may decide to move in objective domain into the direction he wishes to 'improve' this solution, while minimal loss in the other objectives occurs. Clearly, the consideration whether the former or the latter solution is better matching the decisionmakers preferences requires instantiation of the new solution in VR, too.

However, in complex problems the amount of solutions a decision maker needs to consider may be high in order to approach to his favourite solution, so that it becomes desirable to start the exploration from a solution among the Pareto solutions that is preferable in an unbiased sense. This is possible due to the involvement of fuzzy modelling in this work.

Although Pareto optimal solutions are equivalent in Pareto sense, it is noted that the solutions may still be distinguished. At the root node, the performance score is computed by the defuzzification process given by:

$$w_1 f_1 + w_2 f_2 + w_3 f_3 = p$$

where f_1 is the output of the node technical performance; f_2 of node utility performance; f_3 of node experiential performance. That is, they denote the performance values for these aspects of the design, which are subject to maximization. The variable p denotes the design performance which is also requested to be maximized. In w_1, w_2, and w_3 denote the weights associated to the connections from f_1, f_2 and f_3 to the design performance. It is noted that $w_1 + w_2 + w_3 = 1$.

In many real-world optimization tasks the cognitive viewpoint plays an important role. This means it is initially uncertain what values $w_1, ... w_3$ should have. Namely, the node outputs $f_1, ..., f_3$ can be considered as the design feature vector, and the reflection of these features can be best performed if the weights $w_1 ; ...; w_3$ define the same direction as that of the feature vector. This implies that the performance p_{max} for each genetic solution is given by:

$$p_{max} = \frac{f_1^2 + f_2^2 + f_3^2}{f_1 + f_2 + f_3}$$

Therefore, the above equation is computed for all the design solutions on the Pareto front. Then the solution having maximal value of p_{max} is selected among the Pareto solutions. This way the particular design is identified as a solution candidate with the corresponding w_1, w_2, ..., w_n weights. These weights form a priority vector w^*. If for any reason this candidate solution is not appealing, the next candidate is searched among the available design solutions with a desired design feature vector and the relational attributes, i.e., w_1, w_2, ..., w_n. One should note that, although performance does not play role in the genetic optimization, Pareto front offers a number of design options with fair performance leaving the final choice dependent on other environmental preferences. Using the above equation, second-order preferences are identified that are most promising for the task at hand, where ultimately maximal design performance is pursued.

To this end, to make the analysis explicit we consider a two-dimensional objective space. In this case, equation $P_{max} = \dfrac{f_1^2 + f_2^2 + f_3^2}{f_1 + f_2 + f_3}$ becomes:

$$P_{max} = \dfrac{f_1^2 + f_2^2}{f_1 + f_2}$$

which can be put into the form:

$$f_1^2 + f_2^2 - pf_1 + pf_2 = 0$$

that defines a circle along which the performance is constant. To obtain the circle parameters in terms of performance, we write:

$$f_1^2 + f_2^2 - pf_1 + pf_2 \equiv (x - x_1)^2 + (y - y_1)^2 - R^2$$

From the above equation we obtain the center coordinates x_1, y_1 and the radius R of the circle in terms of performance as:

$$x_1 = p/2$$
$$y_1 = p/2$$
$$R = p/\sqrt{2}$$

The performance circle with the presence of two different Pareto fronts are schematically. It is seen that the maximum performance is at the locations where either of the objectives is maximal at the Pareto front. If both objectives are equal, the maximal performance takes its lowest value and the degree of departing from the equality means a better performance in Pareto sense. This result is significant since it reveals that, a design can have a better performance if some measured extremity in one way or other is exercised. It is meant that, if a better performance is obtained, then most presumably extremity will be observed in this design. It is noted that the location of an expected superior Pareto optimal solution in this unbiased sense depends on the shape of the Pareto front, in particular on the degree of symmetry the Pareto front has w.r.t. the line passing from the origin of the objective space through the ideal point. Where it is seen that for a Pareto front that is asymmetrical w.r.t. to this diagonal a unique location of a solution with a superior performance may exist.

Implementation Number 1

This implementation of the system in VR concerns the design of an interior space.

The space is based on the main hall of the World Trade Centre in Rotterdam in the Netherlands. The aim is to optimally position a number of design objects in this space. The objects are a vertical building core hosting the elevators, a mezzanine, stairs, and two vertical ducts. The perception of a virtual observer plays a role in this task, because the objective involves a number of perception-based requirements. The function $f_x(x)$ shown in figure is a probability density function (pdf) and given by equation $f_x(x) = \dfrac{2}{\pi} \dfrac{1}{\left(l_0^2 + x^2\right)}, -l_0 < x < l_0$. It models the visual attention of an unbiased virtual observer along a plane perpendicular to the observer's frontal direction. The unbiasedness refers that the observer has no a-priori preference for any particular direction within his visual scope over another one. Integral of the pdf over a certain length domain, i.e. of an object, yields perception expressed via a probability in this approach. The probability expresses the degree by which the observer is aware of the object.

The implementation of this model in virtual reality using a virtual observer termed avatar is illustrated in figure. From the figure it is noted that the avatar pays attention to the objects in the space equally in all directions in his visual scope. This is illustrated by means of the rays sent from the eyes of the avatar in random directions and intersecting the objects in the scene. The randomness has a uniform probability density w.r.t. the angle θ in figure. In virtual reality implementation the amount of rays impinging on an object are counted and averaged in real time to approximate the perception expressed by a probability.

$$f_x(x) = \frac{2}{\pi} \frac{1}{\left(l_0^2 + x^2\right)}, -l_0 < x < l_0$$

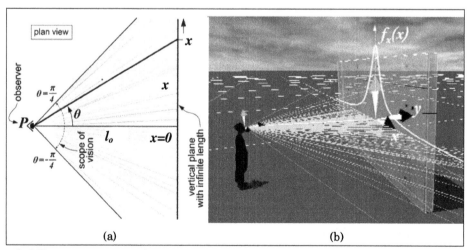

Probabilistic perception model for a basic geometric situation, where the probability density fx(x) models visual attention along a plane object. Plan view (a); perspective view (b).

The perception model requires instantiation of objects to obtain the probability quantifying perception. That is, the GA determines the position of the objects, however their geometric extent is responsible for the perception of the observer. So, once a candidate scene is instantiated in virtual reality, the perception computations involving the geometric features of the scene objects are executed.

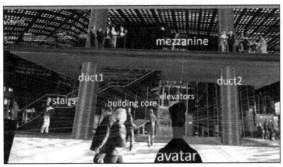

Perception measurement by means of an avatar in virtual reality
based on a probabilistic theory of perception.

The results from the perception measurement are probabilities associated with the objects of the scene, that indicate to what extend an object comes to the awareness of an observer paying unbiased visual attention to the scene. This crisp information needs to be further evaluated with regards to the satisfaction of the goals at hand. The present design task involves several perceptual requirements. Two of them are shown in figure as examples. One example is that the stairs should not be very noticeable from the avatar's viewing position, in order to increase the privacy in terms of access to the mezzanine floor. At the same time the stairs should not be overlooked too easily for people who do need to access the mezzanine floor. This is seen from the mf in figure, where x_{12} denotes the perception degree and $w_o 12$ denotes the fuzzy membership degree. A second example is that the elevators should be positioned in such a way that they are easily noticed from the avatar's viewing position, so that people who wish to access the office floors above the entrance hall easily find the elevators. This requirement is expressed by means of the fuzzy membership function in figure, where increasing perception denoted by x_3 yields increasing membership degree $w_o 3$.

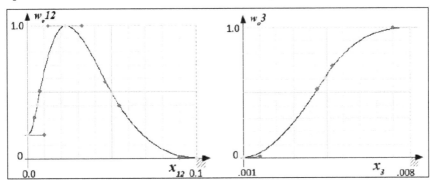

Two requirements subject to satisfaction: perception of the stairs (a) and elevators (b).

It is noted that the perception computation using the probabilistic perception model yields x_{12} in figure. The task is to optimally place the design objects satisfying a number of such perception requirements, and also some functionality requirements.

The functionality requirements concern for instance the size of the space, which is influenced by the position of the building core object. The elemental requirements and their relation with the ultimate goal are seen from the fuzzy neural tree structure shown in figure. From the structure we note that the performance of the entrance hall depends on the performance of the design objects forming the scene. From this we note that the amount of objectives to be maximized is four, namely the outputs of nodes 4-7, whereas the elemental requirements total an amount of 12.

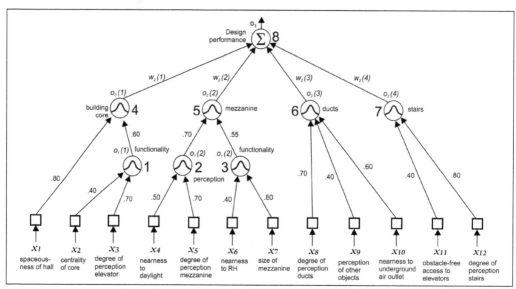

Neural tree structure for the performance evaluation.

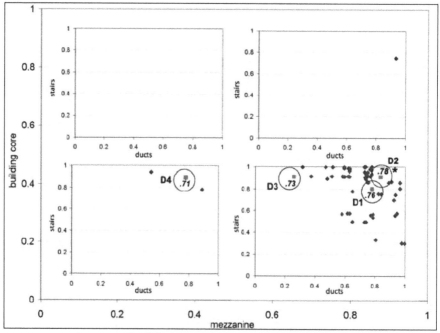

Pareto optimal designs with respect to the four objective dimensions using relaxed Pareto ranking.

The results from the relaxed Pareto ranking approach. It is noted that the objective space has four dimensions, one for the performance of every design object. The representation is obtained by first categorizing the solutions as to which of the four quadrants in the two-dimensional objective space formed by the building core and mezzanine performance they belong, and then representing in each quadrant a coordinate system showing the stairs and ducts performance in this very quadrant. This way four dimensions are represented on the two-dimensional page.

Two Pareto optimal designs are shown in figures for comparison. The maximal performance score as well as the performance feature vector for these solutions is shown in table.

Table: Performance of design D2 versus D4.

	core	mezzanine	ducts	stairs	pmax
D2	0.27	0.73	0.83	0.93	0.78
D4	0.48	0.49	0.78	0.89	0.71

From the table it is seen that design D2 outperforms design D4 with respect to the maximal performance p_{max} obtained using equation $p_{max} = \dfrac{f_1^2 + f_2^2 + f_3^2}{f_1 + f_2 + f_3}$. It is also noted that the performance of D4 as to its features varies less compared to D2. The fact that D2 has a greater p_{max} confirms the theoretical expectation illustrated by figure that solutions with more extreme features generally have a greater maximal performance compared to solutions with little extremity. The greatest absolute difference among D2 and D4 is the performance of the mezzanine. In D2 the mezzanine is located closer to associated functions, and this turns out to be more important compared to the fact that D4 yields more daylight on the mezzanine. Therefore D2 scores higher that D4 regarding the mezzanine. Additionally D2 slightly outperforms D4 regarding the performance of the ducts. This is because the ducts do not penetrate the mezzanine in D2, whereas in D4 they do. The latter is undesirable, as given by the requirements. Regarding the building core D2 is inferior to D4, which is because the spaciousness in D4 is greater and also the elevators are located more centrally. Regarding the stairs' performance, the difference among D2 and D4 is negligible. The latter exemplifies the fact that an objective may be reached in different ways, i.e. solutions that are quite different regarding their physical parameters may yield similar scores as to a certain goal. In the present case the greater distance to the stairs in D2 compared to D4 is compensated by the fact that the stairs is oriented sideways in D2, so that the final perception degree is almost the same. It is noted that D2 is the solution with the greatest maximal performance p_{max}, so that from an unbiased viewpoint it is the most suitable solution among the Pareto optimal ones. This solution is most appealing to be selected for construction. This result is an act of machine cognition, as it reveals that pursuing maximal performance in the present task the stairs and ducts are more important compared to the building core from an unbiased viewpoint. This information was not known prior to the execution of the computational design process. It is interesting to note that the solution that was chosen by a human architect in a conventional design process without computational support was also similar to solution D2. The benefit of the computational approach is that it ensures identification of most suitable solutions, their unbiased comparison, and precise information on their respective trade-off as to the abstract objectives. This is difficult to obtain using conventional means. The diversity of solutions along the Pareto front, which is due to the relaxation of the Pareto concept is significant especially in order to facilitate the process of ensuing validation.

Implementation Number 2

In the second implementation of the computational design system, object instantiation in VR is used for evaluation of solutions in a layout problem of a building complex for a performance measurement involving multiple objectives. In this task the spatial arrangement of a number of spatial units is to be accomplished in such a way that three main goals are satisfied simultaneously. These goals are maximizing the building's functionality and energy performance, as well as its performance regarding form related preferences. It is noted that the spheres represent the performance of a number of alternative solutions for the three objectives of the design task.

The building subject to design consists of a number of spatial units, referred to as design objects, where every unit is designated to a particular purpose in the building. The task is to locate the objects optimally on the building site with respect to the three objectives forming suitable spatial arrangements. The objects and their properties, which play role during the fitness evaluation of solutions generated by the algorithm, are given in table.

Table: Properties of the design objects.

	floorsurface (m²)	ceiling height (m)	Specific power q_I of inner heat sources (W/m²)	surface amount of glass in façades (%)
apt_a_1	22000	2.7	2.1	30
apt_a_2	22000	2.7	2.1	30
apt_a_3	18500	3.2	2.1	40
apt_a_4	22000	2.7	2.1	30
apt_a_5	22000	2.7	2.1	30
apt_b_1	45000	2.7	2.1	30
apt_b_2	37000	3.2	2.1	40
apt_b_3	45000	2.7	2.1	30
hotel	74000	3	2.1	40
care	32000	3	2.1	20
shops	34000	5	4	50

offices	115000	3.5	3.5	70
sport	28000	6	3.5	70

The attributes given in table play an important role in particular in the evaluation of the energy performance of the solutions, which is described in the Appendix A. It is noted that the site is located in Rotterdam in the Netherlands, so that climate data from this location is used in the energy computations. It is further noted that the energy computations require information of the insulation value of the facades expressed by the U-value of the walls, Uvalue of windows and glass façade, as well as the g-value of the glass. In this task the Uvalue of the walls is 0.15 W/m²K; U-value of windows is 1.00W/m²K; and g-value of the glass is 0.5.

In order to let the computer generate a building from the components, i.e. for a solution to be feasible, it is necessary to ensure that all solutions have some basic properties. These are that spaces should not overlap, and objects should be adjacent to the other objects around and above; also the site boundaries should be observed, in particular on the ground floor to permit pedestrian traffic along the waterfront. This is realized in the present application by inserting the objects in a particular sequential manner into the site. Starting from the same location, one by one the objects are moved forward, i.e. in southern direction, until they reach an obstacle. An obstacle may be the site boundary or another object previously inserted. When they touch an object they change their movement direction from the southern to the eastern direction, moving east until they again reach the site boundary or another object. As a final movement step the object will move down until it touches the ground plane, which is in order to account for different heights the objects have. Packing objects in two dimensions in this way is known as bottom-left two heuristic packing routine in literature. After the final object has been placed in this way, due to the fact that the sum of the objects' groundplanes exceeds the available surface on the site, some objects will overlap the site boundary or be situated entirely outside the site boundary.

The objects exceeding the site will be inserted using a second movement procedure, where first the object is moved forward until it reaches an obstacle; then it is moved upwards until it reaches an upper boundary for the building, which is set to 140m. Then the object is moved forward again, until it touches an obstacle. Thereafter it is moved in eastern direction until touching an obstacle, and then down, so that it comes to rest on top the building below it.

It is noted that the decision from which side to insert the building components, and which location to use as the starting point for insertion is a matter of judgement, and it will strongly influence the solutions obtained. The insertion used in this application is due to the preference of the architect is to have the objects line up along the street, which is in northern boundary of the site.

In this task object instantiation is required for several reasons. One of the reasons can be already noted considering the above insertion process during the generation of feasible solutions. Namely, during the movement of an object into the site it is formidable to establish a formalism that can be used to predict the exact geometric condition of the configuration that is already found on the site when the object moves into it. The reason is that the amount of possible geometric configurations is excessive due to the amount of objects and also due to the fact that two of the objects, namely the offices and the hotel unit are permitted to have different amounts of floor levels, which is a parameter in the GA. As the floor surface amount is requested to remain constant, consequently both the object's height and floor plan is variable for these two objects.

Effectively, the spatial configuration an object will encounter during its insertion into the scene can only be known through execution of the insertion process, i.e. through instantiation of the objects on site as well as letting objects move into the site and testing for collisions during the movement. In this respect it is noted that the accuracy of placement is subject to determination, where the step length of the movement at every time frame during object insertion should be set to a small value, however not too small to avoid that the collision detection routine is called excessively. Next to the need for VR during this solution generation procedure, the instantiation is needed to execute the measurements indicated by the letter m in figure as follows.

For the evaluation of the energy performance of the building it is necessary to compute the transmission heat loss denoted by Q_T. Q_T quantifies how much energy will be lost through the facades of every building component over the period of one year due to temperature difference between inside and outside air temperature. In order to obtain this value it is necessary to verify for every façade of a building unit, whether it is adjacent to another building component, or adjacent to outside air. Also it is necessary to compute the solar gain Q_S, which quantifies the amount of solar energy that penetrates into the building unit through the glazing of the facades. For a certain façade surface, Q_S depends, among other factors, on the distance from another building unit located in front of the facade causing a shadow. Therefore, to accomplish computation of Q_T and Q_S it is necessary to measure if another object is adjacent to the façade in question, located in front of the facade at some distance close enough to cause a shadow, or if there is no object in front of the façade causing a shadow on it.

For this purpose a test procedure is executed in the virtual reality, where for every façade the distance to objects in front of it is measured. It is clear that this test requires object instantiation due to the manifold possible geometric configurations in the search. The test is executed by means of rays that are emitted from the centre point of the building component in question and the intersection with other objects is detected. The resulting information is then used in the computations of Q_T and Q_S in order to compute the heat energy Q_H required to heat the building over the period of one year per m² of floor surface area. The output Q_H is the result from energy computations using a steady state model given in the appendix. From the neural tree in figure it is seen that the energy performance evaluation involves a single fuzzy membership function, i.e. it does not involve inner nodes.

It is seen that the input information for the energy evaluation is the heat energy Q_H expressed as energy per m² of floor surface area and per year. That the satisfaction of the energy requirement increases with decreasing energy, and that the satisfaction, expressed by the membership degree μ reaches its maximum for heat energy consumption below 2.2 kWh/m²a, and satisfaction diminishes for energy amount beyond 4.4 kWh/m²a. It is noted that this range concerns relatively low amount of energy compared to most contemporary building projects. This mainly due to the large size of the building units, where the amount of exterior surfaces with respect to the floor is relatively small.

For the evaluation of the performance regarding form preferences for the building, object instantiation in VR is required in order to execute other measurements.

The evaluation of the form preferences has two major aspects, the first one concerns the variations of heights in the building's skyline; the second one concerns the average height of the building. For both aspects two sub-aspects are distinguished in the model: the situation along the side facing the street (along the southern site boundary), and the side along the waterfront (along the northern boundary).

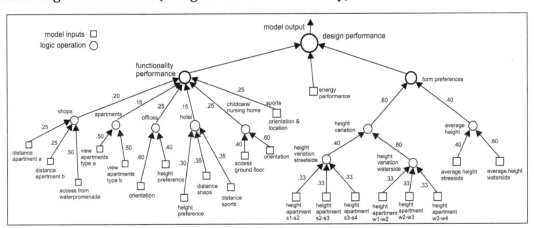

Fuzzy neural tree for performance evaluation of the candidate solutions.

Concerning the requirements on average height of the building the architect prefers to have a high average height along the street side and a low average height at the waterfront. This is to emphasize the urban character of the street, whereas the lower height along the waterfront is to give the building a more accessible expression when perceived by people walking along the waterfront. The requirement for a high average height along the street side is seen from the membership function in figure, yielding maximum membership degree at 100m and diminishing as the height reduces. The requirement for a low average height along the water-front is seen from the membership function in figure, where the membership degree diminishes with increasing height.

In the same way, during evaluation of a design alternative the tree is provided with input values obtained from the virtual building instantiated in VR, and the fuzzification processes are carried out at the terminal nodes. The fuzzification yields the degree of satisfaction for the elemental at the terminal nodes of the neural tree.

The root node of the neural tree shown in figure describes the ultimate goal subject to maximization, namely the design performance and the tree branches form the objectives constituting this goal. The connections among the nodes have a weight associated with them, as seen from the figure. In the same way as the membership functions at the terminals, the weights are given by a designer as an expression of knowledge, and the latter specify the relative significance a node has for the node one level closer to the root node. In particular the weights connecting the nodes on the penultimate level of the model indicate how strongly the output of these nodes influences the output at the root node. It is noted that in the multi-objective optimization case the latter weights are not specified a-priori, but they are subject to determination after the optimization process is accomplished.

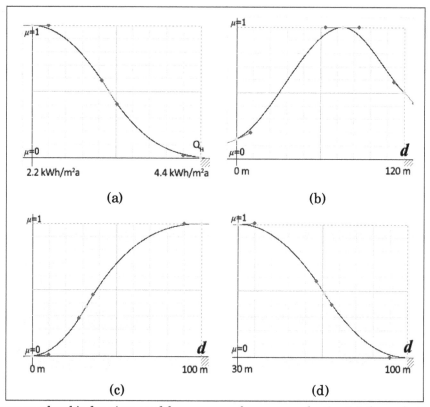

Fuzzy membership functions used for energy performance evaluation (a); for evaluation of the height variation in the building's skyline (b); for evaluation of the average height along the street-side (c); along the waterfront (d).

The fuzzified information is then processed by the inner nodes of the tree. These nodes perform the AND operations using Gaussian membership functions as described above, where the width-vector of the multi-dimensional Gaussian reflects the relative importance among the inputs to a node. Finally this sequence of logic operations starting from the model input yield the performance at the penultimate node outputs of the model. This means the more satisfied the elemental requirements at the terminal level are, the higher the outputs will be at the nodes above, finally increasing the design performance at the root node of the tree. Next to the evaluation of the design performance score, due to the fuzzy logic operations at the inner nodes of the tree, the performance of any sub-aspect is obtained as well. This is a desirable feature in design, which is referred to as transparency.

The multi objective optimization is accomplished using a multi-objective genetic algorithm with adaptive Pareto ranking. It is used to determine the optimal sequence of insertion, so that the three objectives are maximally fulfilled. Every chromosome contains the information for every object, at which rank in the insertion sequence it is to be inserted, as well as the information for the relaxation angle to use during the Pareto ranking for the particular solution. It is noted that the information a chromosome contains in order to determine the sequence of insertion is in the form of float numbers, where one float number is assigned to every object. The objects are then sorted based on the size of the float numbers, so that an object with a higher number will be inserted before one with a lower number. Using float numbers in the chromosome, as opposed to e.g. an integer number denoting a unique sequence of insertion, allows a genetic algorithm with conventional crossover procedure to generate more suitable solutions from the genetic combination of two successful ones. This is because the float number sequence is unbiased with respect the objects to be inserted, whereas an integer coding of the sequences has an inherent bias making it necessary to reflect this bias in the crossover procedure.

The performance evaluation model is used during the evolutionary search process aiming to identify designs with maximal design performance. In the present case we are interested in a variety of alternative solutions that are equivalent in Pareto sense. The design is therefore treated as a multi-objective optimization as opposed to a single-objective optimization. In single-objective case exclusively the design performance, i.e. the output at the root node of the neural tree, would be subject to maximization. In the latter case, the solution would be the outcome of a mere convergence and any cognition aspect would not be exercised. In the multi-objective implementation the outputs of the nodes functionality, energy, and form preferences, which are the penultimate nodes, are subject to maximization. Their values are used in the fitness determination procedure of the genetic algorithm. Employing the fuzzy neural tree in this way the genetic search is equipped with some human-like reasoning capabilities during the search. The part of the tree beyond the penultimate nodes is for the de-fuzzification process, which models cognition, so that ultimately the design performance is obtained at the root node.

Energy Computations

The input of the fuzzy membership function expressing the energy performance shown in the neural tree in figure requires as input the energy demand for heating over the period of one year and per floor surface area. This value is denoted by Q_H and given in the unit kWh/m²a. The size of the floor surface areas are. Q_H is computed as follows:

$$Q_H = Q_L - Q_G$$

where Q_L denotes the sum of the energy losses and QG denotes the sum of energy gains of the building unit. Let us first consider the losses:

$$Q_L = Q_T + Q_V$$

In above equation Q_T denotes losses through transmission via the building envelope, and QV denotes losses through ventilation. Q_T is computed by for every façade element n delimiting the unit as given by:

$$Q_T = \sum_n A_n \cdot U_n \cdot f_t \cdot G_t$$

where A_n denotes the surface amount of the n-th façade element in m²; U_n denotes the Uvalue of the façade element given in the unit W/m²K; ft denotes a temperature factor to account for reduced losses when a façade is touching the earth (.65) versus the normal condition of outside air (1.0); G_t denotes the time-integral of the temperature difference between inside and outside air temperature given in the unit kKh/a. In this implementation G_t=79.8 kKh/a.

Q_V is computed for a building unit by:

$$Q_V = V \cdot n_V \cdot c_{air} \cdot G_t$$

where V denotes the air volume enclosed within the unit given in m³; n_V denotes the energetically effective air exchange rate of the ventilation system during the heating period given in the unit 1/h, which is n_V=0.09/h in this implementation; c_{air} denotes the heat capacity of air c_{air}=0.33 Wh/m³K.

Considering the energy gain: Q_G is obtained by:

$$Q_G = \eta_G \cdot Q_F$$

where η_G is a factor denoting the effectiveness of the heat gains, and Q_F denotes the free heat energy due to solar radiation and internal gains, given by:

$$Q_F = Q_S + Q_I$$

where Q_S denotes the gain due to solar radiation and Q_I denotes the internal gain:

$$Q_s = \sum_n f_r \cdot g_w \cdot A_{n,w} \cdot G_d$$

In above equation for the n-th façade of a building unit f_r denotes a reduction factor that models the effect of a shadow on the façade. In the present implementation this factor is computed online using a measurement in VR. The factor g_w in above equation denotes the g-value of the window glazing used in the façade. This value expresses the total heat energy flux rate permitted through the glass. In the present case g_w=0.5. $A_{n,w}$

denotes the amount of window surface in the façade in m²; G_d denotes the direction dependent solar radiation energy given in the unit kWh/m²a. In the present climatic situation G_{south}=321 kWh/m²a; G_{north}=145 kWh/m²a; G_{east}=270 kWh/m²a and G_{west}=187 kWh/m²a.

Q_I in equation $Q_F = Q_S + Q_I$ is given by:

$$Q_I = 0.024 \cdot q_I \cdot A_f$$

where the number 0.024 is a conversion factor having the unit kh/d; t denotes the length of the heating period in days. In the present case t=205d. P_S denotes the specific power q_I of inner heat sources like people, lighting, computers, etc. given in the unit W/m². For the different building units subject to positioning in this task the different values for qI are. The factor η_G in equation $Q_G = \eta_G \cdot Q_F$ is obtained by:

$$\eta_G = \frac{1 - \left(Q_F / Q_V \right)^5}{1 - \left(Q_F / Q_V \right)^6}$$

Tools for VR Development

VR can offer plenty of value for your business, however, virtual reality app development can be tricky. Robust virtual reality tools assume importance.

Unity

Unity is famous for game development, however, it helps you to build VR solutions for many other sectors too. E.g., you can create VR solutions for automotive, transportation, manufacturing, media and entertainment, engineering, construction, etc. with Unity.

You can get a valuable set of tools when you use Unity, e.g.:

- A powerful editor to create VR assets.

- Artist and designer tools.

- CAD tools.

- Collaboration tools.

Unity offers a portal to learn its products where a VR developer can access courses like "Getting started with Unity", and many more.

Amazon Sumerian

Amazon Sumerian is the VR engine from AWS, and you don't need 3D graphics or VR programming skills to use it. Sumerian works with all popular VR platforms like Oculus Go, Oculus Rift, HTC Vive, HTC Vive Pro, Google Daydream, and Lenovo Mirage, moreover, it works with Android and iOS mobile devices too.

Amazon Sumerian supports various VR use cases like employee education, training simulation, field services productivity, retail and sales, and virtual concierge. It has powerful features, e.g.:

- Sumerian editor.

- Sumerian hosts.

- Asset management.

- An ability to script the logic in the scenes you create.

Google VR for Everyone

Google, the technology giant offers a wide range of VR development tools, and you can use them to create immersive VR experience for your stakeholders. You can access these tools on the Google VR developer portal.

You can use these tools to develop VR apps for multiple platforms, e.g., Unity, Unreal, Android, iOS, and web. To access the guides to develop VR apps for each of these platforms, first navigate to "Choose your development environment" on the Google VR developer portal.

The Google VR developer platform has software development kits (SDKs) for all VR platforms it supports, e.g., Unity, Android, iOS, etc.

Unreal Engine 4 (UE4)

Unreal Engine 4 (UE4) offers a powerful set of VR development tools. With UE4, you can build VR apps that will work on a variety of VR platforms, e.g., Oculus, Sony, Samsung Gear VR, Android, iOS, Google VR, etc.

The UE4 platform has many features, e.g.:

- It offers access to its C++ source code and Python scripts; therefore, any VR developer in your team can study the engine in detail and learn how to use it.

- UE4 has a multiplayer framework, real-time rendering of visuals, and a flexible editor.

- With the Blueprint visual scripting tool offered by UE4, you can create prototypes quickly.

- It's easy to add animation, sequence, audio, simulation, effects, etc.

CRYENGINE

Well-known to game developers, CRYENGINE is a robust choice for a VR software development tool. You can build virtual reality apps with it that will work with popular VR platforms like Oculus Rift, PlayStation 4, Xbox One, etc.

CRYENGINE offers various features, examples:

- You can incorporate excellent visuals in your app.

- Creating a VR app is easy with CRYENGINE since it offers sandbox and other relevant tools.

- You can easily create characters.

- There are built-in audio solutions.

- You can build real-time visualization and interaction with CRYENGINE, which provides an immersive experience to your stakeholders.

CRYENGINE offers excellent documentation, moreover, you can get its entire source code.

Blender

Blender is an open-source 3D creation suite, and it's free. At the time of writing, Blender 2.80 is its latest release. The Blender Foundation, an independent organization for public benefit governs the development of Blender.

Blender offers the following features and capabilities:

- You can create your 3D pipeline with modeling, rigging, animation, simulation, rendering, composing, and motion tracking.

- Blender supports video editing and game creation.

- If you have an experienced VR developer in your team, then he/she can use its API for Python scripting to customize the application. This allows you to create specialized tools.

3ds Max

3ds Max is a popular 3D modeling and rendering software from Autodesk, and you can use it for design visualization, game creation, etc. This powerful software offers a wide range of features, examples:

- You can create professional-quality 3D animations with it.

- 3ds Max offers an efficient and flexible toolset to produce high-quality 3D models.

- There are various options to create textures and effects.

- You get an impressive array of 3D rendering, UI, workflow, pipeline, 3D animation, and other capabilities with 3ds Max.

SketchUp Studio

SketchUp Studio is a powerful 3D modeling tool focused on the construction industry and architecture, and you can use it for virtual reality app development. It's useful for use cases like architecture, commercial interior design, landscape architecture, residential construction, 3D printing, and urban planning.

You can get its powerful desktop tool with easy-to-use UI, and designing your building in 3D will be easier with it. The tool allows you to use compelling graphics, moreover, SketchUp Studio offers construction industry-specific features. You can build both VR and Augmented Reality (AR) apps using this tool.

Maya

Maya is yet VR software development tool from Autodesk. With Maya, you can create 3D animations, motion graphics, and VFX software.

Maya is a powerful software that offers tools for dynamics, effects, 3D animation, 3D rendering, 3D shading, 3D modeling, pipeline integration, motion graphics, etc.

Oculus Medium

Oculus, the well-known provider of VR platforms like Oculus Rift S, Oculus Quest, and Oculus Go also offers powerful VR development software, named Medium. It's a comprehensive tool, which allows you to create 3D assets.

You can sculpt, model, and paint the VR assets you create. Even if you are a beginner, with Oculus Medium you can quickly create an immersive environment.

VR Development with InTml

VR applications are very interesting pieces of technology, not only from the point of view of final users who are immersed in a compelling experience, but also to developers. VR applications are a real challenge in terms of development constraints: they gather information from users through several and possibly redundant input devices, they have to compute a simulation in the order of miliseconds, and they have to deliver output through several devices and modalities at interactive rates. In terms of APIs, VR applications are built on top of a wide variety of software technologies in order to accomplish their goals: from low level drivers that communicate with devices to specialized 3D render APIs, from sockets to real time geometrical algorithms, from XML readers to streaming technologies. Developers should also know about several fields related to computing such as networking, data mangling, simulation, computer graphics, haptics, and human factors. There are several toolkits, libraries, and frameworks that developers could use in this endeavor, so applications can benefit from previous solutions.

However, to this date, VR development is still a challenge. On top of the steepy learning curve of most VR development toolkits, final applications may be unstable, prone to errors, hard to customize to particular user needs and features, difficult to deploy, and technology dependent, among other concerns. Part of these issues is related to the inherent complexity of the technologies involved in development, where the lack of standards and the wide variety of providers make work harder. Part is also related to the inherent focus of a particular VR application, which usually concentrates resources in certain goals (i.e. a particular user study), while treating others as not as important (i.e. code reusability).

Common solutions in VR development are VR toolkits and APIs, which may offer standard solutions to certain problems. Although there are examples of mature tools in the field, some of these may be too difficult, too limiting, or too low level for novices. Some researchers have tried to use tools and techniques from the game industry, which by far exceeds the size and economic force of its VR ancestor. Most of the success of the game industry is due to the vast amount of resources dedicated to improve gamer's experience, but it is also important to notice the availability of powerful game engines which help developers to handle complexity. A game engine allows developers to create compelling results in a short time, by hiding complex parts of a solution under specialized APIs. However, some solutions, shortcuts, and workarounds in games are not adequate for VR, where simulation fidelity and device support are very important.

Our long term goal is to facilitate VR and Mixed Reality (MR) development, by dividing its complexity among several people with different roles. For this reason we created the Interaction Techniques Markup Language (InTml) and a set of tools around this concept. InTml allows us to divide concerns in two main categories, one directed to architectural design, and the other related to code; one high level abstraction, and the other low level implementation. InTml offers an abstraction for the description of VR applications, independent from a particular set of device drivers, VR toolkits, libraries, and programming languages; an abstraction powerful enough to describe a wide variety of applications in the VR domain. This could make VR applications more portable in the future, since their abstract description in InTml may be ported to several technologies. Finally, InTml makes easier to identify particular devices and interaction techniques in an application, so they can be replaced if it is important to port an application to a new hardware environment. We call this process application retargeting, and we hope that in the future it will be an important element of VR application maintenance and evolution.

An InTml application is basically a set of components connected between them. Such components are called filters, which may represent devices, content, or behavior in an application. There is a library of available filter classes, and it is possible to add new classes to the system. This system can be executed in several runtime implementations, based on generic programming languages. We show first an abstract example of an InTml application and later we describe the concept of a filter class. Then, we show how such applications are created and executed in our IDE. Finally, we present the InTml's abstract execution model and an example of an execution, which can be implemented in both a parallel or sequential fashion. In general, InTml hides from designers certain elements of complexity, so developers can use or improve technologies behind the scene.

InTml Application

Our first example is shown in figure, an application that allows a user to move a virtual hand with a tracker and touch virtual objects. In this example, a device (handTracker) gives position and orientation information to an object (handRepr). The behavior filter SelectByTouching receives the actual handRepr and scene objects, and any changes in position or orientation from handRepr. Once a collision is detected the selected objects are passed to Feedback, which activates a white bounding box around such objects. At the end of each execution step, console will render all objects in the scene (both handRepr and objects inside scene).

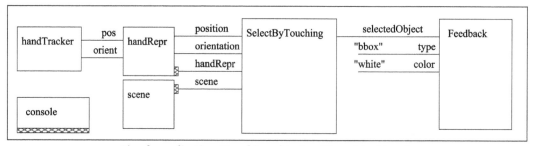

Simple application. Touching objects with a virtual hand.

An InTml application is composed of instances of filter classes, constants, and object holders. Constants can give initial values to selected input ports in the system, and object holders are used as an indirection mechanism. Filters can also be sent as events through the dataflow, which is shown as an output port with a special decoration. We also use a special decoration for an output device (i.e. console), in order to avoid line cluttering of connections from all objects to the output device.

Object holders are an indirection mechanism inside InTml. They are placeholders that can hold any piece of content in an application, i.e. any filter that represents content. They have an special input port that is used to change the contained object, and an output port that informs interested filters about changes in the contained object. Other filters can connect to and from an object holder, and those connections will be attached to the contained object during execution. Figure shows examples of object holders inside a composite filter. GoGoIT, a composite filter that models the Go Go selection technique by Poupyrev, consists of three object holders (cube, current, previous) and three behaviors (gogo, SelectByTouching, FeedbackOne). gogo takes two configuration parameters (K,D) plus position and orientation of the user's head and hand in order to compute a virtual hand's position and orientation plus the visibility of a cube, that represents a user's real hand. SelectByTouching takes a computed virtual hand position, a virtual hand geometry, and a set of selectable objects in the scene in order to compute a selected object. Finally, FeedbackOne uses two object holders in order to modify color and bounding box of the current and previous selected objects. These two last object holders are a good example of the indirection mechanism: no matter which object is selected at any time, FeedbackOne can refer to it and send it events.

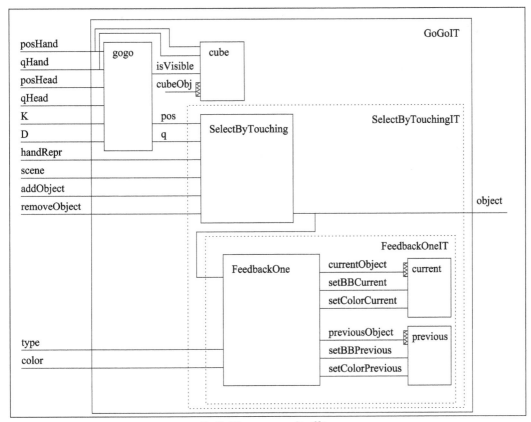

GoGoIT, a composite filter.

Filter Classes

Each filter class defines a type of component that can be instantiated in an InTml application. A filter class' instance is a particular element in an application that receives the required information for its computation and produces certain information. Both required and produced information are modeled as a set of ports, which define the set of chunks of information the filter can receive or produce. Each port is defined in terms of a unique name and the type of information it may receive or produce. At any particular time, a filter can receive zero or more events in each one of its input ports, and produce zero or more events in its output ports.

Simple filter classes should encapsulate just one of the following elements: a piece of content, a behavior, or a device. A piece of content could be an interactive object in the 3D scene, a widget in the interface, a sound effect, or a haptic effect, with ports that allow developers to configure its initial state of modify such content during execution, i.e. activating an effect or changing an object's color. A behavior could be either the core algorithm for an interaction technique or an animation effect, with input ports for receiving the required information for its computation and output ports that carry the result of its computation. A device represents a physical device that users can see and manipulate, i.e. a joystick or a tracking system, with input ports for device configuration and output ports that capture and discriminate the information produced.

Instances of simple filters can be used to create applications or composite filters. A composite filter is a special type of filter class that can be used to hide complexity, and it can contain a set interconnected instances of simple or composite filters.

Abstract Execution Model

The abstract execution of an InTml application follows a pipeline model, with the following stages per execution frame:

- Data gathering: All data from input devices are gathered during a certain period of time. All events gathered during that period are considered simultaneous.

- Data propagation: Gathered information is propagated through the dataflow. All filters compute their output data from events in their input ports. Filters that represent content accumulate changes without affecting the object's state. This is to assure that any read operation over content will read a consistent state during an execution frame.

- Object holder's execution: If required, object holders change their contained objects first. After, they propagate received events to their contained filters.

- Changes in content: All content filters collect input events, compute their new state, and propagate changes through their output ports. Those changes will be received by interested filters in the coming frame of execution.

The computation of a filter, which occurs inside the data propagation stage or inside the changes in content stage, is divided in three main stages:

- Data gathering: All information generated in a certain time interval is collected. This stage is considered a preprocessing stage, in which filters select and manipulate the information they have received, in order to prepare for the next stage.

- Processing: In this stage a filter executes, given the collected input information and its internal state. Output information is generated, but not propagated

- Output propagation: Output information is propagated to all interested filters.

This model allows the parallel execution of filters, if the required computational resources are available.

Design and Execution of InTml Applications

By means of our IDE, an application is created by instantiating the appropriate filter classes. Filters may come from the predefined libraries of classes, organized by the three main categories: objects, devices, and behaviors. Developers can also add their own libraries of filter classes, if necessary, by creating the abstract description of each filter class (name, input and output ports). Figure shows the application view the InTml IDE, that allows designers to load new libraries, create new filter instances, constants, filter holders, or links between filters. Figure shows the library editor that allows the definition of new filter classes, by means of the specification of its input and output ports. This editor also allows code generation for each filter class in each one of the run-time environments Applications can be run inside the IDE with the common method in eclipse, by the `Run As...` wizard.

The library of filter classes has been designed with reusability in mind, from a subset of interaction techniques presented in Bowman. However, this requires rethinking applications to an order that maximizes reuse. For example, figure shows a version of the application, with maximum reuse and extra functionality in mind. The trackerdevice receives a configuration string and outputs streams of positions and orientations, from all tracker elements it may have. The handSelector and headSelector filters separate from these streams the trackers with ids 0 and 1, and values from those devices can be transformed (i.e. moved, rotated, or scales) at handOffset and headOffset.

The output of these two filters transform a virtualHand object and the system's camera. The scene filter loads and separates objects from an input file, and some of them are identified for selection at objectsForSelection. Finally, collision receives the virtualHand and the objects for selection and outputs objects that are collided by the virtual hand, which are visually enhanced by feedback. This diagram may be reduced to the one in figure, by encapsulating tracker, handSelector, and handOffset into a composite filter, by eliminating the filters involved in camera movement, and by making explicit the console filter.

IDE Development

Our current IDE is based in the concepts of Model Driven Architecture by Stahl and

Veolter and Software Product Lines by Clements and Northrop; and it uses technologies such as The Eclipse Foundation's IDE for the basic but extendable environment, EMF and GMF as frameworks inside eclipse for the visual programming environment and the openArchitectureWare.org's oAW for code generation in Java, ActionScript, and C++. This IDE has been developed as follows: first, an eCore3 model of InTml is developed. Such model includes model constraints that help designers to identify errors during development. Then, graphic elements, graphic tools, and interface code are defined for the core model, as it is required by GMF. Based on this output, oAW's templates and constraints are defined in order to generate code for the targeted platforms. It is interesting to notice that both GMF and oAW provide mechanisms for constraint description, which provide a better interface and error feedback to designers. A side effect of this last development is a change in the final XML format for an InTml application: Initially we had defined our own format and DTD. With this final development, we have to use the XML format generated by GMF. This is a minor issue, since the visual programming environment provides a much better experience to designers than our previous XML editor.

During development we have performed two usability tests, the first one with VR developers and the second with non-programmers. In the first test we showed our IDE to 4 students with previous experience in VR development. Subjects received a short introduction to the IDE, see how a small example was developed, and were asked to answer some questions regarding the interface. Those comments were used in order to produce and improved version. In the second experiment 26 graduate students in an extension course of our Arts Department received training in InTml, and produced two designs in which they could optionally use our IDE. Finally, they were asked to fill a questionnaire about InTml's ease of learning, IDE's feedback, restrictions, consistency, and functionality. After 9 hours of exposure, they found InTml easy to learn, although some problems in understanding the execution model were detected. We believe this is due to the lack of experience they had with the actual application in execution, since they were required to design an application, not to execute it. In terms of the IDE they found issues with feedback, which are part of further changes to the environment.

Example of InTml's Operational Semantics

We have developed in the Z formal notation by Spivey a language and platform independent description of the InTml model. We describe in such a notation the concept of a filter, how filters can be composed of filters that hide complexity, how filters process information at any time step, how information gets propagated thoughout a dataflow of filters, and controlled ways to change the dataflow at runtime. The details of the formal description are mentioned in Figueroa et al. Although this description requires a good understanding of Z as a formal language and in consequence it may not be suited for general communication of the InTml capabilities, it is very precise and programming–language neutral. In particular, it has been used as blueprints for both C++ and Java implementations. Here we show with an example the main features that such a model gives to our VR applications. It is possible to find this description plus some motivations for this model.

Figure shows an example of a state of an InTml application in a particular time step, in which we consider H an object holder, E and F two content objects. This example shows the following features of an InTml application during execution:

- A filter can have several input and output ports, which may or may not be connected to other filters. In this way, filters can be reused in different scenarios without common restrictions imposed by standard function calls, which parameters are always mandatory.

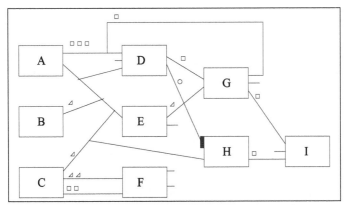

A Time Step in an InTml Application. By convention,
events are propagated from left to right.

- Different filter types such as devices, interactive content, and behavior are first class citizens of this description. Apart from the details already described in the execution of object holders and content objects, all filters seem equal from the design point of view.

- A time step defines a lapse of time in which all events from input devices are considered simultaneous. If A, B, and C are devices, all events they generate during such a small lapse of time will be processed together, no matter the particular generation rates from each device. In this example, A has generated three events in one of its output ports, B just one, and C outputs five events in total.

- Cycles are allowed in the description of an application, but they are broken for the execution of a time step. In the case of this example, the cycle DGD is broken and treated in a special way, i.e. delaying events from G to D to the next time step.

- Filters execute at most once in a time step, and the information they produce is considered simultaneous. A topological sort can be used in order to find a sequential execution order, i.e. ADBCEGHFI in the example. Such an order could be paralelized in the subsets [{A, B, C}, {D, E, F}, {G, H}, {I}], without any effect on the inputs and outputs of each filter. In this regard, InTml guarantees a consistent execution no matter the number of execution threads.

- An object holder has a special input port that allows to replace the contained object (i.e. the connection from D to H will provide objects to be contained in H). Events received in other ports are propagated to the contained object (i.e. events from C to H), and events generated from the contained object are propagated to registered filters (i.e. events from H to I).

- Since content objects can be related in structures that are not evident from the InTml dataflow (i.e. in a scene graph), which may require rule checking and change validation, and since content objects can be queried by several filters in the dataflow, all changes in objects are queued until the end of a time step. For example, E, F, and the object inside H could be parts of the same animated avatar, which have to fulfill certain rules and restrictions in its movements. Again in our example, this means that although all filters will execute at most once in a time step, output events from E and H will be delayed one step. and the entire dataflow will require two frames of execution in order to execute each filter at least once.

Development Process

Our development process is depicted in figure. We divide tasks between two roles: a designer and a developer. A designer is a novice or non-programmer that is interested in developing novel applications based on a set of predefined filters. A developer is a programmer that knows how to create novel filters and novel applications, or it could also be a support asset for a designer that requires to implement novel filter classes. We show here how we used this process from a designer's point of view for a family of applications described at Figueroa et al., a matching test that shows three objects and three copies of such objects, to be executed in four VR hardware setups.

- Identify application goals: We identify the set of use cases that the application has to fulfill: In this example it could be to select an object, move an object to the position and orientation of its copy, remove matched objects, define an initial state for objects, and save chronology of interesting events.

- Describe application requirements in InTml documents: For this stage we define a dataflow that fulfills all goals. We have found that it is more readable for designers to make one dataflow per goal, with cross references between them. Each dataflow is a subset of the entire application, and it is called a Task View. We do not show here the task views for this application.

- Are current libraries enough: Members of this family of applications were consecutively developed. The first application of this family was developed from scratch, so there was no library at that time and all filters were application dependant. From this version on, each new application adapted existing filters in order to make them more reusable, or created new ones when necessary. In this case, the entire set of tasks for developers were performed as part of this step.

- Check correctness in InTml documents: Basic checking of InTml documents can be automatically done by tools: types and names of ports in instanced filters, type correspondence in port connections, or validity of filter classes, among other things. We have developed some tools in order to identify initial problems.

- Execute/Test InTml application: Once filter classes are implemented by developers, designers can run their design and test its usability. In our case we tested our prototypes with users from our staff, in order to identify improvements in their user interfaces.

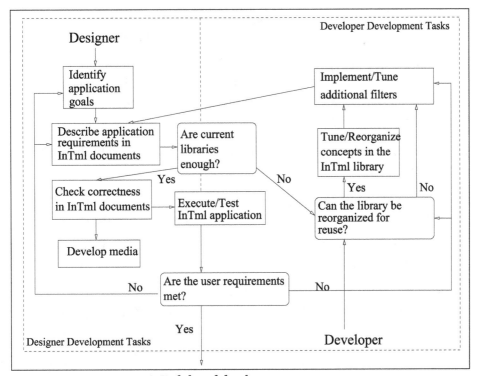

InTml–based development process.

- Develop media: If required, specific application media should be developed in this step. Since it is possible to use basic models as surrogates in initial stages of development, it is possible to delay this task until the end, or even make this task in parallel. In the case of our example, 3D objects were obtained from public repositories.

- Are the user requirements met: Once usability tests are performed, it is possible to identify improvements. Here such improvements are defined in terms of new goals, which are input for the new cycle in the development process.

Variability in Application Families

Variability is what makes different a set of applications with the same functionality but in different hardware setups. Variability's description in novel applications is very complex, due to the big variety of user types, devices, interaction techniques, visualization aids, frameworks, and libraries that may be used. We decided to ease development of non–programmers by dividing the variability spectrum in issues at the level of InTml language and issues at the level of the InTml implementation. An InTml family of applications consists of the following elements:

- A common set of basic types: Basic types in InTml are the equivalent of basic types in common programming languages, such as int or float. They have to be instantiated to available types in a particular InTml implementation.

- A library of filter types: Filter classes are reuse units. Such classes can use qualifiers in order to group them, in a similar way as packages can group Java classes.

- Applications: An InTml application is a set of interconnected instances of filter classes, constants and object holders. An application is divided in tasks, a subset of the application's dataflow. Each application can copy and redefine tasks from other applications in the family.

These elements allow us to address the following types of variability among applications in the same family:

- Devices: Each input and output device is represented by a filter in InTml, which may be instantiated or replaced in an application as desired.

- User types: Support for several user types is represented as different applications in the family, which may share common tasks.

- Interaction techniques: Developers can (and should) change the interaction techniques of a particular application depending on the type of user and devices in use. Such a change consists in the replacement of devices, behavior, or content related to a particular technique from one application to another. This replacement is feasible because filters clearly separate interaction techniques from the rest of the application.

Although also important, the following variation points in a MR application family are hidden from the InTml designer, and should be implemented one level below by an experienced programmer:

- Levels of detail and performance: A particular content could be shown at different levels of detail, depending on the capabilities of the available hardware. In the same way, a particular behavior could be adapted to the particular computational power of the underlying hardware.

- Context awareness: Devices could adapt their behavior to environmental factors, such as light conditions.

- Runtime adaptation: Several InTml applications can be combined in just one executable, which may switch between implementations depending on external factors such as user types.

- Particular APIs and frameworks: InTml can be implemented on top of a wide variety of APIs and frameworks, depending on the desired functionality at the high level and how convenient is to reuse a particular piece of software. A programmer should take into consideration reuse tradeoffs and integrate new elements when feasible.

This separation of variation points allows non–programmers to define by themselves their own prototypes, without special considerations about the InTml implementation. It is up to programmers at the InTml's implementation level to exercise low level variations.

Example:

We show now examples of how application families can be designed by highlighting three main concepts: The design of an application in terms of Task Views, the variability of a task among several applications in a family, and the basic software support for a prototype of a MR platform.

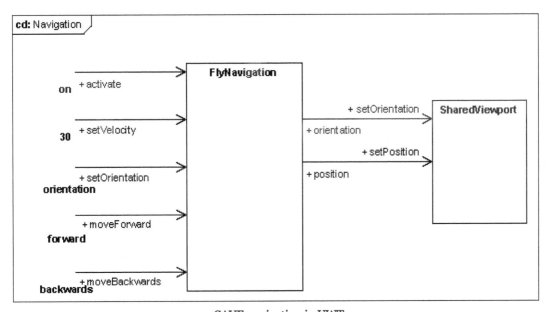

CAVE navigation in VWT.

Client for a Virtual Steering Application

We are collaborating in the development of heterogeneous and distributed clients for a virtual wind tunnel (VWT), that uses massive paralelism and fast algorithms for computational fluid dynamics by Boulanger et al. figures show InTml diagrams for the following tasks: navigation in a CAVE environment, sharing viewpoints between clients, and control from a bluetooth–enable device. This application is going to be implemented in the following environments: a personal environment with a HMD and a

Phantom, a Geowall–like environment, and a CAVE–like environment. Figures apply to all implementations, while figure defines the navigation technique in a CAVE.

Navigation in a CAVE environment uses a simple flying metaphor, in which a head tracker defines move direction, and wand buttons move backwards and forwards.

Shared Viewpoint in figure describes the task of sharing a representation of a user's viewpoint to all clients in a simulation. It shows the local viewpoint (SharedViewport) and how it is added to a pull of viewports, managed by ViewportManager. The implementation of this last filter handles the required networking, and the avatars' representation.

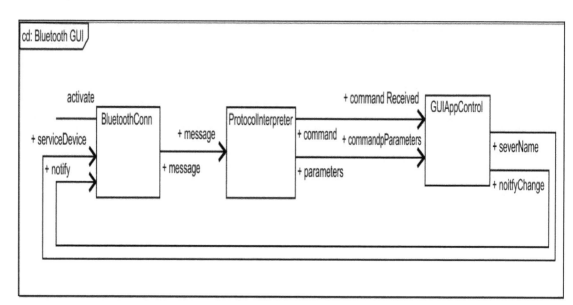

VWT control from a bluetooth device.

Finally, we have a PDA with a bluetooth connection, that allows us to send commands to the control of the application, represented by GUIAppControl in figure.

Navigation Tasks in a Family

We are interested in navigating and showing information about objects in a small but complex VR office, in three hardware platforms: a CAVE, a PC with a joystick, and a cell phone with graphics acceleration. If we concentrate on the navigation task, it is possible to think on interesting and different implementations for such a task in each platform, as follows:

- In a CAVE, a user can navigate to an interesting object by pointing to such an object and selecting it. The system should compute a path from the current viewpoint position to a position in front of such an object. This technique is similar to Fixed–Object Manipulation in, with extra behavior for path planning.

- In a PC with a joystick, a navigation technique that resembles the WALK mode in VRML could be used (P2D2NavInPlane). This mode features collision detection between the avatar and objects in the environment.

- In a cell phone, due to computation restrictions and limitations on the input device, it is more convenient to select pre–recorded viewpoints and paths than using the previous navigation techniques. It could be also important to reduce the complexity of the scene as possible.

The InTml diagrams of such navigation techniques.

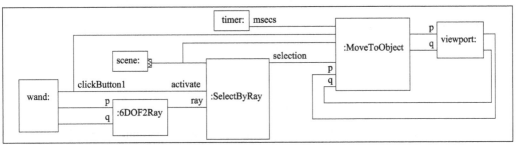

Navigation in a Cave.

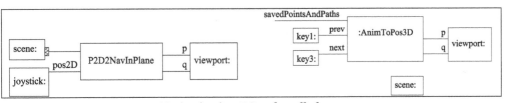

Navigation in a PC and a cell phone.

Software Support for a new MR Platform

We are developing an integrated MR platform based on the ARToolkit and VRPN, and we are designing a set of reusable filter classes as an API for developers. Such an API will facilitate development to a family of applications in that particular domain, and corresponds to the concept of core assets in the Software Product Line literature such as Clements and Northrop. Figures show some of the current set of platform-independent filter types, which correspond the following functionality:

- MappedVRPNTracker, which gives 6DOF data from an identified pattern and a definition of its local coordinate system.

- Switch, which sends as output one of the predefined inputs once a signal is received.

- Scene, which allows to select and copy an object by giving an id.

- Map2DtoTerrain, which outputs a 3D position over a terrain from a 2D one.

- Collision, which identify a collision between two objects.

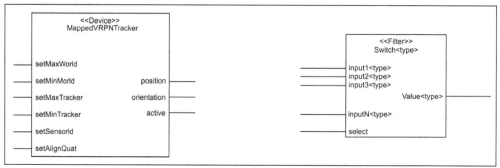

A tracker for ARToolkit patterns and a switch filter.

These filters were identified in a study of three concepts in interior design, and we plan to validate this API with other applications.

References

- 5-types-virtual-reality-affect-the-future-4030: datafloq.com, Retrieved 26 April, 2020

- Shih, Y.-H., & Liu, M. (2007). The importance of emotional usability. Journal of Educational Technology Usability, 36(2), 203–218

- 3-benefits-virtual-reality: livetiles.nyc, Retrieved 08 June, 2020

- 10-great-tools-for-vr-development: devteam.space, Retrieved 11 August, 2020

- Virtual-reality, vr-development-with-intml: intechopen.com, Retrieved 05 May, 2020

2
Types of Virtual Reality

There are three major types of virtual reality that are used to transform the world. It includes non-immersive, semi-immersive and fully-immersive simulations. This chapter has been carefully written to provide an easy understanding of these types of virtual reality.

Immersive

Immersive virtual reality (immersive VR) is the presentation of an artificial environment that replaces users' real-world surroundings convincingly enough that they are able to suspend disbelief and fully engage with the created environment. Immersiveness is an important element of virtual reality applications, such as VR gaming and VR therapy.

Immersiveness is usually considered on a scale or along a continuum, from least immersive to fully immersive. Typically, user engagement will vary accordingly, although to some extent dependent on individual differences. An inadequately immersive environment will not engage the user, while one that completely replicated the real world could have unpredictable psychological effects. To date, the latter scenario is not an issue because that level of immersiveness has not been achieved.

Elements of virtual environments that increase the immersiveness of the experience:

- Continuity of surroundings: The user must be able to look around in all directions and have continuity of the environment.

- Conformance to human vision: Visual content must conform to elements that allow humans to understand their environments, so that, for example, objects in the distance are sized appropriately to our understanding of their size and distance from us. Motion parallax ensures that our view of objects changes appropriately as our perspective changes.

- Freedom of movement: It's important that the user can move about normally within the confines of the environment. That capacity can be achieved in room-scale

VR and dedicated VR rooms but requires complicated hardware for stationary VR and is impossible for seated VR.

- Physical interaction: A user should be able to interact with objects in the virtual environment similarly to the way they do with real life ones. Data gloves, for example, can allow the user to make motions like pushing or turning to interact with objects in a natural way – turning a doorknob or picking up a book.

- Physical feedback: The user should receive haptic feedback to replicate the feel of real-world interaction. So, for example, when a user turns a doorknob, they not only replicate the movement but experience the feeling of having that object in their hand.

- Narrative engagement: The user should have the ability to decide the flow of the narrative. The environment should include cues that lead the user to create interesting developments.

- 3D audio: For immersiveness, VR environments should be able to replicate natural positioning of sounds relative to people and objects in the environment and the position of the user's head.

Non-immersive

Non-immersive VR is a type of the virtual reality technology that provides users with a computer-generated environment without a feeling of being immersed in the virtual world. The main characteristic of a non-immersive VR system is that users can keep control over physical surrounding while being aware of what's going on around them: sounds, visuals, and haptics.

Non-immersive virtual reality systems rely on a computer or video game console, display, and input devices like keyboards, mice, and controllers. Unlike semi-immersive VR based on hard simulators also known as cockpits, gaming non-immersive VR systems also can use racing wheels, pedals, and speed shifters to provide users with an enhanced gaming experience. Using various input devices, users can interact with digital content on a display.

Fully Immersive VR vs Non-immersive VR

The main difference between immersive and non-immersive virtual reality is in the 3D content delivery method. Fully immersive virtual reality is a realistic simulation technology that enables users to interact with a 3D virtual environment with special haptic devices. Unlike non-immersive VR based on typical displays, fully immersive VR provides computer-generated surroundings via head-mounted displays (HMDs) that isolate users from the real world. Thus, they become unaware of physical objects and sounds.

VR headsets have two displays that generate digital content on each user's eye separately. It ensures a binocular image perceived as a real-world environment. HMDs have built-in head tracking systems that can determine the orientation of the user's head to ensure the interactivity of a virtual world. These systems provide a sense of presence within VR environments and allow users to feel engaged in it like in a physical environment.

Non-immersive virtual reality is the least immersive and interactive type of immersive technologies. Instead of VR headsets, it uses a single display to provide computer-generated content. In order to ensure an additional level of immersion, some video games provide a first-person view for players to associate themselves with their game avatar.

One of the significant differences between fully immersive and non-immersive VR technologies lays in digital content perception. Unlike fully immersive virtual reality, non-immersive VR transmits the same image for both users' eyes. Therefore, users perceive this image only in two dimensions: height and width while fully immersive VR technology provides a digital image perceived in three dimensions that include height, width, and depth.

Example:

Like augmented and mixed reality technologies, virtual reality has a wide range of possible applications in various industries. The list of non-immersive VR examples is obviously shorter, but it still brings valuable benefits to sectors like gaming, healthcare, and design.

Gaming

A video game is one of the most representative examples of non-immersive virtual reality. Players experience a virtual environment, which can either be unreal or duplicate a real-world city, country, or a specific location, through a TV or computer display. Within a video game, users can interact with virtual objects or other playable characters using a keyboard and mouse. Some online video games like The Elder Scrolls Online enable users to interact with other players' avatars within a computer-generated environment.

Healthcare

VR technologies are currently much more than just gaming and entertainment. Within the last decade, they have become an innovative instrument used in medical research studies. Immersive techniques have turned out to be effective techniques capable to replace or at least decrease the need for taking medicines in order to reduce physical pain or improve patient's psychological health without any interventions.

A study conducted by scientists from medical universities located in Canada and Iran showed that the use of non-immersive virtual reality can significantly reduce pain on a molecular level. The researchers used the functional magnetic resonance imaging system to track how patients perceive pain caused by high temperature while experiencing non-immersive VR. Their results revealed that virtual reality reduced the subjective pain perception as well as decreased the activity of involved brain regions.

Furthermore, the final report showed that watching a movie or playing a video game in a typical way deals with the subjective pain reduction in a more efficient way compared to the use of computer-generated environments transmitted via a head-mounted display. Therefore, non-immersive virtual reality turned out to be even more effective than fully immersive VR when it comes to pain reduction.

Watching a Movie

During the above-mentioned experiment, researchers asked both male and female patients to watch a movie in 2D and 3D. Their results showed that male patients experienced a lower level of pain and unpleasantness when watching a 3D video while women felt less pain due to watching a 2D video. Moreover, the second group needed a significantly lower dose of sedative medication required to kill their acute pain while enjoying a movie than before.

Playing a Game

Rehabilitation is an intensive and time-consuming task that requires a lot of efforts from both patients and medical specialists. The destination of any rehabilitation is a successful recovery after a disease or injury. However, a full health recovery can be impossible because of the negative impact of the patient's trauma. In this case, therapists strive to ensure patients to be able to live a full and minimize the effect of the injury or disease in the long-term perspective.

The rehabilitation process also requires repetitive and goal-oriented measures to improve cortical reorganization and motor function of patients with either acute or chronic pain. So British scientists from Cambridge University created a non-immersive VR rehabilitation system based on the Unity engine. They developed a video game that helps patients recover faster and in a more enjoyable way compared to traditional physical exercises.

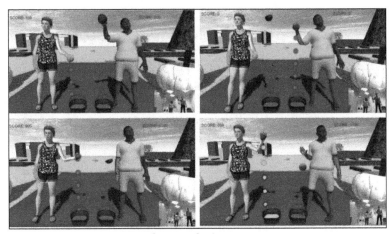

ReHubgame playing process.

When playing ReHabgame, patients virtually reach and catch fruits appeared in the computer-generated environment. Then they release these fruits above the 3D basket in order to gain points. This game uses Microsoft Kinect, a motion sensing input device that tracks user movements. Therefore, players have to move their arms in a specific way to perform the necessary manipulations in the game.

The use of Kinect controllers allows patients to undergo rehabilitation at home without the need for visiting a therapist at the clinic. Furthermore, using a video game as a means of a recovery measure increases patient's motivation to keep performing physical exercises thus retaining their adherence. By presenting points for correct manipulations, the game encourages players to improve their results thus speeding up the rehabilitation process.

The non-immersive virtual reality system also allows therapists to monitor patient progress in the game. Medical specialists can check the number of points gained by players. As a result, a therapist can adjust the overall rehabilitation program and provide individual recommendations to make it more efficient for each particular patient. This game-based therapy ensures a suitable physical and mental engagement using visual feedback during each rehabilitation session.

Design

Designers used to manually draw their prototypes using a pencil and paper. Many automotive designers still use these old-school methods to inspire themselves and quickly visualize their idea. At the next stage of the development process, non-immersive VR comes into action. This technology is now widely used in design and prototyping.

By creating a 3D image of any item, designers can better visualize what they want to build thus providing other experts like engineers with detailed visual information of what they need to assemble. Both designers and engineers use special software to develop prototypes. Autodesk software is one of the most popular prototyping tools. For example, architects can use ArchiCAD to design buildings while automotive designers from Nissan and Aston Martin use such tools as Alias, VRED, and Maya.

Despite being the least immersive type of virtual reality, non-immersive VR brings significant benefits to various industries like healthcare and design. In medicine, this technology reveals to be an effective alternative of conventional pain reduction therapy while designers can use it for visualizing purposes. However, non-immersive VR has gained its popularity through gaming where players can experience virtual environments as well as interact with them using various input devices.

Augmented Reality

Augmented reality (AR) is an interactive experience of a real-world environment where the objects that reside in the real world are enhanced by computer-generated perceptual information, sometimes across multiple sensory modalities, including visual, auditory, haptic, somatosensory and olfactory. An augogram is a computer generated image that is used to create AR. Augography is the science and practice of making augograms for AR. AR can be defined as a system that fulfills three basic features: a combination of real and virtual worlds, real-time interaction, and accurate 3D registration of virtual and real objects. The overlaid sensory information can be constructive (i.e. additive to the natural environment), or destructive (i.e. masking of the natural environment). This experience is seamlessly interwoven with the physical world such that it is perceived as an immersive aspect of the real environment. In this way, augmented reality alters one's ongoing perception of a real-world environment, whereas virtual reality completely replaces the user's real-world environment with a simulated one. Augmented reality is related to two largely synonymous terms: mixed reality and computer-mediated reality.

Virtual Fixtures – first AR system.

The primary value of augmented reality is the manner in which components of the digital world blend into a person's perception of the real world, not as a simple display of data, but through the integration of immersive sensations, which are perceived as natural parts of an environment. The earliest functional AR systems that provided

immersive mixed reality experiences for users were invented in the early 1990s, starting with the Virtual Fixtures system developed at the U.S. Air Force's Armstrong Laboratory in 1992. Commercial augmented reality experiences were first introduced in
entertainment and gaming businesses. Subsequently, augmented reality applications
have spanned commercial industries such as education, communications, medicine,
and entertainment. In education, content may be accessed by scanning or viewing an
image with a mobile device or by using markerless AR techniques. An example relevant
to the construction industry is an AR helmet for construction workers which displays
information about construction sites.

Augmented reality is used to enhance natural environments or situations and offer perceptually enriched experiences. With the help of advanced AR technologies (e.g. adding
computer vision, incorporating AR cameras into smartphone applications and object
recognition) the information about the surrounding real world of the user becomes interactive and digitally manipulated. Information about the environment and its objects
is overlaid on the real world. This information can be virtual or real, e.g. seeing other
real sensed or measured information such as electromagnetic radio waves overlaid in
exact alignment with where they actually are in space. Augmented reality also has a lot
of potential in the gathering and sharing of tacit knowledge. Augmentation techniques
are typically performed in real time and in semantic contexts with environmental elements. Immersive perceptual information is sometimes combined with supplemental
information like scores over a live video feed of a sporting event. This combines the
benefits of both augmented reality technology and heads up display technology (HUD).

Difference between Virtual Reality and Augmented Reality

In Virtual Reality (VR), the users' perception of reality is completely based on virtual
information. In Augmented Reality (AR) the user is provided with additional computer
generated information that enhances their perception of reality. For example, in architecture, VR can be used to create a walk-through simulation of the inside of a new
building; and AR can be used to show a building's structures and systems super-im-
posed on a real-life view. Another example is through the use of utility applications.
Some AR applications, such as Augment, enable users to apply digital objects into real
environments, allowing businesses to use augmented reality devices as a way to preview
their products in the real world. Similarly, it can also be used to demo what products
may look like in an environment for customers, as demonstrated by companies such as
Mountain Equipment Co-op or Lowe's who use augmented reality to allow customers
to preview what their products might look like at home through the use of 3D models.

Augmented Reality (AR) differs from Virtual Reality (VR) in the sense that in AR part
of the surrounding environment is actually 'real' and just adding layers of virtual objects to the real environment. On the other hand, in VR the surrounding environment
is completely virtual. A demonstration of how AR layers objects onto the real world
can be seen with augmented reality games. WallaMe is an augmented reality game

application that allows users to hide messages in real environments, utilizing geolocation technology in order to enable users to hide messages wherever they may wish in the world. Such applications have many uses in the world, including in activism and artistic expression.

Possible Applications

Augmented reality has been explored for many applications, from gaming and entertainment to medicine, education and business. Example application areas described below include archaeology, architecture, commerce and education. Some of the earliest cited examples include augmented reality used to support surgery by providing virtual overlays to guide medical practitioners, to AR content for astronomy and welding.

Archaeology

AR has been used to aid archaeological research. By augmenting archaeological features onto the modern landscape, AR allows archaeologists to formulate possible site configurations from extant structures. Computer generated models of ruins, buildings, landscapes or even ancient people have been recycled into early archaeological AR applications. For example, implementing a system like, VITA (Visual Interaction Tool for Archaeology) will allow users to imagine and investigate instant excavation results without leaving their home. Each user can collaborate by mutually "navigating, searching, and viewing data". Hrvoje Benko, a researcher in the computer science department at Columbia University, points out that these particular systems and others like them can provide "3D panoramic images and 3D models of the site itself at different excavation stages" all the while organizing much of the data in a collaborative way that is easy to use. Collaborative AR systems supply multimodal interactions that combine the real world with virtual images of both environments.

Architecture

AR can aid in visualizing building projects. Computer-generated images of a structure can be superimposed onto a real-life local view of a property before the physical building is constructed there; this was demonstrated publicly by Trimble Navigation in 2004. AR can also be employed within an architect's workspace, rendering animated 3D visualizations of their 2D drawings. Architecture sight-seeing can be enhanced with AR applications, allowing users viewing a building's exterior to virtually see through its walls, viewing its interior objects and layout.

With continual improvements to GPS accuracy, businesses are able to use augmented reality to visualize georeferenced models of construction sites, underground structures, cables and pipes using mobile devices. Augmented reality is applied to present new projects, to solve on-site construction challenges, and to enhance promotional materials. Examples include the Daqri Smart Helmet, an Android-powered hard hat used to create augmented reality for the industrial worker, including visual instructions, real-time alerts, and 3D mapping.

Following the Christchurch earthquake, the University of Canterbury released City View AR, which enabled city planners and engineers to visualize buildings that had been destroyed. This not only provided planners with tools to reference the previous cityscape, but it also served as a reminder of the magnitude of the resulting devastation, as entire buildings had been demolished.

STEM Education

In educational settings, AR has been used to complement a standard curriculum. Text, graphics, video, and audio may be superimposed into a student's real-time environment. Textbooks, flashcards and other educational reading material may contain embedded "markers" or triggers that, when scanned by an AR device, produced supplementary information to the student rendered in a multimedia format. 2015's Virtual, Augmented and Mixed Reality: 7th International Conference mentioned Google Glass as an example of augmented reality that can replace the physical classroom. First, AR technologies help learners engage in authentic exploration in the real world, and virtual objects such as texts, videos, and pictures are supplementary elements for learners to conduct investigations of the real-world surroundings. As AR evolves, students can participate interactively and interact with knowledge more authentically. Instead of remaining passive recipients, students can become active learners, able to interact with their learning environment. Computer-generated simulations of historical events allow students to explore and learning details of each significant area of the event site.

In higher education, Construct3D, a Studierstube system, allows students to learn mechanical engineering concepts, math or geometry. Chemistry AR apps allow students to visualize and interact with the spatial structure of a molecule using a marker object held in the hand. Others have used HP Reveal, a free app, to create AR notecards for studying organic chemistry mechanisms or to create virtual demonstrations of how to use laboratory instrumentation. Anatomy students can visualize different systems of the human body in three dimensions. Using AR as a tool to learn anatomical structures has been shown to increase the learner knowledge and provide intrinsic benefits, such as increased engagement and learner immersion.

Industrial Manufacturing

AR is used to substitute paper manuals with digital instructions which are overlaid on the manufacturing operator's field of view, reducing mental effort required to operate. AR makes machine maintenance efficient because it gives operators direct access to a machine's maintenance history. Virtual manuals help manufacturers adapt to rapidly-changing product designs, as digital instructions are more easily edited and distributed compared to physical manuals.

Digital instructions increase operator safety by removing the need for operators to look at a screen or manual away from the working area, which can be hazardous. Instead, the instructions are overlaid on the working area. The use of AR can increase operators' feeling of safety when working near high-load industrial machinery by giving operators additional information on a machine's status and safety functions, as well as hazardous areas of the workspace.

Commerce

AR is used to integrate print and video marketing. Printed marketing material can be designed with certain "trigger" images that, when scanned by an AR-enabled device using image recognition, activate a video version of the promotional material. A major difference between augmented reality and straightforward image recognition is that one can overlay multiple media at the same time in the view screen, such as social media share buttons, the in-page video even audio and 3D objects. Traditional print-only publications are using augmented reality to connect different types of media.

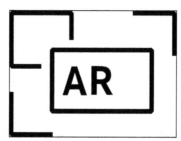

The AR-Icon can be used as a marker on print as well as on online media.
It signals the viewer that digital content is behind it. The content
can be viewed with a smartphone or tablet.

AR can enhance product previews such as allowing a customer to view what's inside a product's packaging without opening it. AR can also be used as an aid in selecting products from a catalog or through a kiosk. Scanned images of products can activate views of additional content such as customization options and additional images of the product in its use.

By 2010, virtual dressing rooms had been developed for e-commerce.

In 2012, a mint used AR techniques to market a commemorative coin for Aruba. The coin itself was used as an AR trigger, and when held in front of an AR-enabled device it revealed additional objects and layers of information that were not visible without the device.

In 2018, Apple announced USDZ AR file support for iPhones and iPads with iOS12. Apple has created an AR QuickLook Gallery that allows masses to experience augmented reality on their own Apple device.

In 2018, Shopify, the Canadian e-commerce company, announced ARkit2 integration. Their merchants are able to use the tools to upload 3D models of their products. Users will be able to tap on the goods inside Safari to view in their real-world environments.

In 2018, Twinkl released a free AR classroom application. Pupils can see how York looked over 1,900 years ago. Twinkl launched the first ever multi-player AR game, Little Red and has over 100 free AR educational models.

Augmented reality is becoming more frequently used for online advertising. Retailers offer the ability to upload a picture on their website and "try on" various clothes which are overlaid on the picture. Even further, companies such as Bodymetrics install dressing booths in department stores that offer full-body scanning. These booths render a 3-D model of the user, allowing the consumers to view different outfits on themselves without the need of physically changing clothes. For example, JC Penney and Bloomingdale's use "virtual dressing rooms" that allow customers to see themselves in clothes without trying them on. Another store that uses AR to market clothing to its customers is Neiman Marcus. Neiman Marcus offers consumers the ability to see their outfits in a 360-degree view with their "memory mirror". Makeup stores like L'Oreal, Sephora, Charlotte Tilbury, and Rimmel also have apps that utilize AR. These apps allow consumers to see how the makeup will look on them. According to Greg Jones, director of AR and VR at Google, augmented reality is going to "reconnect physical and digital retail".

AR technology is also used by furniture retailers such as IKEA, Houzz, and Wayfair. These retailers offer apps that allow consumers to view their products in their home prior to purchasing anything. In 2017, Ikea announced the Ikea Place app. It contains a catalogue of over 2,000 products—nearly the company's full collection of sofas, armchairs, coffee tables, and storage units which one can place anywhere in a room with their phone. The app made it possible to have 3D and true-to-scale models of furniture in the customer's living space. IKEA realized that their customers are not shopping in stores as often or making direct purchases anymore.

Literature

The first description of AR as it is known today was in Virtual Light, the 1994 novel by William Gibson. AR was blended with poetry by ni ka from Sekai Camera in Tokyo, Japan. The prose of these AR poems come from Paul Celan, Die Niemandsrose, expressing the aftermath of the 2011 Tōhoku earthquake and tsunami.

An example of an AR code containing a QR code.

Visual Art

AR applied in the visual arts allows objects or places to trigger artistic multidimensional experiences and interpretations of reality.

10.000 Moving Cities.

Augmented reality can aid in the progression of visual art in museums by allowing museum visitors to view artwork in galleries in a multidimensional way through their phone screens. The Museum of Modern Art in New York has created an exhibit in their art museum showcasing AR features that viewers can see using an app on their smartphone. The museum has developed their personal app, called MoMAR Gallery, that museum guests can download and use in the Augmented Reality specialized gallery in order to view the museum's paintings in a different way. This allows individuals to see hidden aspects and information about the paintings, and to be able to have an interactive technological experience with artwork as well.

AR technology was also used in two of the public art pieces in the 2019 Desert X exhibition.

AR technology aided the development of eye tracking technology to translate a disabled person's eye movements into drawings on a screen.

Mixed Reality

Mixed reality (MR) is the merging of real and virtual worlds to produce new environments and visualizations, where physical and digital objects co-exist and interact in real time. Mixed reality does not exclusively take place in either the physical or virtual world, but is a hybrid of reality and virtual reality, encompassing both augmented reality and augmented virtuality via immersive technology.

The first immersive mixed reality system that provided enveloping sight, sound, and touch was the Virtual Fixtures platform, which was developed in 1992 at the Armstrong

Laboratories of the United States Air Force. The project demonstrated that human performance could be significantly amplified, by overlaying spatially registered virtual objects on top of a person's direct view of a real physical environment.

An example of mixed reality, showing virtual
characters mixed into a real-world live stream.

Mixed reality refers to a continuum that encompasses both virtual reality (VR) and augmented reality (AR):

- Virtual reality immerses users in a fully artificial digital environment.

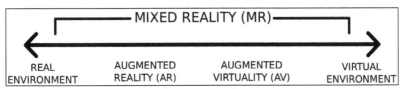

The reality-virtuality continuum.

- Augmented reality overlays virtual objects on the real-world environment with spatial registration that enables geometric persistence concerning placement and orientation within the real world. Prior technologies that overlaid data or images not spatially registered to real-world geometries are referred to as heads-up display technologies.

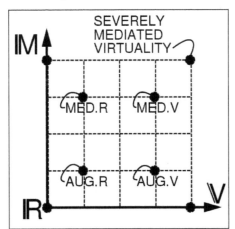

Mediated reality continuum (horizontal axis: virtuality; vertical axis: mediality). Four points are
shown for augmented reality, augmented virtuality, mediated reality, and mediated virtuality.

Virtuality Continuum and Mediality Continuum

In 1994, Paul Milgram and Fumio Kishino defined a mixed reality as "anywhere between the extrema of the virtuality continuum" (VC), where the virtuality continuum extends from the completely real through to the completely virtual environment, with augmented reality and augmented virtuality ranging between. The first fully immersive mixed reality system was the Virtual Fixtures platform, which was developed in 1992 by Louis Rosenberg at the Armstrong Laboratories of the United States Air Force. It enabled human users to control robots in real-world environments that included real physical objects and 3D virtual overlays ("fixtures") that were added enhance human performance of manipulation tasks. Published studies showed that by introducing virtual objects into the real world, significant performance increases could be achieved by human operators.

The continuum of mixed reality is one of the two axes in Steve Mann's concept of mediated reality as implemented by various welding helmets, wearable computers, and wearable photographic systems he created in the 1970s and early 1980s. The second axis was the mediality continuum, which includes Diminished Reality, such as implemented in a welding helmet or eyeglasses that can block out advertising or replace real-world ads with useful information.

"The conventionally held view of a Virtual Reality (VR) environment is one in which the participant-observer is immersed in, and able to interact with, a completely synthetic world. Such a world may mimic the properties of some real-world environments, either existing or fictional; however, it can also exceed the bounds of physical reality by creating a world in which the physical laws ordinarily governing space, time, mechanics, material properties, etc. no longer hold. What may be overlooked in this view, however, is that the VR label is also frequently used in association with a variety of other environments, to which total immersion and complete synthesis do not necessarily pertain, but which fall somewhere along a virtuality continuum. In this paper, we focus on a particular subclass of VR related technologies that involve the merging of real and virtual worlds, which we refer to generically as Mixed Reality (MR)."

Interreality Physics

In a physics context, the term "interreality system" refers to a virtual reality system coupled with its real-world counterpart. An interreality system comprising a real physical pendulum coupled to a pendulum that only exists in virtual reality. This system has two stable states of motion: a "Dual Reality" state in which the motion of the two pendula are uncorrelated, and a "Mixed Reality" state in which the pendula exhibit stable phase-locked motion, which is highly correlated. The use of the terms "mixed reality" and "interreality" is clearly defined in the context of physics, but may be slightly different in other fields.

Mixed Reality

Augmented virtuality (AV) is a subcategory of mixed reality that refers to the merging of real-world objects into virtual worlds.

A person is in a virtual environment, with a
camera acting as a third-person point of view.

As an intermediate case in the virtuality continuum, it refers to predominantly virtual spaces, where physical elements (such as physical objects or people) are dynamically integrated into and can interact with the virtual world in real time. This integration is achieved with the use of various techniques, such as streaming video from physical spaces, like through a webcam, or using the 3D digitalization of physical objects.

The use of real-world sensor information, such as gyroscopes, to control a virtual environment is an additional form of augmented virtuality, in which external inputs provide context for the virtual view.

Applications

Mixed reality has been used in applications across fields including art, entertainment, and military training.

Interactive Product Content Management (IPCM)

Moving from static product catalogs to interactive 3D smart digital replicas, this solution consists of application software products with scalable license models.

Simulation-based Learning (SBL)

Moving from e-learning to s-learning, simulation-based learning includes VR-based training and interactive, experiential learning. This also includes software and display solutions with scalable licensed curriculum development model.

Military Training

Combat reality is simulated and represented in complex, layered data through HMD. Military training solutions are often built on commercial off-the-shelf (COTS) technologies, such as Virtual Battlespace 3 and VirTra, both of which are used by the United States Army. As of 2018, VirTra is being used by both civilian and military law enforcement to train personnel in a variety of scenarios, including active shooter, domestic violence, and military traffic stops. Mixed reality technologies have been used by the United States Army Research Laboratory to study how this stress affects decision-making. With mixed reality, researchers may safely study military personnel in scenarios where soldiers would not likely survive.

In 2017, the U.S. Army was developing the Synthetic Training Environment (STE), a collection of technologies for training purposes that was expected to include mixed reality. As of 2018, STE was still in development without a projected completion date. Some recorded goals of STE included enhancing realism and increasing simulation training capabilities and STE availability to other systems.

It was claimed that mixed-reality environments like STE could reduce training costs, such as reducing the amount of ammunition expended during training. In 2018, it was reported that STE would include representation of any part of the world's terrain for training purposes. STE would offer a variety of training opportunities for squad brigade and combat teams, including Stryker, armory, and infantry teams. STE is expected to eventually replace the U.S. Army's Live, Virtual, Constructive – Integrated Architecture (LVC-IA).

Remote Working

Mixed reality allows a global workforce of remote teams to work together and tackle an organization's business challenges. No matter where they are physically located, an employee can wear a headset and noise-canceling headphones and enter a collaborative, immersive virtual environment. As these applications can accurately translate in real time, language barriers become irrelevant. This process also increases flexibility.

While many employers still use inflexible models of fixed working time and location, there is evidence that employees are more productive if they have greater autonomy over where, when, and how they work. Some employees prefer loud work environments, while others need silence. Some work best in the morning; others work best at night. Employees also benefit from autonomy in how they work because of different ways of processing information. The classic model for learning styles differentiates between visual, auditory, and kinesthetic learners.

Machine maintenance can also be executed with the help of mixed reality. Larger companies with multiple manufacturing locations and a lot of machinery can use mixed reality to educate and instruct their employees. The machines need regular check-ups and have to be adjusted every now and then. These adjustments are mostly done by humans, so employees need to be informed about needed adjustments. By using mixed reality, employees from multiple locations can wear headsets and receive live instructions about the changes. Instructors can operate the representation that every employee sees, and can glide through the production area, zooming in to technical details and explaining every change needed. Employees completing a five-minute training session with such a mixed-reality program has been shown to yield the same results as reading a 50-page training manual.

Functional Mockup

Mixed reality can be used to build mockups that combine physical and digital elements. With the use of simultaneous localization and mapping (SLAM), mockups can interact with the physical world to utilize features like object permanence.

Consciousness

It has been hypothesized that a hybrid of mixed and virtual reality could pave the way for human consciousness to be transferred into a digital form entirely—a concept known as Virternity, which would leverage blockchain to create its main platform.

Medical

Mixed reality can combine smartglasses with surgical processes.

Simulated Reality

Simulated reality is the hypothesis that reality could be simulated—for example by quantum computer simulation—to a degree indistinguishable from "true" reality. It could contain conscious minds which may or may not be fully aware that they are living inside a simulation.

This is quite different from the current, technologically achievable concept of virtual reality. Virtual reality is easily distinguished from the experience of actuality; participants are never in doubt about the nature of what they experience. Simulated reality, by contrast, would be hard or impossible to separate from "true" reality. There has been much debate over this topic, ranging from philosophical discourse to practical applications in computing.

Simulation Argument

A version of the simulation hypothesis was first theorised as a part of a philosophical argument on the part of René Descartes, and later by Hans Moravec. The philosopher Nick Bostrom developed an expanded argument examining the probability of our reality being a simulation. His argument states that at least one of the following statements is very likely to be true:

- Human civilization or a comparable civilization is unlikely to reach a level of technological maturity capable of producing simulated realities or such simulations are physically impossible to construct.

- A comparable civilization reaching aforementioned technological status will likely not produce a significant number of simulated realities (one that might push the probable existence of digital entities beyond the probable number of "real" entities in a Universe) for any of a number of reasons, such as diversion of computational processing power for other tasks, ethical considerations of holding entities captive in simulated realities, etc.

- Any entities with our general set of experiences are almost certainly living in a simulation.

- We are living in a reality in which posthumans have not developed yet and we are actually living in reality.

Bostrom's argument rests on the premise that given sufficiently advanced technology, it is possible to represent the populated surface of the Earth without recourse to digital physics; that the qualia experienced by a simulated consciousness are comparable or equivalent to those of a naturally occurring human consciousness, and that one or more levels of simulation within simulations would be feasible given only a modest expenditure of computational resources in the real world.

If one assumes first that humans will not be destroyed nor destroy themselves before developing such a technology, and that human descendants will have no overriding legal restrictions or moral compunctions against simulating biospheres or their own historical biosphere, then, Bostrom argues, it would be unreasonable to count ourselves among the small minority of genuine organisms who, sooner or later, will be vastly outnumbered by artificial simulations.

Epistemologically, it is not impossible to tell whether we are living in a simulation. For example, Bostrom suggests that a window could pop up saying: "You are living in a simulation. Click here for more information." However, imperfections in a simulated environment might be difficult for the native inhabitants to identify and for purposes of authenticity, even the simulated memory of a blatant revelation might be purged programmatically. Nonetheless, should any evidence come to light, either for or against the skeptical hypothesis, it would radically alter the aforementioned probability.

Computationalism

Computationalism is a philosophy of mind theory stating that cognition is a form of computation. It is relevant to the Simulation hypothesis in that it illustrates how a simulation could contain conscious subjects, as required by a "virtual people" simulation. For example, it is well known that physical systems can be simulated to some degree of accuracy. If computationalism is correct and if there is no problem in generating artificial consciousness or cognition, it would establish the theoretical possibility of a simulated reality. Nevertheless, the relationship between cognition and phenomenal qualia of consciousness is disputed. It is possible that consciousness requires a vital substrate that a computer cannot provide and that simulated people, while behaving appropriately, would be philosophical zombies. This would undermine Nick Bostrom's simulation argument; we cannot be a simulated consciousness, if consciousness, as we know it, cannot be simulated. The skeptical hypothesis remains intact, however, and we could still be envatted brains, existing as conscious beings within a simulated environment, even if consciousness cannot be simulated. It has been suggested that whereas virtual reality would enable a participant to experience only three senses (sight, sound and optionally smell), simulated reality would enable all five (including taste and touch).

Some theorists have argued that if the "consciousness-is-computation" version of computationalism and mathematical realism (or radical mathematical Platonism) are true then consciousnesses is computation, which in principle is platform independent and thus admits of simulation. This argument states that a "Platonic realm" or ultimate ensemble would contain every algorithm, including those which implement consciousness. Hans Moravec has explored the simulation hypothesis and has argued for a kind of mathematical Platonism according to which every object (including, for example, a stone) can be regarded as implementing every possible computation.

Dreaming

A dream could be considered a type of simulation capable of fooling someone who is asleep. As a result, the "dream hypothesis" cannot be ruled out, although it has been argued that common sense and considerations of simplicity rule against it. One of the first philosophers to question the distinction between reality and dreams was Zhuangzi, a Chinese philosopher from the 4th century BC. He phrased the problem as the well-known "Butterfly Dream," which went as follows:

> "Once Zhuangzi dreamt he was a butterfly, a butterfly flitting and fluttering around, happy with himself and doing as he pleased. He didn't know he was Zhuangzi. Suddenly he woke up and there he was, solid and unmistakable Zhuangzi. But he didn't know if he was Zhuangzi who had dreamt he was a butterfly or a butterfly dreaming he was Zhuangzi. Between Zhuangzi and a butterfly there must be some distinction! This is called the Transformation of Things."

The philosophical underpinnings of this argument are also brought up by Descartes, who was one of the first Western philosophers to do so. In Meditations on First Philosophy, he states "There are no certain indications by which we may clearly distinguish wakefulness from sleep", and goes on to conclude that "It is possible that I am dreaming right now and that all of my perceptions are false".

Chalmers discusses the dream hypothesis and notes that this comes in two distinct forms:

- That he is currently dreaming, in which case many of his beliefs about the world are incorrect.

- That he has always been dreaming, in which case the objects he perceives actually exist, albeit in his imagination.

Both the dream argument and the simulation hypothesis can be regarded as skeptical hypotheses; however in raising these doubts, just as Descartes noted that his own thinking led him to be convinced of his own existence, the existence of the argument itself is testament to the possibility of its own truth. Another state of mind in which some argue an individual's perceptions have no physical basis in the real world is called psychosis though psychosis may have a physical basis in the real world and explanations vary.

The dream hypothesis is also used to develop other philosophical concepts, such as Valberg's personal horizon: what this world would be internal to if this were all a dream.

Existence of Simulated Reality Unprovable in any Concrete Sense

Known as the idea of Nested Simulations: The existence of simulated reality is seen to be unprovable in any concrete sense as there is an infinite regress problem with the argument: any evidence that is directly observed could be another simulation itself.

Even if we are a simulated reality, there is no way to be sure the beings running the simulation are not themselves a simulation and the operators of that simulation are not a simulation.

"Recursive simulation involves a simulation or an entity in the simulation, creating another instance of the same simulation, running it and using its results."

In August 2019, philosopher Preston Greene suggested that it may be best not to find out if we're living in a computer simulation since, if it were found to be true, such knowing may end the simulation.

Greene's suggestion is not dissimilar to Douglas Adams' humorous idea that if anyone in the Universe should actually work out 'The Meaning of Life, the Universe and Everything ', it would instantly disappear and be immediately replaced with something 'even more complex and inexplicable'.

Collaborative

Information sharing is central to collaborative work. Collaborative virtual environments (CVEs) are distributed virtual reality systems that offer graphically realized, potentially infinite, digital landscapes. Within these landscapes, individuals can share information through interaction with each other and through individual and collaborative interaction with data representations.

Virtual environments offer the potential for much flexibility in the way the landscape(s), data and individuals are represented. For example, representations of data or of individuals may utilize sophisticated 3D graphical representations, be 2D 'flat' representations or be simply text flows pasted onto planes. Landscapes can be large or small, coloured planes, complex meshed surfaces, detailed fantastic vistas or photo-realistic backdrops.

Most virtual environments support user representations, although none are shown in figure. Such representations of actants or users are called "avatars" or "embodiments". Interactions between users can be achieved through auditory or visual (textual or graphical) communication channels. Interaction between users and the system can be effected through a variety of means (e.g. mouse-driven, speech driven, typed command driven).

Adding the C to VE: Designing to Support Collaborative Work

In addition to their immediate aesthetic appeal, systems and applications are designed to serve a purpose. To be fit for their intended purpose(s), systems must be designed with intended user's tasks explicitly considered. Specifically, in order to support collaborative and cooperative activities, it is important that virtual environments provide task appropriate information representation and communication tools, and appropriately designed landscapes in which activities can occur.

Observations of Co-operative and Collaborative Work

When designing systems to support collaborative work we can learn a great deal from observations of people working and collaborating together in conventional settings. A number of field studies in recent years have offered insights into the nature of collaborative work. We also acknowledge that cooperative and collaborative activities involve considerable negotiation, and teams vary tremendously in their negotiation strategies as well as in their task accomplishment processes. Thus, the design of a CVE for any task context would require further investigation of that task context within a formative design framework.

Characterizing Collaborative Work

Transitions between Shared and Individual Activities

Work by numerous researchers testifies that in all 'real world' domains, collaborative work involves the interleaving of individual and group effort. Collaborative work thus involves considerable complex information exchange. These interleaved, singular-to-shared activities require considerable explicit and tacit communication between collaborators to be successful. Individuals need to negotiate shared understandings of task goals, of task decomposition and sub-task allocation and of task/sub-task progress. It is important that collaborators know what is currently being done and what has been done in the context of the task goals.

Most CVEs have been used as meeting places where group activities are the central task. However, it is easy to imagine situations where more complex, interleaved individual and collaborative activities would be carried out within one VE with team members moving continually between individual and collaborative activities.

Flexible and Multiple Viewpoints

Tasks often require use of multiple representations, each tailored to a different points of view and different subtasks. For example, Bellotti and Rogers offer a detailed analysis of the production of a daily newspaper. In this process many different representations are used to design the layout of the paper; these vary from hand-drawn to computer generated and reflect different task requirements. In certain cases, one individual may require multiple representations to reflect different aspects of their task(s), whilst in other cases different individuals may require tailored representations to provide information specific to their tasks. For example, consider an architectural design review of a building. Whilst the people taking part in the review would need an overview of the building they might only want to see features relating to their specialty in detail. Thus, an electrician might only want to see wiring plans in detail, but not necessarily see the plans for the plumbing, except in cases where there was a potential conflict. Smith offers another example. Multi-lingual text displays in virtual environments enables users to explore the same basic environment whilst seeing all textual annotations in their preferred language.

There is also a broader social context within which visualizations may need to vary; if the data being visualized is commercially sensitive, then viewing of certain pieces of information might need to be restricted to a subset of the user population. If the virtual environment does not support subjective views then the users are forced to agree on a common (possibly non-optimal) visualization style.

Sharing Context

Shared context is crucial for collaborative activities. 'Shared context' can mean many things; it can mean shared knowledge of each other's current activities, shared knowledge of others' past activities, shared artifacts and shared environment. Together, these lead to shared understandings.

Shared physical space facilitates or 'affords' shared understandings. As Gaver states, "in the everyday world, collaboration is situated within a shared, encompassing space, one which is rich with perceptual information about objects and events that can be explored and manipulated". Within these shared spaces, focused and unfocussed collaboration is accomplished through alignment towards the focal area of the shared activity, such as a shared document and through gestures like pointing toward portions of the document for added emphasis and clarity. When artifacts are shared not only do they become the subject of communication between users, but also the medium of communication; as one user manipulates an object, changes to it are visible to others in an externalization of processes of change. For the design of systems to support collaborative work, this means that shared artifacts should be visible and available for local negotiation and often the current focus of attention should be indicated. This can drive subsequent activities.

Where actions are not physically collocated and co-temporal providing shared context is more difficult. Work within CSCW has stressed the importance of tools for providing shared context in asynchronous work contexts (meeting capture, version control and so on); such tools provide activity audits and provide 'awareness' of others' activities which in turn provides a sense of shared context.

Awareness of Others

There are several ways of conceptualizing 'awareness'. One view is that reflected above, awareness as knowledge of task related activities. For example, Dourish and Bellotti state that awareness is an "understanding of the activities of others, which provides a context for your own activity". This is awareness as an audit of activity, and is the predominant notion of awareness in groupware where activities are often asynchronous and tasks are 'handed off' between team members. Such a view of awarenesscentralises intentional awareness. Awareness has also been discussed in terms of feelings of 'co-presence'. Notably this sense of awareness intersects with work by Slater and Usoh on sense of presence, where 'presence' refers to a sense of immersion in an environment. Awareness as co-presence involves consideration of peripheral as well as focussed attention and more accurately characterises what occurs when team members are engaged in parallel but independent ongoing activities. In contrast to intentional awareness, such tasks often require moment-to-moment, peripheral co-ordination. For example air traffic controllers are not aware of each other's moment-to-moment activities but peripheral vision and background sound all provide information such that if a disruption occurs, unplanned collaborative activities can ensue. Some consideration of providing such moment-to-moment awareness or sense of copresence exists in work on video portholes and video tunnels where offices are linked with video cameras and monitors.

Awareness can also relate to activities outside of the current task context where one is interested in the activities of a collaborator who is not currently present and who may not be working on the shared task. Often we need to know where to get hold of someone and need to adjust our plans on the basis of when someone will be back. In everyday life,.plan files, answerphones and a vacation email messages play this role.

Negotiation and Communication

Negotiation through talk is important for collaboration. Collaborative work requires the negotiation not only of task related content, but also of task structure in terms roles and activities and task/sub-task allocations.

Conversation analytic studies of negotiation at work have detailed how subtle verbal and nonverbal contribute to such negotiations. Nonverbal cues are crucial for most conversations. Studies of nonverbal behavior suggest facial expression, body posture and gesture carry from 60%-90% of the information in the verbal message being conveyed. Finally, cues from evaluation of dress, posture, behavioral traits and mannerisms provide much framing context for interpretations of verbal negotiations.

CVEs as a Paradigm Shift in Computer Supported Collaborative Work (CSCW)

A number of features are central to CVEs. These features distinguish CVEs from CSCW applications and Groupware applications like Lotus Notes which also provide distributed access to shared contexts. Other examples of groupware are desktop conferencing, video conferencing, co-authoring features and applications, bulletin boards, email, meeting support systems, workflow systems, group calendars, meeting support systems and voice applications. These applications focus on providing team members with access to the same information and a sense of what has been achieved within a collaborative or co-operative task. We focused on complex, highly negotiated and interwoven collaborative tasks, some collaborative and co-operative activities are more are routine cases of information exchange or task execution. For these routine activities where clear categories for hand-off are available traditional systems work well. Participants can check into a system, see what has been entered since the last occasion, enter comments and then depart. However, Grinter has shown how such systems are often designed to incorporate models of work flow; such models sometimes constrain communication rather than facilitate it. There are numerous examples, where such systems do not work effectively; arguably these occasions are those that require more complex negotiation and interaction, Specifically, early on in task decomposition and in less well structured tasks like collaborative design activities, co-workers spend more time in negotiations, discussion and task specification. At these stages offering structure prematurely can cause frustration and reduce creativity.

We believe that CVEs can support many forms of communication both to support routinised tasks but also negotiated, interwoven tasks for which a more fine-grained collaboration is ideal.

CVEs and the Concept of Space

CVEs represent a paradigm shift in that they provide a space that contains or encompasses data representations and users. To illustrate, offer three central metaphors that have accompanied the development of computer use. The first metaphor is the computer as a tool that literally computes, where program and data are fed into computing machinery on cards and tape. The second metaphor is the computer as container, where the programs and data are held in the machine (often displayed on a desktop) and files can be 'downloaded into' the computer, by ftp for example. Their third metaphor, and the predominant metaphor in CSCW applications, is the computer as window, where we can "view and converse with distant people and objects".

However, rather than a window, CVEs represent the computer as a malleable space, a space in which to build and utilize shared places for work and leisure. CVEs provide a terrain or digital landscape that can be 'inhabited' or 'populated' by individuals and data, encouraging a sense of shared space or place. Users, in the form of embodiments or avatars, are free to navigate through the space, encountering each other, artifacts and data objects and are free to communicate with each using verbal and non-verbal communication through visual and auditory channels.

Although conceptually simpler and technologically much lighter weight, this notion of providing places for interaction is also reflected within environments like MUDs and MOOs despite the lack of sophisticated graphics. This is carried into simple graphical MUDs and MOOs (e.g. The Palace) which offer limited avatar or embodiment representations which are generally limited, acting more as "placeholders" than active, gesturing embodiments.

CVEs and Collaborative Work

Having laid out this conceptual ground, we shall now consider how 3D graphical CVEs can support collaborative work by considering some of the issues raised above. The possibilities for flexibility in representation specification and in the establishment of shared virtual spaces means that CVEs are able to support many of the activities.

It is clear that CVEs should allow users to switch smoothly between individual and collaborative tasks. This means being able to alter representations and navigate easily, as well as being able to communicate quickly and efficiently regarding current activities. Currently many systems are rather clumsy in the way interaction and modality shifts are handled, and the tools for navigation do not always provide the easiest mapping from 'real world' to VE movement, but research developments are improving this situation. For example, investigations into the use of speech input for altering views and the use of a bicycle as an input device in Diamond Park.

Sharing a space with others can facilitate communication and collaboration. It has been argued that a shared virtual space that adheres to shared conventions (in this case real world spatial conventions although this need not necessarily be the case) thus provides a natural and intuitive way to navigate and to interact with individuals and groups. Certainly, research from many disciplines confirms that the design of spaces affects and is affected by human social action, social interaction, perception and cognition. A potentially infinite virtual space provides potentially infinite opportunities for individuals to define and delimit regions for particular activities. Such collaboratively defined, bordered places within the virtual space provide the possibility of framing social behaviours and social interactions.

The flexibility of virtual environments thus supports flexible, negotiated interactions. By contrast, traditional CSCW applications and more spatially oriented applications like shared drawing tools (e.g. VideoDraw and Clearboard offer a shared window onto a shared task, usually on a point-to-point basis. They offer less support for the flexible and 11 spontaneous altering of shared frames of reference or the redrawing of shared places and regions in which renegotiated activities can take place. Similarly, the negotiation of multiple places within the VE for multiple groups to collaborate in parallel is not as easily established. As such, along with video conferencing and video awareness tools, these offer what has been called "discontinuous and arbitrary space". Virtual environments potentially provide many places within one encompassing space or place where many groups can define regions of activity or one group can define regions for different activities, all within one continuous space which adheres to shared conventions drawn from the physical world.

Further, the flexibility of virtual environments enables flexibility in the design of shared data representations. It is clear that tasks often require many levels of expertise and different levels of information. Although most current multi-user virtual reality systems provide a highly 'objective' virtual environment where all users see the environment in the same way (albeit from different viewpoints) and all users see the same objects in the same places with the same appearances, this need not be the case. The current predominance of the objective view is partly due to the fact that multi-user VR systems evolved from single-user systems that have been extended to support a number of users. This aspect of the evolution of VR systems is similar to the way that groupware systems evolved from systems such as Shared X, that simply replicated an application's user interface to multiple users.

However, visualizations of abstract information are not fixed; the choice of visualization style can vary widely since the source data has no intrinsic appearance. Given this freedom of choice it is likely that users will form their own preferences for the display of particular datasets for particular tasks. However, if the virtual environment is capable of supporting subjective views then users are free to choose their own preferred visualization style. Subjective or differing views may also be appropriate for other cognitive reasons. These requirements can be accommodated with CVEs if each user has an independently controlled viewpoint from which they can inspect the virtual environment. This corresponds to our experience of the real world and as such we expect people to be skilled at relating to viewpoints and reasoning about these kinds of subjective effects. One way of achieving this individuality in representation whilst maintaining an easily accessible shared context is through level-of-detail (LOD) effects. LOD effects represent a common technique in interactive computer graphics and act to provide several different representations of a single artifact each with a different level of complexity. When viewing the object from a distance the user is shown a simple version of the artifact which is replaced by more detailed representations as the user approaches.

Similarly, flexibility in the design of embodiments means that embodiments can be tailored to task requirements, particularly the degree of interaction between users. Within CVEs, auditory and visual channels support real-time conversation and within 3D graphical CVEs embodiments support the use of gesture and non-verbal cues to support interactions. Gesture and facial play an important role in human interaction. Benford et. al. state that "the inhabitants of collaborative virtual environments (and other kinds of collaborative systems) ought to be visible to themselves and to others through a process of direct and sufficiently rich embodiment". Simply, individuated, gesturing embodiments combined with good information channels (visual and auditory) enable us to know who's who, where they are and what they're doing. Users have to recognize who someone is from their embodiment(s), and be able to differentiate between autonomous software agents for example and 'avatars' in the true sense (embodiments behind which are users in 'live' interaction). Embodiments provide a sense of location within the shared space, acting as 'placeholders' as mentioned above, but also providing dynamic cues as to current foci and activities. Thus, embodiments within a spatial framework provide a sense of awareness of others through cues akin to those in the physical world. For example, they offer proximity cues through use of auditory and visual cues, activity cues through their movements and informational cues through gesture, speech and intonation.

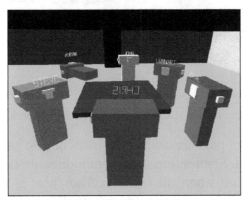

Embodiments in MASSIVE-1.

In contrast to video technologies that offer 'a talking heads' vision of one's collaborators (ideally reciprocal), embodiments within CVEs offer greater scope for use of body movements and spatial orientation. These offer complex cues for interaction and for development of shared contexts; such cues are critical in our everyday interactions in the 'real' world when we are physically collocated with others. Collaborators can, for example, point to objects or to portions of objects and move around objects to have multiple shared viewpoints. In many CSCW systems this process becomes more cumbersome because users have to point to objects via input devices and using complex sentences, but this issue is being addressed in current research. Notably, this capability is not available within telephone conferencing or within textual MUDs and MOOs. Graphical MOOs provide only limited possibilities for this.

Currently facial expressions and fine grained limb movements are not well developed for CVE embodiments. However, we believe that tailorable representations will be offered in the future; these will have possibilities for more individuation, greater scope for self representation and increasingly fine-tuned non verbal behaviours. Even at the current level of embodiment design however, it is possible to use conventions to signify certain things. For example, embodiments can convey information about the availability for interaction. This is illustrated in figure. Here several embodiments are shown, positioned around a table. One embodiment is 'lying down'; within this group, this position is a convention that indicates that the person behind the embodiment is not present. The embodiment owner is engaged elsewhere. This allows the other group members to know there will be no input from that person. Similarly, the 'faces' of the embodiments indicate the communication capabilities of different team members. The embodiment with a 'T' indicates this user has only text and not audio chat capabilities.

Embodiments in MASSIVE-1 around a shared blackboard.

Embodiments can also support historical awareness of who has been present and what activities they performed. Semi-autonomous embodiments can act on a user's behalf, offering useful information when the owner/author/user is not currently present. A user can also leave many embodiments around the VE; thus people can be in several places in one CVE, or in several CVEs at the same time. Users can also support asynchronous interactions by leaving each other messages within the VE. In figure, several embodiments are shown standing around a virtual blackboard on which a message is etched. Similarly in Laurel and Strickland's art installation Placeholder, visitors were able to leave voicemail for later review by themselves or others. These examples show the capabilities for supporting asynchronous activities as well as synchronous activities.

Example Systems

A small number of existing systems and applications, each chosen to highlight a particular point of interest and illustrate the range of applications for which CVEs are being employed which include. These include information visualization (VR-VIBE), tele-conferencing (MASSIVE-1), battlefield simulation (NPSNET) and social and artistic events (MASSIVE/MASSIVE-2 and 15 Diamond Park/SPLINE).

DIVE

DIVE is a multi-user virtual environment developed at the Swedish Institute of computer science. DIVE is one of the more mature multi-user virtual environments and is being used worldwide for developing VE applications. DIVE 3 supports scripting using Tcl/Tk. This is a powerful feature and allows DIVE objects to have associated behaviour without the need for a heavyweight process to control it. Another more interesting feature is the capability for one DIVE process to send a Tcl/Tk script to be executed in another DIVE process. This allows, for example, a DIVE application to send a script to the DIVE user client which extends the user interface to add application specific controls.

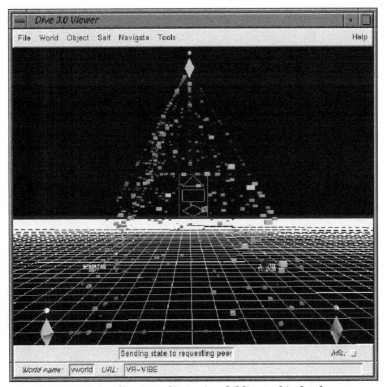

VR-VIBE visualization of items in a bibliographic database.

A number of applications have been constructed using DIVE, one of these is VR-VIBE which provides a multi-user visualization of bibliographic data and allows users to browse and search the corpus of documents. Developments reflected in DIVE 3 are exploited by the latest version of VR-VIBE, which provides a variety of visualizations and user-interface styles. The main application process is only concerned with providing services for managing visualization and all the user interface components are entirely separate and written in Tcl/Tk. It is therefore possible to completely replace the VR-VIBE interface without changing the main application at all.

Figure shows a VR-VIBE 3D representation of items in a database. The green octahedrons (shown at the top centre and bottom left and right of the figure) represent points of interest that have been specified by a user. The blue items in between represent documents in the database. User can navigate through the space of these document icons, and can view the documents by clicking on an icon.

User studies of VR-VIBE have shown promising results; users are able to issue complex queries, navigate successfully through the space and select appropriate items. Although to date all published work has concerned single user search and browse tasks, current work centres on collaborative search and browse tasks using VR-VIBE visualizations as shared, distributed environments.

MASSIVE

MASSIVE-1 is a distributed VR system targeted initially at teleconferencing applications. MASSIVE currently runs on Sun and Silicon Graphics workstations. The main 17 feature of MASSIVE-1 is that it supports multiple users, applications and worlds that are connected by portals. A noteworthy feature of MASSIVE is that a user of a powerful workstation running graphical, audio and text interfaces can interact, albeit in a limited way, with another user who has only a vt100 running a text interface. The text user is represented in the graphical medium and vice versa. The users can communicate by emoting, by typed text, and the text adapters (text to speech and text to graphics) allow graphical users to follow the activities of text-only users. For users with more technological capabilities, it is possible to employ an arbitrary combination of graphics, text and audio interfaces.

The COMIC spatial model of interaction controls all interactions. This model is intended to support interaction and cooperation in heavily populated virtual spaces. To this end, MASSIVE1 concentrates on facilitating user-user interaction, while user-object interaction is relatively undeveloped. This spatial model of interaction uses the concepts of aura, focus and nimbus. Users can explicitly control their interactions with other objects; specifically, users are able to control how aware they are of other objects or users, and how aware those objects or users are of them.

MASSIVE currently supports up to about 10 mutually aware users in a given world. It has been used over the LAN for internal research group meetings, and has been used over the UK's SuperJANET network to hold three site meetings between Nottingham, Lancaster and QMW in London and over the internet to hold five-site meetings between Nottingham, Lancaster, Stockholm (2 sites) and Bonn.

MASSIVE-2 combines ideas from MASSIVE-1 and AVIARY. From MASSIVE-1 is borrowed the use of the COMIC spatial model of interaction. From AVIARY is borrowed the architecture based on a distributed object system. MASSIVE-2 also adds some novel functionality. This includes hierarchical compositions of regions in virtual worlds which can be mapped to separated multicast groups, different media which can either share or use separate multicast groups, support for the new extended spatial model of interaction which includes third parties, regions and abstractions and an extensible object oriented (class-based) developers API.

A number of evaluations of the MASSIVE distributed environment have been conducted. Early evaluation studies concentrated on group collaborative and competitive games. These indicated that users were able to easily manipulate aspects of the spatial model to control awareness of others and to vary levels of privacy in conversations. Having explicit control over these levels of interaction proved much less frustrating for users than when no such control was provided. In the everyday world, we have control over the level of privacy of any utterance by whispering or shouting. This expectation was clear amongst our users. The studies also indicated a need to support clear, moment-to-moment communication between team members and to consider what information needed to be shared and how quickly, reinforcing the user centred design perspective.

A more extensive but less formal evaluation was the MASSIVE VR/poetry performance which took place as part of the Nottingham NOW ninety6 arts festival. This event was an experiment in using a CVE as a performance space. Four rap poets performed (in sequence) on a stage to a live audience. Position trackers were attached to the poets' heads and hands and used to control the embodiment representing the poet in a virtual space. In a separate room 10 Silicon Graphics workstations running the MASSIVE-2 system allowed members of the public to see and hear the virtual representation of the poet, to explore the virtual environment and to talk with one another via a real-time audio connection. Views from the virtual environment were projected onto screens in both rooms so that people not currently logged on could follow the activity in the virtual environment. The results indicated that users enjoyed the event very much and were able to easily navigate the fairly extensive virtual environment. Communication was also easy. Navigation and communication were so easy in fact that the virtual audience members spent more time communicating with each other and navigating the space than they did watching the poetry event. The poets themselves were not aware of the activities of the virtual audience members, as they were engaged in performing to the ëliveí audience.

A number of design recommendations deriving from this event are detailed by Benford et al. These mainly concern the level of control embodiment are granted regarding the use of the spatial model of interaction. Notably the recommendations offered are pertinent to the specific type of event considered, in this case a public performance with a stage and with virtual audience members.

NPSNET

NPSNET is a networked VR system designed for military training and simulation with the goal of supporting large numbers of participants. NPSNET is a single application rather than a general 19 purpose system intended to support applications. Its eventual goal is to support hundreds of users. The means by which it attempts to do this are therefore of interest to the designers of large scale multi-user VR systems. NPSNET uses the standard DIS (Distributed Interactive Simulation) protocol to communicate between entities taking part in the simulation (IEEE, 1993). IP- MULTICAST is used to transmit updates to reduce bandwidth requirements.

SPLINE

SPLINE is a CVE system that supports both audio and video interaction between users and is designed to support large numbers of users. The principle application for SPLINE so far has been to create Diamond Park, a social virtual environment containing a square mile of terrain. In addition to a desktop workstation based interface, Diamond Park supports a novel user interface based on modified recumbent exercise bicycles which allows users to cycle around the environment. To date no formal user testing has been done of Diamond Park or other applications based in SPLINE (W. Yerazunis, Mitsubishi Electric, personal communication).

References

- Immersive-virtual-reality-immersive-VR: whatis.techtarget.com, Retrieved 13 March, 2020

- Ma, Minhua; C. Jain, Lakhmi; Anderson, Paul (2014). Virtual, Augmented Reality and Serious Games for Healthcare 1. Springer Publishing. p. 120. ISBN 978-3-642-54816-1

- What-is-non-immersive-virtual-reality-definition-examples: cyberpulse.info, Retrieved 17 July, 2020

- Hut, P.; Alford, M.; Tegmark, M. (2006). "On Math, Matter and Mind". Foundations of Physics. 36 (6): 765–794. arXiv:physics/0510188. Bibcode:2006FoPh...36..765H. doi:10.1007/s10701-006-9048-x

- Collaborative-virtual-environments-An-introductory-review-of-issues-and-systems-220530352: researchgate.net, Retrieved 16 January, 2020

- Stuart Eve (2012). "Augmenting Phenomenology: Using Augmented Reality to Aid Archaeological Phenomenology in the Landscape" (PDF). Journal of Archaeological Method and Theory. 19 (4): 582–600. doi:10.1007/s10816-012-9142-7

3
Hardware and Software

Different kinds of software and hardware are used for the working and operations of the virtual reality systems. Some of them are head mounted display, EyeTap, contact lens, virtual retinal display, etc. The topics elaborated in this chapter will help in gaining a better perspective of various VR hardware and software.

User Input

The input channels of a virtual reality application are those with which humans emit information and interact with the environment. We interact with the world mainly through locomotion and manipulation, and we communicate information mostly by means of voice, gestures, and facial expressions.

Gestural communication as well as locomotion makes full body motion analysis desirable, while verbal communication with the computer or other users makes voice input an important option.

However, for practical purposes, it is possible to limit user input to a few selected channels. As the hand offers many more degrees of freedom concentrated in a small area than any other part of the body, hand motion tracking is sufficient for most applications. Moreover, the fact that the hand is our privileged manipulation tool makes hand motion tracking a critical input for interacting with virtual worlds. Viewpoint specification requires real time motion tracking of the user's head, and possibly eyes, in order to update displayed stereo images in coordination with user movements.

Sensory Feedback

Our sense of physical reality is a construction derived from the symbolic, geometric, and dynamic information directly presented to our senses. The output channels of a virtual reality application correspond thus to our senses: vision, touch and force perception, hearing, smell, taste. Sensory simulation is thus at the heart of virtual reality technology.

Visual Perception

Vision is generally considered the most dominant sense, and there is evidence that human cognition is oriented around vision. High quality visual representation is thus critical for virtual environments. The major aspects of the visual sense that have an impact on display requirements are the following:

- Depth perception: Stereoscopic viewing is a primary human visual mechanism for perceiving depth. However, because human eyes are located only on average 6.3 centimeters apart, the geometric benefits of stereopsis are lost for objects more distant than 30 meters, and it is most effective at much closer distances. Other primary cues (eye convergence and accommodation) and secondary cues (e.g. perspective, motion parallax, size, texture, shading, and shadows) are essential for far objects and of varying importance for near ones.

- Accuracy and field-of-view: The total horizontal field of vision of both human eyes is about 180 degrees without eye/head movement and 270 with fixed head and moving eyes. The vertical field of vision is typically over 120 degrees. While the total field is not necessary for a user to feel immersed in a visual environment, 90 to 110 degrees are generally considered necessary for the horizontal field of vision; when considering accuracy, the central fovea of a human eye has a resolution of about 0.5 minutes of arc.

- Critical fusion frequency: Visual simulations achieve the illusion of animation by rapid successive presentation of a sequence of static images. The critical fusion frequency is the rate above which humans are unable to distinguish between successive visual stimuli. This frequency is proportional to the luminance and the size of the area covered on the retina. Typical values for average scenes are between 5 and 60 Hz. A rule of thumb in the computer graphics industry suggests that below about 10-15 Hz, objects will not appear to be in continuous motion, resulting in distraction. High-speed applications, such as professional flight simulators, require visual feedback frequencies of more than 60 Hz.

Sound Perception

Analyzing crudely how we use our senses, we can say that vision is our privileged mean of perception, while hearing is mainly used for verbal communication, to get information from invisible parts of the world or when vision does not provide enough information. Audio feedback must thus be able to synthesize sound, to position sound sources in 3D space and can be linked to a speech generator for verbal communication with the computer. In humans, the auditory apparatus is most efficient between 1000 and 4000 Hz, with a drop in efficiency as the sound frequency becomes higher or lower. The synthesis of a 3D auditory display typically involves the digital generation of stimuli using location-dependent filters. In humans, spatial hearing is performed by evaluating monaural clues, which are the same for both ears, as well as binaural ones, which differ between the two eardrum signals. In general, the distance between a sound source and the two ears is different for sound sources outside the median plane. This is one reason for interaural time, phase and level differences that can be evaluated by the auditory system for directivity perception. These interaural clues are mainly used for azimuth perception (left or right), which is usually quite accurate (up to one degree). Exclusively interaural levels and time differences do not allow univocal spatial perceptions. Monaural cues are mainly used for perceiving elevation. These are amplifications and attenuations in the so-called directional (frequency) bands. Particularly the presence of the external ear (consisting of head, torso, shoulders and pinnae) has decisive impact on the eardrum signals.

Position, Touch and Force Perception

While the visual and auditory systems are only capable of sensing, the haptic sense is capable of both sensing what it is happening around the human being and acting on the environment. This makes it an indispensable part of many human activities and thus, in order to provide the realism needed for effective applications, VR systems need to provide inputs to, and mirror the outputs of, the haptic system. The primary input/output variables for the haptic sense are displacements and forces.

Haptic sensory information is distinguished as either tactile or proprioceptive information. The difference between these is the following. Suppose the hand grasps an object. The initial feeling (contact) is provided by the touch receptors in the skin, which also provide information on the shape of the object and its texture. If the hand applies more force, proprioceptive (or kinesthetic) information provides details about the position and motion of the hand and arm, and the forces acting on these, to give a sense of total contact forces, surface compliance, and, very often, weight. In general tactile and kinesthetic sensing occur simultaneously.

To manipulate an object, say move it, rotate it, or pinch it, the haptic system must issue motor action commands that exert forces on the object. These forces are highly dependent on the type of grasping that is used. Power grasping employs all the fingers and the palm, whereas precision grasping uses only the finger-tips.

Two important aspects in force simulation that have an impact on the requirements of a VR systems are the maximum force magnitude and the frequency of force feedback. These depend heavily on application, and research on human factors related to these issues is active. Typical values for simulating interaction with a good variety of objects is at least 10 N at 1 KHz.

Another important variable to take in account in VR environments is the human's capability to sense motion and control posture (orientation and balance). The two primary systems playing a role in this perception are the visual and the vestibular systems. In its role as a sensory system, the vestibular system provides information about movement of the head and the position of the head with respect to gravity and any other acting inertial forces. As a motor system, the vestibular system plays an important role in posture control, that is, orienting to the vertical, controlling center of mass, and stabilizing the head.

Olfactory Perception

It exists specialized applications where olfactory perception is of importance. One of these is surgical simulation, which need to provide the proper olfactory stimuli at the appropriate moments during the procedure. Similarly, the training of emergency medical personnel operating in the field should bring them into contact with the odors that would make the simulated environment seem more real and which might provide diagnostic information about the injuries that simulated casualty is supposed to have incurred.

The main problem about simulating the human olfactory system is, indeed, that a number of questions on how it works remain unanswered. It is certain that the stimuli to the brain cortex are originated in the nose when molecules carrying odors are caught by the receptors neurons, but it is still unknown how the brain generates a recognition pattern isolating some scents from others and reconstructing missing parts. Other sensory systems are strictly tangled with olfaction. It is reported that humans may identify barely one third of the odors while lacking inputs from other senses, like vision. Appropriate color cues improve both accuracy and speed of identification of odors. Human capability of detective odors is quite sensitive, capable of detecting smells in concentration from one part per million to one part per billion, depending on the odor in question. It is much easier to detect increases than decreases in concentration and the magnitude perceived is not linear with changes but closer to a logarithmic relation. A VR environment giving olfactory cues should provide the possibility to diffuse the odors when needed and purify and filter the air when the cue is no longer required.

Spatiotemporal Realism

Virtual reality applications typically offer multiple input/output modalities and that for each of these modalities timing constraints have to be met in order for applications to be usable (e.g. visual feedback rate > 10 Hz, haptic feedback rate > 1 KHz).

Additional performance constraints derive from the fact that multimodal outputs have to be integrated into a single system. This task is particularly difficult for the following reasons:

First, the various devices need to display information in tight synchronization, since human tolerances of synchronization errors are quite small. Second, varying delays in the various output devices makes proper synchronization even harder. Worse, synchronization errors also result from varying distances between user and devices. (Modern movie soundtracks must take into account the distance sound travels in an average movie theatre before reaching the audience.) Third and last, synchronization is not always beneficial. For example, in limited bandwidth, computer-supported cooperative work applications, it is preferable to sacrifice synchronization to enable low-latency, audio only communication.

Even mono-modal VR applications (e.g. applications with only visual feedback) have to face similar problems, and low-latency constraints have to be met. In this case, synchronization is between synthesized and real-world sensory input. Human beings are very sensitive to these problems. For instance, it has been reported that, depending on the task and surrounding environment, lag of as little as 100 ms degrades human performance and, if lag exceeds 300 ms, humans start to dissociate their movements from the displayed effects, thus destroying any immersive effects.

Immersion in virtual reality environments has been shown to result in problems of disorientation and nausea similar to the symptoms of motion sickness, and it has been demonstrated that lag and synchronization problems are a major influencing factor. Simulator and motion sickness are generally considered to be caused by conflicts between the information received from two or more sensory systems. Sensory conflict alone is not sufficient to explain the development of simulator sickness, since it takes no account of the adaptive capabilities of the human body. To take account of habituation, the concept of sensory conflict has been extended into a theory of sensory rearrangement, which states that all situations which provoke motion sickness are characterized by a condition of sensory rearrangement in which the motion signals transmitted by the eyes, the vestibular system and the non-vestibular proprioceptors are at variance either with one another or with what is expected from previous experience.

This means that spatio-temporal realism, i.e. the ability to meet synchronization, lag, and accuracy constraints within low tolerances, is a required feature for all virtual reality system. Quantifying exactly absolute and taskdepending tolerance limits is an open research subject.

The analysis of the requirements in terms of input and output channels has highlighted fidelity and performance requirements for the bare simulation of existence of synthetic objects.

Successful virtual reality applications must combine new input and output devices in ways that provide not only such an illusion of existence of synthetic objects, but also the interaction metaphors for interacting with them. An ACM CHI workshop on the challenges of 3D interaction has identified five types of characteristics that 3D user interfaces must have to exploit the perceptual and spatial skills of users. These are:

- Multiple/integrated input and output modalities: User interfaces should be able to use more than just the visual channel for communications.

- Functional fidelity: Taken together, the various sensory cues provided by an interface must be appropriate to the task being performed.

- Responsiveness: 3D user interfaces must be very quick to respond to user actions so that natural and explorative behavior can occur. This introduces important timing constraints on the applications.

- Affordances: Affordances allow the creation of objects that have meaningful properties and provide clues about how to interact with 3D objects and environments.

- Appeal to mental representation: User interfaces must be organized in a way that they are recognizable by users. Real-world metaphors and physical simulation techniques are especially helpful with this respect.

These characteristics pose important challenges both to the hardware side of virtual reality systems, in terms of devices that have to be used to communicate to and with users, and to the software side, in terms of techniques that have to be developed to efficiently support multimodal interaction in a time-critical setting.

Hardware

User Input

Position/Orientation Tracking

Head tracking is the most valuable input for promoting the sense of immersion in a VR system. The types of trackers developed for the head also can be mounted on glove or body suit devices to provide tracking of a user's hand or some other body part. Many different technologies can be used for tracking. Mechanical systems measure change in position by physically connecting the remote object to a point of reference with jointed linkages; they are quite accurate, have low lag and are good for tracking small volumes but are intrusive, due to tethering and subject to mechanical part wear-out. Magnetic systems couple a transmitter producing magnetic fields and a receiver capable to determine the strength and angles of the fields; they are quite inexpensive and accurate and accommodate for larger ranges, the size of a small room, but they are subject to field distortion and electromagnetic interference. Optical systems can use a variety of detectors, from ordinary video cameras to LED's, to detect either ambient light or light emitted under control of the position tracker (infrared light is often used to prevent interference with other activities); they can work over a large area, are fast and are not subject to interferences but are heavy and expensive. Acoustic (ultrasound) systems use three microphones and three emitters to compute the distance between a source and receiver via triangulation; they are quite inexpensive and lightweight but subject to noise interference and yield low accuracy since speed of sound in air varies and there can be echoes. Inertial systems use accelerometers and gyroscopes to compute angular velocity about each axis and changes in position; they are unlimited in range and fast but can detect only 3 DOF and are not accurate for slow position changes. The price range of these systems is quite large: from less than 1,000 ECU for the cheapest acoustic and magnetic systems to more than 60,000 ECU of the most sophisticated ones. The resolution offered is, typically, around 0.1 mm for translations and 0.1° for rotations.

Eye Tracking

Eye trackers work somewhat differently: they do not measure head position or orientation but the direction at which the users' eyes are pointed out of the head. This information is used to determine the direction of the user's gaze and to update the visual display accordingly. The approach can be optical, electroocular, or electromagnetic. The first of these, optical, uses reflections from the eye's surface to determine eye gaze. Most commercially available eye trackers are optical, they usually illuminate the eye with IR LED's, generating corneal reflections. Electroocular approaches use an electrooculogram (EOG) via skin electrodes that provide measurement of the corneoretinal potential generated within the eyeball by the metabolically active retinal epithelium. There is availability of, at least, one commercial product based on this approach. It has the advantage to be totally non-invasive, but it is less stable and needs more often to be recalibrated. Electromagnetic approaches determine eye gaze based on measurement of magnetically induced voltage on a coil attached to a lens on the eye. All the commercial products are quite expensive, ranging from approximately 15,000 ECU up to almost 100,000 and offer good frequency response (up to 500 Hz).

Full Body Motion

There are two kinds of full-body motion to account for: passive motion, and active self-motion. The first is quite feasible to simulate vehicles with current technology. The usual practice is to build a "cabin" that represents the physical vehicle and its controls, mount it on a motion platform, and generate virtual window displays and motion commands in response to the user's operation of the controls. They are usually specialized for particular application (e.g., flight simulators) and they represented the first practical VR applications for military and pilots' training use. More recently this technology have been extensively used by the entertainment industry. Selfmotion interfaces, instead, are defined as those cases where the user moves himself through a VR environment. This is typically performed linking the body to a gyroscope, giving a 3600 range of motion in pitch, roll and yaw. All these systems are usually quite expensive, from 6,000 ECU to 50,000 ECU.

Sensory Feedback

Visual Feedback

Humans are strongly oriented to their visual sense: they give precedence to the visual system if there are conflicting inputs from different sensory modalities. Visual displays used in a VR context should guarantee stereoscopic vision and the ability to track head movements and continually update the visual display to reflect the user's movement through the environment. In addition, the user should receive visual stimuli of adequate resolution, in full color, with adequate brightness, and high-quality motion representations.

Many different techniques provide stereoscopic vision: head mounted displays (HMDs), shutter glasses, passive glasses, and booms. Currently HMDs use separate displays mounted in a helmet for each eye. New versions of HMDs, still under development, are based on the creation of the image directly on the retina, using a beam of light. With shutter glasses the user wear a pair of glasses where each lens is substituted with an electronic shutter (a monochrome LCD). Looking at a CRT showing left and right images synchronized with them, the shutters are alternatively opaque or transparent. Passive glasses use an approach in which perspective views for each eye are encoded in the form of either color or polarization of the light, with the "lens" for each eye containing a filter that passes only the appropriate image intended for each eye. A boom is a system using two monitors (CRT or LCD) and special optics to present a different image to each eye, mounted in a device suspended from a boom in front of the user.

The vast majority of current commercial products are HMDs ranging from high-end, expensive products priced around 50,000 ECU to quite inexpensive consumer product displays costing less than 1,000 ECU. Shutter glasses are generally inexpensive and booms are definitely the more expensive, reaching prices over 80,000 ECU. The resolution range from 320×400 of the cheapest devices to the 1280×1024 with a horizontal field of view up to 140°.

Haptic Feedback

At the current time, tactile feedback is not supported in practical use, that is, tactile systems are not in everyday use by users (as opposed to developers). Tactile stimulation can be achieved in a number of different ways. Those presently used in VR systems include mechanical pins activated by solenoid, piezoelectric crystal where changing electric fields causes expansion and contraction, shape-memory alloy technologies, voice coils vibrating to transmit low amplitude, high frequency vibrations to the skin, several kinds of pneumatic systems (air-jets, air-rings, bladders), and heat pump systems. Other technologies, such as electrorheological fluids that harden under the application of an electric field are currently being investigated. Only one commercial system is known to provide temperature feedback, not coupled to tactile. The maximum resolution obtainable is around 1 mm and the price range is between 1,000 ECU and 10,000 ECU.

Kinesthetic interfaces, instead, are much more developed and in common use. Essentially, there are three components to providing a force feedback interface for VR systems: measurement of the movement of the user's fingers, hand, and arm, and sensing any forces he exerts; calculation of the effect of the exerted forces on objects and the resultant forces that should act on the user; and presentation of these resultant forces to the user's fingers, wrist, and arm as appropriate. The technologies in current use to provide force feedback are: electromagnetic motors that produce torque with two time-varying magnetic fields, hydraulics systems where a hydraulic fluid is pressurized and, under the control of valves, delivered to actuators and pneumatics systems using pressurized gases. Piezoelectric and magnetorestrictive technologies are still the subject of research and development. The available systems can offer from 3 up to 8 DOF, simulate forces up to 10 N (peak) and, for the ones for which price is available, cost from 6,000 ECU to 20,000 ECU.

Sound Feedback

The commercial products available for the development of 3-D sounds (sounds apparently originating from any point in a 3-D environment) are very different in quality and price. They range from low-cost, PC-based, plug-in technologies that provide limited 3-D capabilities to professional quality, service-only technologies that provide true surround audio capabilities. Applications for them range from video games to military simulations, from consumer electronic to professional post-processing.

Some of these systems can generate multiple sounds at a time, possibly 2-D and 3-D together. Other interesting features are: Doppler shifts simulation with the sounds changing while travelling past the listener, control of reverb reflections, possibility to perform an acoustic ray-tracing of rooms and environments. Depending upon the chosen systems, the sounds are delivered to the user by speakers or earphones. The prices range from 1,000 ECU to 10,000 ECU and the quality of the sampling is typically the CD one (44.1 KHz).

Olfactory Feedback

Devices used to collect and interpret odors are usually referred to as artificial or electronic noses and use three basic technologies: gas chromatography, mass spectrometry and chemical array sensors.

Among the various technologies used to deliver odors, perhaps the most mature is odorant storage. Odorants can be stored under several different forms: liquid, gels or waxes. Most usually they are microencapsulated on flat surfaces. The system releases the odors scratching the desired amount of capsules, so discretely metering the dosage. Capsules can contain droplets of liquid ranging from 10 to 1000 µm in a neutral layer of gelatin.

Current market available systems use air streams to actually deliver the smell to the user. The odorants are dissolved in a solvent gas, such as carbon dioxide, and then directed to the user's nose through a hose. Several available technologies are considered to be used for odor delivery inside a HMD. Such portable system has to be miniaturized and lightweight and have low power requirements. Ink-jet printer nozzles are good candidates since they allow precise control of some odorants. The number of odors currently available in a single system ranges from 6-7 to almost 20 and there are researches trying to simulate special odors needed for particular application like human odors (e.g., blood, liver) in surgical simulation.

Head Mounted Display

A head-mounted display (HMD) is a display device, worn on the head or as part of a helmet, that has a small display optic in front of one (monocular HMD) or each eye (binocular HMD). An HMD has many uses including gaming, aviation, engineering, and medicine. Head-mounted Displays are the primary components of virtual reality headsets. There is also an optical head-mounted display (OHMD), which is a wearable display that can reflect projected images and allows a user to see through it.

British Army Reserve soldier demonstrates a virtual reality headset.

An eye tracking HMD with LED illuminators and cameras to measure eye movements.

A typical HMD has one or two small displays, with lenses and semi-transparent mirrors embedded in eyeglasses (also termed data glasses), a visor, or a helmet. The display units are miniaturized and may include cathode ray tubes (CRT), liquid-crystal displays (LCDs), liquid crystal on silicon (LCos), or organic light-emitting diodes (OLED). Some vendors employ multiple micro-displays to increase total resolution and field of view.

HMDs differ in whether they can display only computer-generated imagery (CGI), or only live imagery from the physical world, or combination. Most HMDs can display only a computer-generated image, sometimes referred to as virtual image. Some HMDs can allow a CGI to be superimposed on real-world view. This is sometimes referred to as augmented reality (AR) or mixed reality (MR). Combining real-world view with CGI can be done by projecting the CGI through a partially reflective mirror and viewing the real world directly. This method is often called optical see-through. Combining re-al-world view with CGI can also be done electronically by accepting video from a cam-era and mixing it electronically with CGI.

Optical HMD

An optical head-mounted display uses an optical mixer which is made of partly silvered mirrors. It can reflect artificial images, and let real images cross the lens, and let a user look through it. Various methods have existed for see-through HMD's, most of which can be summarized into two main families based on curved mirrors or waveguides. Curved mirrors have been used by Laster Technologies, and by Vuzix in their Star 1200 product. Various waveguide methods have existed for years. These include diffraction optics, holographic optics, polarized optics, and reflective optics.

Applications

Major HMD applications include military, government (fire, police, etc.), and civilian-commercial (medicine, video gaming, sports, etc.).

Aviation, Tactical and Ground

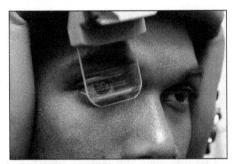

U.S. Air Force flight equipment technician testing a Scorpion helmet mounted integrated targeting system.

In 1962, Hughes Aircraft Company revealed the Electrocular, a compact CRT(7" long), head-mounted monocular display that reflected a TV signal in to transparent eyepiece. Ruggedized HMDs are increasingly being integrated into the cockpits of modern helicopters and fighter aircraft. These are usually fully integrated with the pilot's flying helmet and may include protective visors, night vision devices, and displays of other symbology.

Military, police, and firefighters use HMDs to display tactical information such as maps or thermal imaging data while viewing a real scene. Recent applications have included the use of HMD for paratroopers. In 2005, the Liteye HMD was introduced for ground combat troops as a rugged, waterproof lightweight display that clips into a standard U.S. PVS-14 military helmet mount. The self-contained color monocular organic light-emitting diode (OLED) display replaces the NVG tube and connects to a mobile computing device. The LE has see-through ability and can be used as a standard HMD or for augmented reality applications. The design is optimized to provide high definition data under all lighting conditions, in covered or see-through modes of operation. The LE has a low power consumption, operating on four AA batteries for 35 hours or receiving power via standard Universal Serial Bus (USB) connection.

The Defense Advanced Research Projects Agency (DARPA) continues to fund research in augmented reality HMDs as part of the Persistent Close Air Support (PCAS) Program.

Vuzix is currently working on a system for PCAS that will use holographic waveguides to produce see-through augmented reality glasses that are only a few millimeters thick.

Engineering

Engineers and scientists use HMDs to provide stereoscopic views of computer-aided design (CAD) schematics. Virtual reality, when applied to engineering and design, is a key factor in integration of the human in the design. By enabling engineers to interact with their designs in full life-size scale, products can be validated for issues that may not have been visible until physical prototyping. The use of HMDs for VR is seen as supplemental to the conventional use of CAVE for VR simulation. HMDs are predominantly used for single-person interaction with the design, while CAVEs allow for more collaborative virtual reality sessions.

Head Mounted Display systems are also used in the maintenance of complex systems, as they can give a technician a simulated x-ray vision by combining computer graphics such as system diagrams and imagery with the technician's natural vision (augmented or modified reality).

Medicine and Research

There are also applications in surgery, wherein a combination of radiographic data (X-ray computed tomography (CAT) scans, and magnetic resonance imaging (MRI) imaging) is combined with the surgeon's natural view of the operation, and anesthesia, where the patient vital signs are within the anesthesiologist's field of view at all times.

Research universities often use HMDs to conduct studies related to vision, balance, cognition and neuroscience. As of 2010, the use of predictive visual tracking measurement to identify mild traumatic brain injury was being studied. In visual tracking tests, a HMD unit with eye tracking ability shows an object moving in a regular pattern. People without brain injury are able to track the moving object with smooth pursuit eye movements and correct trajectory.

Gaming and Video

Low-cost HMD devices are available for use with 3D games and entertainment applications. One of the first commercially available HMDs was the Forte VFX1 which was announced at Consumer Electronics Show (CES) in 1994. The VFX-1 had stereoscopic displays, 3-axis head-tracking, and stereo headphones. Another pioneer in this field was Sony, which released the Glasstron in 1997. It had as an optional accessory a positional sensor which permitted the user to view the surroundings, with the perspective moving as the head moved, providing a deep sense of immersion. One novel application of this technology was in the game MechWarrior 2, which permitted users of the Sony Glasstron or Virtual I/O's iGlasses to adopt a new visual perspective from inside the cockpit of the craft, using their own eyes as visual and seeing the battlefield through their craft's own cockpit.

Many brands of video glasses can be connected to modern video and DSLR cameras, making them applicable as a new age monitor. As a result of the glasses ability to block out ambient light, filmmakers and photographers are able to see clearer presentations of their live images.

The Oculus Rift is a virtual reality (VR) head-mounted display created by Palmer Luckey that the company Oculus VR is developing for virtual reality simulations and video game. The HTC Vive is a virtual reality head-mounted display. The headset is produced by a collaboration between Valve and HTC, with its defining feature being precision room-scale tracking, and high-precision motion controllers. The PlayStation VR is the only virtual reality headset for gaming consoles, dedicated for the PlayStation 4. Windows Mixed Reality is a platform developed by Microsoft which includes a wide range of headsets produced by HP, Samsung, and others and is capable of playing most HTC Vive games. It uses only inside-out tracking for its controllers.

Sports

A HMD system has been developed for Formula One drivers by Kopin Corp. and the BMW Group. The HMD displays critical race data while allowing the driver to continue focusing on the track as pit crews control the data and messages sent to their drivers through two-way radio. Recon Instruments released on 3 November 2011 two head-mounted displays for ski goggles, MOD and MOD Live, the latter based on an Android operating system.

Training and Simulation

A key application for HMDs is training and simulation, allowing to virtually place a trainee in a situation that is either too expensive or too dangerous to replicate in real-life. Training with HMDs covers a wide range of applications from driving, welding and spray painting, flight and vehicle simulators, dismounted soldier training, medical procedure training, and more. However, a number of unwanted symptoms have been caused by prolonged use of certain types of head-mounted displays, and these issues must be resolved before optimal training and simulation is feasible.

Performance Parameters

- Ability to show stereoscopic imagery: A binocular HMD has the potential to display a different image to each eye. This can be used to show stereoscopic images. It should be borne in mind that so-called 'Optical Infinity' is generally taken by flight surgeons and display experts as about 9 meters. This is the distance at which, given the average human eye rangefinder "baseline" (distance between the eyes or Interpupillary distance (IPD)) of between 2.5 and 3 inches (6 and

8 cm), the angle of an object at that distance becomes essentially the same from each eye. At smaller ranges the perspective from each eye is significantly different and the expense of generating two different visual channels through the computer-generated imagery (CGI) system becomes worthwhile.

- Interpupillary distance (IPD): This is the distance between the two eyes, measured at the pupils, and is important in designing head-mounted displays.

- Field of view (FOV): Humans have an FOV of around 180°, but most HMDs offer far less than this. Typically, a greater field of view results in a greater sense of immersion and better situational awareness. Most people do not have a good feel for what a particular quoted FOV would look like (e.g., 25°) so often manufacturers will quote an apparent screen size. Most people sit about 60 cm away from their monitors and have quite a good feel about screen sizes at that distance. To convert the manufacturer's apparent screen size to a desktop monitor position, divide the screen size by the distance in feet, then multiply by 2. Consumer-level HMDs typically offer a FOV of about 110°.

- Resolution: HMDs usually mention either the total number of pixels or the number of pixels per degree. Listing the total number of pixels (e.g., 1600×1200 pixels per eye) is borrowed from how the specifications of computer monitors are presented. However, the pixel density, usually specified in pixels per degree or in arcminutes per pixel, is also used to determine visual acuity. 60 pixels/° (1 arcmin/pixel) is usually referred to as eye limiting resolution, above which increased resolution is not noticed by people with normal vision. HMDs typically offer 10 to 20 pixels/°, though advances in micro-displays help increase this number.

- Binocular overlap: Measures the area that is common to both eyes. Binocular overlap is the basis for the sense of depth and stereo, allowing humans to sense which objects are near and which objects are far. Humans have a binocular overlap of about 100° (50° to the left of the nose and 50° to the right). The larger the binocular overlap offered by an HMD, the greater the sense of stereo. Overlap is sometimes specified in degrees (e.g., 74°) or as a percentage indicating how much of the visual field of each eye is common to the other eye.

- Distant focus (collimation): Optical methods may be used to present the images at a distant focus, which seems to improve the realism of images that in the real world would be at a distance.

- On-board processing and operating system: Some HMD vendors offer on-board operating systems such as Android, allowing applications to run locally on the HMD, and eliminating the need to be tethered to an external device to generate video. These are sometimes referred to as smart goggles. To make the HMD construction lighter producers may move the processing system to connected smart necklace form-factor that would also offer the additional benefit of larger battery pack. Such solution would allow to design lite HMD with sufficient energy supply for dual video inputs or higher frequency time-based multiplexing.

Support of 3D Video Formats

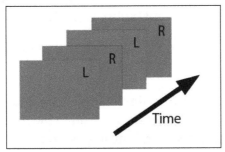

Frame sequential multiplexing.

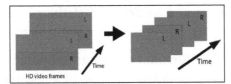

Side-by-side and top-bottom multiplexing.

Depth perception inside an HMD requires different images for the left and right eyes. There are multiple ways to provide these separate images:

- Use dual video inputs, thereby providing a completely separate video signal to each eye.

- Time-based multiplexing: Methods such as frame sequential combine two separate video signals into one signal by alternating the left and right images in successive frames.

- Side by side or top-bottom multiplexing: This method allocated half of the image to the left eye and the other half of the image to the right eye.

The advantage of dual video inputs is that it provides the maximum resolution for each image and the maximum frame rate for each eye. The disadvantage of dual video inputs is that it requires separate video outputs and cables from the device generating the content.

Time-based multiplexing preserves the full resolution per each image, but reduces the frame rate by half. For example, if the signal is presented at 60 Hz, each eye is receiving just 30 Hz updates. This may become an issue with accurately presenting fast-moving images.

Side-by-side and top-bottom multiplexing provide full-rate updates to each eye, but reduce the resolution presented to each eye. Many 3D broadcasts, such as ESPN, chose to provide side-by-side 3D which saves the need to allocate extra transmission bandwidth and is more suitable to fast-paced sports action relative to time-based multiplexing methods.

Not all HMDs provide depth perception. Some lower-end modules are essentially bi-ocular devices where both eyes are presented with the same image. 3D video players sometimes allow maximum compatibility with HMDs by providing the user with a choice of the 3D format to be used.

Peripherals

- The most rudimentary HMDs simply project an image or symbology on a wearer's visor or reticle. The image is not bound to the real world, i.e., the image does not change based on the wearer's head position.

- More sophisticated HMDs incorporate a positioning system that tracks the wearer's head position and angle, so that the picture or symbol displayed is congruent with the outside world using see-through imagery.

- Head tracking: Binding the imagery. Head-mounted displays may also be used with tracking sensors that detect changes of angle and orientation. When such data is available in the system computer, it can be used to generate the appropriate computer-generated imagery (CGI) for the angle-of-look at the particular time. This allows the user to look around a virtual reality environment simply by moving the head without the need for a separate controller to change the angle of the imagery. In radio-based systems (compared to wires), the wearer may move about within the tracking limits of the system.

- Eye tracking: Eye trackers measure the point of gaze, allowing a computer to sense where the user is looking. This information is useful in a variety of contexts such as user interface navigation: By sensing the user's gaze, a computer can change the information displayed on a screen, bring added details to attention, etc.

- Hand tracking: Tracking hand movement from the perspective of the HMD allows natural interaction with content and a convenient game-play mechanism.

EyeTap

An EyeTap is a concept for a wearable computing device that is worn in front of the eye that acts as a camera to record the scene available to the eye as well as a display to superimpose computer-generated imagery on the original scene available to the eye. This structure allows the user's eye to operate as both a monitor and a camera as the EyeTap intakes the world around it and augments the image the user sees allowing it to overlay computer-generated data over top of the normal world the user would perceive.

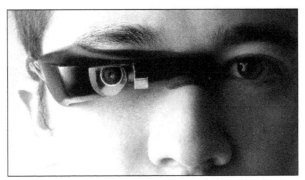

Man wearing a one-eyed injection-molded EyeTap.

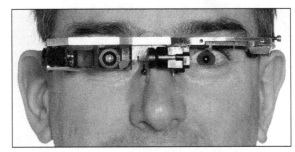

EyeTap inventor Steve Mann wearing a metal frame Laser EyeTap.

In order to capture what the eye is seeing as accurately as possible, an EyeTap uses a beam splitter to send the same scene (with reduced intensity) to both the eye and a camera. The camera then digitizes the reflected image of the scene and sends it to a computer. The computer processes the image and then sends it to a projector. The projector sends the image to the other side of the beam splitter so that this computer-generated image is reflected into the eye to be superimposed on the original scene. Stereo EyeTaps modify light passing through both eyes, but many research prototypes (mainly for reasons of ease of construction) only tap one eye.

EyeTap is also the name of an organization founded by inventor Steve Mann to develop and promote EyeTap-related technologies such as wearable computers.

Possible Uses

An EyeTap is somewhat like a head-up display (HUD). The important difference is that the scene available to the eye is also available to the computer that projects the head-up display. This enables the EyeTap to modify the computer generated scene in response to the natural scene. One use, for instance, would be a sports EyeTap: here the wearer, while in a stadium, would be able to follow a particular player in a field and have the EyeTap display statistics relevant to that player as a floating box above the player. Another practical use for the EyeTap would be in a construction yard as it would allow the user to reference the blueprints, especially in a 3D manner, to the current state of the building, display a list of current materials and their current locations as well perform basic measurements. Or, even in the business world, the EyeTap has great potential, for it would be capable of delivering to the user constant up to date information on the stock market, the user's corporation, and meeting statuses. On a more day-to-day basis some of Steve Mann's first uses for the technology was using it to keep track of names of people and places, his to-do lists, and keeping track of his other daily ordeals. The EyeTap Criteria are an attempt to define how close a real, practical device comes to such an ideal. EyeTaps could have great use in any field where the user would benefit from real-time interactive information that is largely visual in nature. This is sometimes referred to as computer-mediated reality, commonly known as augmented reality.

Inventor Steve Mann using weather-resistant
EyeTap together with a hydraulophone.

Eyetap has been explored as a potential tool for individuals with visual disabilities due to its abilities to direct visual information to parts of the retina that function well. As well, Eyetap's role in sousveillance has been explored by Mann, Jason Nolan and Barry Wellman.

Possible Side Effects

Users may find that they experience side effects such as headaches and difficulty sleeping if usage occurs shortly before sleep. Mann finds that due to his extensive use of the device that going without it can cause him to feel "nauseous, unsteady, naked" when he removes it.

Cyborglogs and EyeTaps

The EyeTap has applications in the world of cyborg logging, as it allows the user the ability to perform real-time visual capture of their daily lives from their own point of view. In this way, the EyeTap could be used to create a lifelong cyborg log or "glog" of the user's life and the events they participate in, potentially recording enough media to allow producers centuries in the future to present the user's life as interactive entertainment (or historical education) to consumers of that era.

Principle of Operation

The EyeTap is essentially a half-silvered mirror in front of the user's eye, reflecting some of the light into a sensor. The sensor then sends the image to the aremac, a display device capable of displaying data at any fitting depth. The output rays from the aremac are reflected off the half-silvered mirror back into the eye of the user along with the original light rays.

In these cases, the EyeTap views infrared light, as well as the overall design schematic of how the EyeTap manipulates lightrays.

A conceptual diagram of an EyeTap:

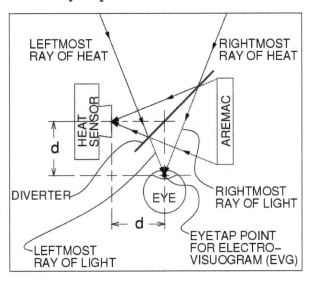

Components

CCD Cameras (Charge-coupled device) are the most common type of digital camera used today.

Head-up Display

A head-up display or heads-up display, also known as a HUD, is any transparent display that presents data without requiring users to look away from their usual viewpoints. The origin of the name stems from a pilot being able to view information with the head positioned "up" and looking forward, instead of angled down looking at lower instruments. A HUD also has the advantage that the pilot's eyes do not need to refocus to view the outside after looking at the optically nearer instruments.

HUD of an F/A-18 Hornet.

Although they were initially developed for military aviation, HUDs are now used in commercial aircraft, automobiles, and other (mostly professional) applications.

HUD mounted in a PZL TS-11 Iskra jet trainer aircraft with a
glass plate combiner and a convex collimating lens just below it.

A typical HUD contains three primary components: a projector unit, a combiner, and a video generation computer.

The projection unit in a typical HUD is an optical collimator setup: a convex lens or concave mirror with a cathode ray tube, light emitting diode display, or liquid crystal display at its focus. This setup (a design that has been around since the invention of the reflector sight) produces an image where the light is collimated, i.e. the focal point is perceived to be at infinity.

The combiner is typically an angled flat piece of glass (a beam splitter) located directly in front of the viewer. Combiners may have special coatings that reflect the monochromatic light projected onto it from the projector unit while allowing all other wavelengths of light to pass through. In some optical layouts combiners may also have a curved surface to re-focus the image from the projector.

The computer provides the interface between the HUD (i.e. the projection unit) and the systems/data to be displayed and generates the imagery and symbology to be displayed by the projection unit.

Types

Other than fixed mounted HUD, there are also head-mounted displays (HMDs). Including helmet mounted displays (both abbreviated HMD), forms of HUD that features a display element that moves with the orientation of the user's head.

Many modern fighters (such as the F/A-18, F-16, and Eurofighter) use both a HUD and HMD concurrently. The F-35 Lightning II was designed without a HUD, relying solely on the HMD, making it the first modern military fighter not to have a fixed HUD.

Generations

HUDs are split into four generations reflecting the technology used to generate the images:

- First Generation: Use a CRT to generate an image on a phosphor screen, having the disadvantage of the phosphor screen coating degrading over time. The majority of HUDs in operation today are of this type.

- Second Generation: Use a solid state light source, for example LED, which is modulated by an LCD screen to display an image. These systems do not fade or require the high voltages of first generation systems. These systems are on commercial aircraft.

- Third Generation: Use optical waveguides to produce images directly in the combiner rather than use a projection system.

- Fourth Generation: Use a scanning laser to display images and even video imagery on a clear transparent medium.

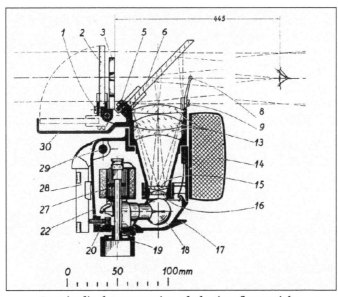

Longitudinal cross-section of a basic reflector sight.

Newer micro-display imaging technologies are being introduced, including liquid crystal display (LCD), liquid crystal on silicon (LCoS), digital micro-mirrors (DMD), and organic light-emitting diode (OLED).

Copilot's HUD of a C-130J.

HUDs evolved from the reflector sight, a pre-World War II parallax-free optical sight technology for military fighter aircraft. The gyro gunsight added a reticle that moved based on the speed and turn rate to solve for the amount of lead needed to hit a target while maneuvering.

During the early 1940s, the Telecommunications Research Establishment (TRE), in charge of UK radar development, found that Royal Air Force (RAF) night fighter pilots were having a hard time reacting to the verbal instruction of the radar operator as they approached their targets. They experimented with the addition of a second radar display for the pilot, but found they had trouble looking up from the lit screen into the dark sky in order to find the target. In October 1942 they had successfully combined the image from the radar tube with a projection from their standard GGS Mk. II gyro gunsight on a flat area of the windscreen, and later in the gunsight itself. A key upgrade was the move from the original AI Mk. IV radar to the microwave-frequency AI Mk. VIII radar found on the de Havilland Mosquito night fighter. This set produced an artificial horizon that further eased head-up flying.

In 1955 the US Navy's Office of Naval Research and Development did some research with a mockup HUD concept unit along with a sidestick controller in an attempt to ease the pilot's burden flying modern jet aircraft and make the instrumentation less complicated during flight. While their research was never incorporated in any aircraft of that time, the crude HUD mockup they built had all the features of today's modern HUD units.

HUD technology was next advanced by the Royal Navy in the Buccaneer, the prototype of which first flew on 30 April 1958. The aircraft was designed to fly at very low altitudes at very high speeds and drop bombs in engagements lasting seconds. As such, there was no time for the pilot to look up from the instruments to a bombsight. This led to the concept of a "Strike Sight" that would combine altitude, airspeed and the gun/bombsight into a single gunsight-like display. There was fierce competition between supporters of the new HUD design and supporters of the old electro-mechanical gun-sight, with the HUD being described as a radical, even foolhardy option.

The Air Arm branch of the UK Ministry of Defence sponsored the development of a Strike Sight. The Royal Aircraft Establishment (RAE) designed the equipment and the earliest usage of the term "head-up-display" can be traced to this time. Production units were built by Cintel, and the system was first integrated in 1958. The Cintel HUD business was taken over by Elliott Flight Automation and the Buccaneer HUD was manufactured and further developed, continuing up to a Mark III version with a total of 375 systems made; it was given a 'fit and forget' title by the Royal Navy and it was still in service nearly 25 years later. BAE Systems, as successor to Elliotts via GEC-Marconi Avionics, thus has a claim to the world's first Head Up Display in operational service. A similar version that replaced the bombing modes with missile-attack modes was part of the AIRPASS HUD fit to the English Electric Lightning.

In the United Kingdom, it was soon noted that pilots flying with the new gun-sights were becoming better at piloting their aircraft. At this point, the HUD expanded its purpose beyond weapon aiming to general piloting. In the 1960s, French test-pilot Gilbert Klopfstein created the first modern HUD and a standardized system of HUD symbols so that pilots would only have to learn one system and could more easily transition between aircraft. The modern HUD used in instrument flight rules approaches to landing was developed in 1975. Klopfstein pioneered HUD technology in military fighter jets and helicopters, aiming to centralize critical flight data within the pilot's field of vision. This approach sought to increase the pilot's scan efficiency and reduce "task saturation" and information overload.

Use of HUDs then expanded beyond military aircraft. In the 1970s, the HUD was introduced to commercial aviation, and in 1988, the Oldsmobile Cutlass Supreme became the first production car with a head-up display.

Until a few years ago, the Embraer 190, Saab 2000, Boeing 727, Boeing 737-300, 400, 500 and Boeing 737 New Generation Aircraft (737-600,700,800, and 900 series) were the only commercial passenger aircraft available with HUDs. However, the technology is becoming more common with aircraft such as the Canadair RJ, Airbus A318 and several business jets featuring the displays. HUDs have become standard equipment on the Boeing 787. Furthermore, the Airbus A320, A330, A340 and A380 families are currently undergoing the certification process for a HUD. HUDs were also added to the Space Shuttle orbiter.

Design Factors

There are several factors that interplay in the design of a HUD:

- Field of View: Also "FOV", indicates the angle(s), vertically as well as horizon-tally, subtended at the pilot's eye, that the combiner displays symbology in relation to the outside view. A narrow FOV means that the view (of a runway, for example) through the combiner might include little additional information beyond the perimeters of the runway environment; whereas a wide FOV would allow a 'broader' view. For aviation applications, the major benefit of a wide FOV is that an aircraft approaching the runway in a crosswind might still have the runway in view through the combiner, even though the aircraft is pointed well away from the runway threshold; where a narrow FOV the runway would be 'off the edge' of the combiner, out of the HUD's view. Because the human eyes are separated, each eye receives a different image. The HUD image is viewable by one or both eyes, depending on technical and budget limitations in the design process. Modern expectations are that both eyes view the same image, in other words a "binocular Field of View (FOV)".

- Collimation: The projected image is collimated which makes the light rays parallel. Because the light rays are parallel the lens of the human eye focuses on infinity to get a clear image. Collimated images on the HUD combiner are perceived as existing at or near optical infinity. This means that the pilot's eyes do not need to refocus to view the outside world and the HUD display the image appears to be "out there", overlaying the outside world. This feature is critical for effective HUDs: not having to refocus between HUD-displayed symbolic information and the outside world onto which that information is overlaid is one of the main advantages of collimated HUDs. It gives HUDs special consideration in safety-critical and time-critical manoeuvers, when the few seconds a pilot needs in order to re-focus inside the cockpit, and then back outside, are very critical: for example, in the final stages of landing. Collimation is therefore a primary distinguishing feature of high-performance HUDs and differentiates them from consumer-quality systems that, for example, simply reflect uncollimated information off a car's windshield (causing drivers to refocus and shift attention from the road ahead).

- Eyebox: The optical collimator produces a cylinder of parallel light so the display can only be viewed while the viewer's eyes are somewhere within that cylinder, a three-dimensional area called the head motion box or eyebox. Modern HUD eyeboxes are usually about 5 lateral by 3 vertical by 6 longitudinal inches. This allows the viewer some freedom of head movement but movement too far up/down left/right will cause the display to vanish off the edge of the collimator and movement too far back will cause it to crop off around the edge (vignette). The pilot is able to view the entire display as long as one of the eyes is inside the eyebox.

- Luminance/contrast: Displays have adjustments in luminance and contrast to account for ambient lighting, which can vary widely (e.g., from the glare of bright clouds to moonless night approaches to minimally lit fields).

- Boresight: Aircraft HUD components are very accurately aligned with the aircraft's three axes – a process called boresighting – so that displayed data conforms to reality typically with an accuracy of ±7.0 milliradians (±24 minutes of arc), and may vary across the HUD's FOV. In this case the word "conform" means, "when an object is projected on the combiner and the actual object is visible, they will be aligned". This allows the display to show the pilot exactly where the artificial horizon is, as well as the aircraft's projected path with great accuracy. When Enhanced Vision is used, for example, the display of runway lights are aligned with the actual runway lights when the real lights become visible. Boresighting is done during the aircraft's building process and can also be performed in the field on many aircraft.

- Scaling: The displayed image (flight path, pitch and yaw scaling, etc.), are scaled to present to the pilot a picture that overlays the outside world in an exact 1:1 relationship. For example, objects (such as a runway threshold) that are 3 degrees below the horizon as viewed from the cockpit must appear at the −3 degree index on the HUD display.

- Compatibility: HUD components are designed to be compatible with other avionics, displays, etc.

Contact Lens

Contact lenses that display AR imaging are in development. These bionic contact lenses might contain the elements for display embedded into the lens including integrated circuitry, LEDs and an antenna for wireless communication. The first contact lens display was reported in 1999, then 11 years later in 2010-2011. Another version of contact lenses, in development for the U.S. military, is designed to function with AR spectacles, allowing soldiers to focus on close-to-the-eye AR images on the spectacles and distant real world objects at the same time.

The futuristic short film Sight features contact lens-like augmented reality devices.

Many scientists have been working on contact lenses capable of different technological feats. A patent filed by Samsung describes an AR contact lens, that, when finished, will include a built-in camera on the lens itself. The design is intended to control its interface by blinking an eye. It is also intended to be linked with the user's smartphone to review footage, and control it separately. When successful, the lens would feature a camera, or sensor inside of it. It is said that it could be anything from a light sensor, to a temperature sensor.

In Augmented Reality, the distinction is made between two distinct modes of tracking, known as marker and markerless. Markers are visual cues which trigger the display of the virtual information. A piece of paper with some distinct geometries can be used. The camera recognizes the geometries by identifying specific points in the drawing. Markerless tracking, also called instant tracking, does not use markers. Instead, the user positions the object in the camera view preferably in a horizontal plane. It uses sensors in mobile devices to accurately detect the real-world environment, such as the locations of walls and points of intersection.

Virtual Retinal Display

A virtual retinal display (VRD) is a personal display device under development at the University of Washington's Human Interface Technology Laboratory under Dr. Thomas A. Furness III. With this technology, a display is scanned directly onto the retina of a viewer's eye. This results in bright images with high resolution and high contrast. The viewer sees what appears to be a conventional display floating in space.

Several of tests were done to analyze the safety of the VRD. In one test, patients with partial loss of vision—having either macular degeneration (a disease that degenerates the retina) or keratoconus—were selected to view images using the technology. In the macular degeneration group, five out of eight subjects preferred the VRD images to the cathode-ray tube (CRT) or paper images and thought they were better and brighter and were able to see equal or better resolution levels. The Keratoconus patients could all resolve smaller lines in several line tests using the VRD as opposed to their own correction. They also found the VRD images to be easier to view and sharper. As a result of these several tests, virtual retinal display is considered safe technology.

Virtual retinal display creates images that can be seen in ambient daylight and ambient room light. The VRD is considered a preferred candidate to use in a surgical display due to its combination of high resolution and high contrast and brightness. Additional tests show high potential for VRD to be used as a display technology for patients that have low vision.

Software

Man-machine Communication

Interactive programs have to establish a bidirectional communication with humans. Not only they have to let humans modify information, but they have to present it in a way to make it simple to understand, to indicate what types of manipulations are permitted, and to make it obvious how to do it. As noted by Marcus, awareness of semiotic principles, in particular the use of metaphors is essential for researchers and developers in achieving more efficient, effective ways to communicate to more diverse user communities. As a common vocabulary is the first step towards effective communication, user-interface software development systems should assist developers by providing implementations of standard interaction metaphors. This has been a very successful approach for 2D interfaces. Recent research in the 3D interaction field has focused on exploring responsive 3D interfaces with better affordances, functional fidelity and mental appeal. Growing the vocabulary of 3D interaction metaphors is an active research subject.

Iterative Construction

Multiple iteration of the classic design-implement-test cycle have to be done, and it is difficult to evaluate the time that has to be spent before validation. A classic survey on user interface programming reports that more than 90% of the projects analyzed that included a user interface used an iterative approach to design and implementation. The same report shows that in today's applications, an average of 48% of the code is devoted to the user interface portion. The report underlines the importance of user interface tools, such as toolkits, user interface management systems, or graphical user interface builders.

In the case of virtual environment, no standard solution exists. The design of software architectures to support construction and rapid prototyping of three dimensional interfaces, interactive illustrations, and three dimensional widgets is an important area of research.

Parallel Programming

Interactive applications have to model user interaction with a dynamically changing world. In order for this to be possible, it is necessary for applications to handle within a short time real-world events that are generated in an order that is not known before the simulation is run. Thus, user interface software is inherently parallel, and some form of parallelism, from quasiparallelism, to pseudo-parallelism to real parallelism has to be used for its development.

All problems inherent to parallel programming have thus to be solved (e.g., synchronization, maintenance of consistency, protection of shared data).

Furthermore, the multimodal aspect of virtual environment applications impose the use of true parallelism, as the various components of an applications have to receive input and produce output at considerably variable rates (e.g., 10 Hz for visual feedback and 1 KHz for haptic feedback).

Performance

Virtual reality applications have very stringent performance requirements. In particular, low visual feedback bandwidth can destroy the illusion of animation, while high latency can induce simulation sickness and loss of feeling of control. In order to be spatio-temporally realistic, and thus effectively useable, applications should meet latency and visual feedback constraints. This high sensitivity of humans to latency and visual feedback rates frequency requires that appropriate techniques be used in VR applications to minimize the latency and maximize the feedback frequency. These two aspects are related but are not the same thing: for instance, using pipelined multiprocessing to increase computation speed is a way to probably increase feedback frequency that is likely to also increase application latency. For this reason, simply optimizing standard applications is not sufficient.

Robustness

The contract model of software programming is a way to specify and understand the behavior of software units. With this model, precondition and postcondition describe the benefits and obligation in the software contract that relates the software unit supplier to its clients. User interface software units are forced to have weak preconditions, since few assumptions can be made on the behavior of the external world. This makes its realization and verification more difficult.

Modularization

The ease of creation and maintenance of a piece of software is improved by decoupling it in units with very weak coupling, so as to develop and test them in isolation. Unfortunately, a complete separation between user interface and application is very difficult to obtain. In particular, the need of semantic feedback associated to the different operation tends to increase the coupling among application and interface components. This fact often forces a change in application parts because of changes in the user interface.

Information Presentation

Presenting information in 3D space introduces problems which are not present in classical 2D interfaces. In particular, occlusion and perspective effects offer both new possibilities and new challenges to visualization. Treating 3D information is more complex than treating the 2D counterpart (e.g., because of the complexity of 3D geometric space) and, in particular, 3D manipulation requires more dexterity. A notable example demonstrating the potential of 3D interfaces for information presentation is Xerox Parc's Information Visualizer. Built using the Cognitive Coprocessor architecture, it takes advantage of the greater possibilities of 3D with novel means of information presentation, such as the cone tree and the perspective wall.

Perceptual Requirements

The perceptual requirements of virtual reality application are more complex to satisfy that those of standard graphical applications.

Software Solutions

The fact that virtual reality software is intrinsically difficult to design and implement emphasizes the importance of user interface tools, such as toolkits, frameworks, user interface management systems, or graphical user interface builders.

Current systems to support virtual reality software construction are subdivided into two categories: toolkits and authoring systems. Toolkits are programming libraries that provide a set of functions for supporting the creation of a virtual reality application. Authoring systems are complete programs with graphical interfaces for creating worlds without resorting to detailed programming. These usually include some sort of scripting language in which to describe complex actions (e.g., VRML, which is becoming a defacto standard for describing virtual worlds). While simpler to use, current authoring system do not offer all the functionalities of toolkits.

At the current state of the art, no single system supports satisfactorily all the aspects of creation of a virtual reality application. Most of the time, different systems have to be combined, and ad-hoc solutions implemented to integrate them in a working application. A typical VR toolkit provides supports for high-speed rendering (mostly through the use of some form of level-of-detail modeling), low-level interfacing with a variety of input devices (at the minimum supporting high frequency sensor reading for input and a variety of graphics display formats for output), a few built-in interaction metaphors (at the minimum for viewpoint/object motion and picking), graphical database support with converters to/from a variety of formats, and an event model for interactive application programming. Tools of this kind range from zero or low-cost solution (e.g., Rend386, Superscape, OpenGL Optimizer) to high-end "professional" packages (e.g., Division dVS and dVise, Sense8 World Tool Kit WTK). The increased power of parallel processing is essential to meet timing constraints in real applications, and for this reason high-end graphics systems are network-parallel or MP-parallel. No system to date, however, incorporates appropriate support to time-critical graphics and low-latency synchronization schemes.

In addition to generic support systems, a variety of software tools exist to solve specific problems. Examples are domain-specific toolkits for supporting distributed application, libraries for implementing high-speed collision detection, and tools for supporting physical simulation with haptic feedback. In parallel, a few toolkits, such as UGA, VB2, Alice, and OpenInventor, provide support for 3D interaction techniques that go beyond the standard picking and viewpoint/object motion, implementing in particular 3D widgets or virtual tools.

References

- Norris, G.; Thomas, G.; Wagner, M. & Forbes Smith, C. (2005). Boeing 787 Dreamliner—Flying Redefined. Aerospace Technical Publications International. ISBN 0-9752341-2-9

- Wagner, Daniel (29 September 2009). First Steps Towards Handheld Augmented Reality. ACM. ISBN 9780769520346. Retrieved 29 September 2009

- Krevelen, Poelman, D.W.F, Ronald (2010). A Survey of Augmented Reality Technologies, Applications and Limitations. International Journal of Virtual Reality. pp. 3, 6

- Dähne, Patrick; Karigiannis, John N. (2002). Archeoguide: System Architecture of a Mobile Outdoor Augmented Reality System. ISBN 9780769517810. Retrieved 6 January, 2010

- Shibata, Takashi (1 April 2002). "Head mounted display". Displays. 23 (1–2): 57–64. doi:10.1016/S0141-9382(02)00010-0. ISSN 0141-9382

- Fred H. Previc; William R. Ercoline (2004). Spatial Disorientation in Aviation. AIAA. p. 452. ISBN 978-1-60086-451-3

4

3D Graphics

3D graphics refers to the use of three-dimensional geometric data and algorithms for rendering 2D images, etc. It makes use of wire-frame model, Schlick's approximation, depth map, false radiosity and smoothing group. All the concepts related to 3D graphics have been carefully analyzed in this chapter.

3D graphics or three-dimensional graphics is a sphere of computer graphics, a set of techniques and tools allowing creating three-dimensional objects using shapes and colors. It differs from the two-dimensional images by the creation of a geometrical projection of a three-dimensional model of the scene (virtual space) in the 2D. This is executed with the help of specialized software. The resulting model can be the same as the real-world objects (e.g., a building, a person, a car, an asteroid), or to be completely abstract (projection of the four-dimensional fractal).

Today, 3D graphics firmly entered many areas of our lives:

- Construction (visualization of volumetric images of architectural buildings, objects, interior and exterior).

- Production (object modeling).

- TV (simulated images in glossy magazines, video clips, special effects in the movie).

- The game industry (3D-animations and virtual worlds, the development of computer games).

- Polygraph (creating the printed products).

- Commercial (electronic presentations and catalogs, billboards, etc.) and so on.

3D graphics is one of the most effective tools in advertising, allowing extending the impact on the potential customer and raise the quality of ads presenting both real and virtual worlds.

3D modeling is the process of creating three-dimensional model of the object. 3D-modeling' goal is to develop a volumetric visual image of the desired object. With the help of three-dimensional graphics, you can create an exact copy of any object, and to develop new, unreal object, which has not existed until now.

Application

Three-dimensional graphics actively used to create the images on the flat screen or sheet of printed materials in science and industry. For example, in the systems of aided design (CAD; to create solid-state elements: buildings, machinery parts, mechanisms), architectural visualization (this includes so-called "virtual archaeology"), in modern systems of medical imaging.

Its widest use is in many modern computer games, as well as an element of film industry, television, and printed products.

Three-dimensional graphics usually deals with a virtual, imaginary three-dimensional space that is to be displayed on a flat, two-dimensional surface or paper. Nowadays there are known several ways to display the three-dimensional information in a volumetric form, although most of them represent three-dimensional characteristics with many conditions, because they work with the stereo images. Stereo glasses, virtual helmets, 3D-displays able to demonstrate the three-dimensional images. Several manufacturers have demonstrated the readiness for serial production of three-dimensional displays. However, they still do not allow you to create a solid-state in physics, tangible copy of a mathematical model that is easily created by three-dimensional graphics. Developing since 1990s, technology of rapid prototyping eliminates this gap. This technology uses a mathematical representation of the object model as a solid-state object (so-called "Voxel model").

3D computer graphics are graphics that utilize a three-dimensional representation of geometric data that is stored in the computer for the purposes of performing calculations and rendering 2D images. Such images may be for later display or for real-time viewing.

Despite these differences, 3D computer graphics rely on many of the same algorithms as 2D computer vector graphics in the wire frame model and 2D computer raster graphics in the final rendered display.

In computer graphics software, the distinction between 2D and 3D is occasionally blurred; 2D applications may use 3D techniques to achieve effects such as lighting, and primarily 3D may use 2D rendering techniques. 3D computer graphics are often referred to as 3D models.

Apart from the rendered graphic, the model is contained within the graphical data file. However, there are differences. A 3D model is the mathematical representation of any three-dimensional object (either inanimate or living). A model is not technically a graphic until it is visually displayed. Due to 3D printing, 3D models are not confined to virtual space. A model can be displayed visually as a two-dimensional image through a process called 3D rendering, or used in non-graphical computer simulations and calculations.

3D graphics techniques and their application are fundamental to the entertainment, games, and computer-aided design industries. It is a continuing area of research in scientific visualization.

Furthermore, 3D graphics components are now a part of almost every personal computer and, although traditionally intended for graphics-intensive software such as games, they are increasingly being used by other applications.

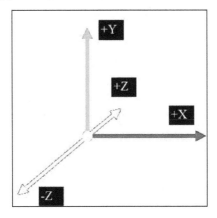

Parallel Projection

Parallel projection discards z-coordinate and parallel lines from each vertex on the object are extended until they intersect the view plane. In parallel projection, we specify a direction of projection instead of center of projection.

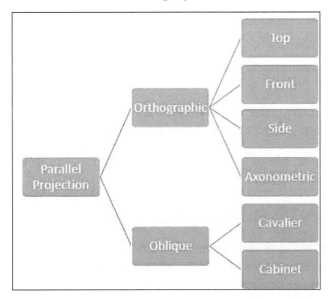

In parallel projection, the distance from the center of projection to project plane is infinite. In this type of projection, we connect the projected vertices by line segments which correspond to connections on the original object.

Parallel projections are less realistic, but they are good for exact measurements. In this type of projections, parallel lines remain parallel and angles are not preserved. Various types of parallel projections are shown in the following hierarchy.

Orthographic Projection

In orthographic projection the direction of projection is normal to the projection of the plane. There are three types of orthographic projections:

- Front Projection.

- Top Projection.

- Side Projection.

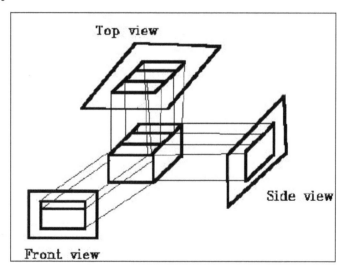

Oblique Projection

In oblique projection, the direction of projection is not normal to the projection of plane. In oblique projection, we can view the object better than orthographic projection.

There are two types of oblique projections – Cavalier and Cabinet. The Cavalier projection makes 45° angle with the projection plane. The projection of a line perpendicular to the view plane has the same length as the line itself in Cavalier projection. In a cavalier projection, the foreshortening factors for all three principal directions are equal.

The Cabinet projection makes 63.4° angle with the projection plane. In Cabinet projection, lines perpendicular to the viewing surface are projected at ½ their actual length. Both the projections are shown in figure.

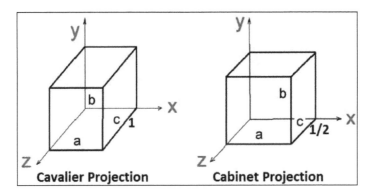

Cavalier Projection   Cabinet Projection

Isometric Projections

Orthographic projections that show more than one side of an object are called axonometric orthographic projections. The most common axonometric projection is an isometric projection where the projection plane intersects each coordinate axis in the model coordinate system at an equal distance. In this projection parallelism of lines are preserved but angles are not preserved. The following figure shows isometric projection:

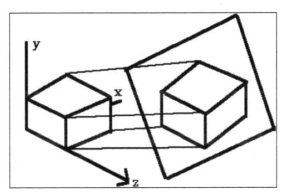

Perspective Projection

In perspective projection, the distance from the center of projection to project plane is finite and the size of the object varies inversely with distance which looks more realistic.

The distance and angles are not preserved and parallel lines do not remain parallel. Instead, they all converge at a single point called center of projection or projection reference point. There are 3 types of perspective projections:

- One point perspective projection is simple to draw.

- Two point perspective projection gives better impression of depth.

- Three point perspective projection is most difficult to draw.

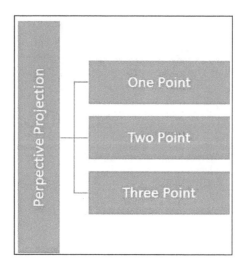

The following figure shows all the three types of perspective projection:

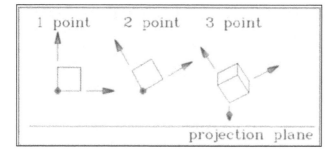

Translation

In 3D translation, we transfer the Z coordinate along with the X and Y coordinates. The process for translation in 3D is similar to 2D translation. A translation moves an object into a different position on the screen.

The following figure shows the effect of translation:

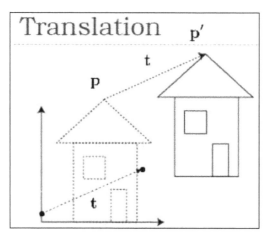

A point can be translated in 3D by adding translation coordinate (t_x, t_y, t_z) to the original coordinate X,Y,Z to get the new coordinate X',Y',Z':

$$T = \begin{bmatrix} 1 & 0 & 0 & 0 \\ 0 & 1 & 0 & 0 \\ 0 & 0 & 1 & 0 \\ t_x & t_y & t_z & 1 \end{bmatrix}$$

$$P' = P \cdot T$$

$$[X'Y'Z'1] = [XYZ1] \begin{bmatrix} 1 & 0 & 0 & 0 \\ 0 & 1 & 0 & 0 \\ 0 & 0 & 1 & 0 \\ t_x & t_y & t_z & 1 \end{bmatrix}$$

$$= [X + t_x \ Y + t_y \ Z + t_z \ 1]$$

3D Modeling

In 3D computer graphics, 3D modeling is the process of developing a mathematical representation of any surface of an object (either inanimate or living) in three dimensions via specialized software. The product is called a 3D model. Someone who works with 3D models may be referred to as a 3D artist. It can be displayed as a two-dimensional image through a process called 3D rendering or used in a computer simulation of physical phenomena. The model can also be physically created using 3D printing devices.

Models may be created automatically or manually. The manual modeling process of preparing geometric data for 3D computer graphics is similar to plastic arts such as sculpting.

3D modeling software is a class of 3D computer graphics software used to produce 3D models. Individual programs of this class are called modeling applications or modelers.

Models

Three-dimensional (3D) models represent a physical body using a collection of points in 3D space, connected by various geometric entities such as triangles, lines, curved surfaces, etc. Being a collection of data (points and other information), 3D models can be created by hand, algorithmically (procedural modeling), or scanned. Their surfaces may be further defined with texture mapping.

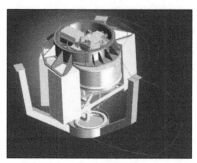

Three-dimensional model of a spectrograph.

3D models are widely used anywhere in 3D graphics and CAD. Their use predates the widespread use of 3D graphics on personal computers. Many computer games used pre-rendered images of 3D models as sprites before computers could render them in real-time. The designer can then see the model in various directions and views, this can help the designer see if the object is created as intended to compared to their original vision. Seeing the design this way can help the designer/company figure out changes or improvements needed to the product.

3D selfie models are generated from 2D pictures taken
at the Fantasitron 3D photo booth at Madurodam.

Today, 3D models are used in a wide variety of fields. The medical industry uses detailed models of organs; these may be created with multiple 2-D image slices from an MRI or CT scan. The movie industry uses them as characters and objects for animated and real-life motion pictures. The video game industry uses them as assets for computer and video games. The science sector uses them as highly detailed models of chemical compounds. The architecture industry uses them to demonstrate proposed buildings and landscapes in lieu of traditional, physical architectural models. The engineering community uses them as designs of new devices, vehicles and structures as well as a host of other uses. In recent decades the earth science community has started to construct 3D geological models as a standard practice. 3D models can also be the basis for physical devices that are built with 3D printers or CNC machines.

Representation

A modern render of the iconic Utah teapot model developed
by Martin Newell. The Utah teapot is one of the most common
models used in 3D graphics education.

Almost all 3D models can be divided into two categories:

- Solid: These models define the volume of the object they represent (like a rock). Solid models are mostly used for engineering and medical simulations, and are usually built with constructive solid geometry.

- Shell/boundary: These models represent the surface, e.g. the boundary of the object, not its volume (like an infinitesimally thin eggshell). Almost all visual models used in games and film are shell models.

Solid and shell modeling can create functionally identical objects. Differences between them are mostly variations in the way they are created and edited and conventions of use in various fields and differences in types of approximations between the model and reality.

Shell models must be manifold (having no holes or cracks in the shell) to be meaningful as a real object. Polygonal meshes (and to a lesser extent subdivision surfaces) are by far the most common representation. Level sets are a useful representation for deforming surfaces which undergo many topological changes such as fluids.

The process of transforming representations of objects, such as the middle point coordinate of a sphere and a point on its circumference into a polygon representation of a sphere, is called tessellation. This step is used in polygon-based rendering, where objects are broken down from abstract representations ("primitives") such as spheres, cones etc., to so-called meshes, which are nets of interconnected triangles. Meshes of triangles (instead of e.g. squares) are popular as they have proven to be easy to rasterise (the surface described by each triangle is planar, so the projection is always convex). Polygon representations are not used in all rendering techniques, and in these cases the tessellation step is not included in the transition from abstract representation to rendered scene.

Modeling Process

There are three popular ways to represent a model:

- Polygonal modeling: Points in 3D space, called vertices, are connected by line segments to form a polygon mesh. The vast majority of 3D models today are built as textured polygonal models, because they are flexible and because computers can render them so quickly. However, polygons are planar and can only approximate curved surfaces using many polygons.

- Curve modelling: Surfaces are defined by curves, which are influenced by weighted control points. The curve follows (but does not necessarily interpolate) the points. Increasing the weight for a point will pull the curve closer to that point. Curve types include nonuniform rational B-spline (NURBS), splines, patches, and geometric primitives.

- Digital sculpting: Still a fairly new method of modeling, 3D sculpting has become very popular in the few years it has been around. There are currently three types of digital sculpting: Displacement, which is the most widely used among applications at this moment, uses a dense model (often generated by subdivision surfaces of a polygon control mesh) and stores new locations for the vertex positions through use of an image map that stores the adjusted locations. Volumetric, loosely based on voxels, has similar capabilities as displacement but does not suffer from polygon stretching when there are not enough polygons in a region to achieve a deformation. Dynamic tessellation is similar to voxel but divides the surface using triangulation to maintain a smooth surface and allow finer details. These methods allow for very artistic exploration as the model will have a new topology created over it once the models form and possibly details have been sculpted. The new mesh will usually have the original high resolution mesh information transferred into displacement data or normal map data if for a game engine.

A 3D fantasy fish composed of organic surfaces generated using LAI4D.

The modeling stage consists of shaping individual objects that are later used in the scene. There are a number of modeling techniques, including:

- Constructive solid geometry.

- Implicit surfaces.

- Subdivision surfaces.

Modeling can be performed by means of a dedicated program (e.g., Cinema 4D, Maya, 3ds Max, Blender, LightWave, Modo) or an application component (Shaper, Lofter in

3ds Max) or some scene description language (as in POV-Ray). In some cases, there is no strict distinction between these phases; in such cases modeling is just part of the scene creation process (this is the case, for example, with Caligari trueSpace and Realsoft 3D).

3D models can also be created using the technique of Photogrammetry with dedicated programs such as RealityCapture, Metashape, 3DF Zephyr, and Meshroom, and cleanup applications such as MeshLab, netfabb or MeshMixer. Photogrammetry creates models using algorithms to interpret the shape and texture of real-world objects and environments based on photographs taken from many angles of the subject.

Complex materials such as blowing sand, clouds, and liquid sprays are modeled with particle systems, and are a mass of 3D coordinates which have either points, polygons, texture splats, or sprites assigned to them.

Human Models

The first widely available commercial application of human virtual models appeared in 1998 on the Lands' End web site. The human virtual models were created by the company My Virtual Mode Inc. and enabled users to create a model of themselves and try on 3D clothing. There are several modern programs that allow for the creation of virtual human models (Poser being one example).

3D Clothing

Dynamic 3D clothing model made in marvelous designer.

The development of cloth simulation software such as Marvelous Designer, CLO3D and Optitex, has enabled artists and fashion designers to model dynamic 3D clothing on the computer. Dynamic 3D clothing is used for virtual fashion catalogs, as well as for dressing 3D characters for video games, 3D animation movies, for digital doubles in movies as well as for making clothes for avatars in virtual worlds such as SecondLife.

Compared to 2D Methods

3D photorealistic effects are often achieved without wireframe modeling and are sometimes indistinguishable in the final form. Some graphic art software includes filters that can be applied to 2D vector graphics or 2D raster graphics on transparent layers.

Advantages of wireframe 3D modeling over exclusively 2D methods include:

- Flexibility, ability to change angles or animate images with quicker rendering of the changes.

- Ease of rendering, automatic calculation and rendering photorealistic effects rather than mentally visualizing or estimating.

- Accurate photorealism, less chance of human error in misplacing, overdoing, or forgetting to include a visual effect.

Disadvantages compare to 2D photorealistic rendering may include a software learning curve and difficulty achieving certain photorealistic effects. Some photorealistic effects may be achieved with special rendering filters included in the 3D modeling software. For the best of both worlds, some artists use a combination of 3D modeling followed by editing the 2D computer-rendered images from the 3D model.

3D Model Market

A large market for 3D models (as well as 3D-related content, such as textures, scripts, etc.) still exists – either for individual models or large collections. Several online marketplaces for 3D content allow individual artists to sell content that they have created, including TurboSquid, CGStudio, CreativeMarket, Sketchfab, CGTrader and Cults. Often, the artists' goal is to get additional value out of assets they have previously created for projects. By doing so, artists can earn more money out of their old content, and companies can save money by buying pre-made models instead of paying an employee to create one from scratch. These marketplaces typically split the sale between themselves and the artist that created the asset, artists get 40% to 95% of the sales according to the marketplace. In most cases, the artist retains ownership of the 3d model; the customer only buys the right to use and present the model. Some artists sell their products directly in its own stores offering their products at a lower price by not using intermediaries.

Over the last several years numerous marketplaces specialized in 3D printing models have emerged. Some of the 3D printing marketplaces are combination of models sharing sites, with or without a built in e-com capability. Some of those platforms also offer 3D printing services on demand, software for model rendering and dynamic viewing of items, etc. 3D printing file sharing platforms include Shapeways, Sketchfab, Pinshape, Thingiverse, TurboSquid, CGTrader, Threeding, MyMiniFactory, and GrabCAD.

3D Printing

3D printing is a form of additive manufacturing technology where a three dimensional object is created by laying down or build from successive layers of material.

3D printing is a great way to create objects because you can create objects that you couldn't make otherwise without having complex expensive molds created or by having the objects made with multiple parts. A 3D printed part can be edited by simply editing the 3D model. That avoids having to do any additional tooling which can save time and money. 3D printing is great for testing out an idea without having to go through the production process which is great for getting a physical form of the person/company's idea.

In recent years, there has been an upsurge in the number of companies offering personalized 3D printed models of objects that have been scanned, designed in CAD software, and then printed to the customer's requirements. 3D models can be purchased from online marketplaces and printed by individuals or companies using commercially available 3D printers, enabling the home-production of objects such as spare parts, mathematical models, and even medical equipment.

Uses

3D modeling is used in various industries like film, animation and gaming, interior design and architecture. They are also used in the medical industry to create interactive representations of anatomy. A wide number of 3D software are also used in constructing digital representation of mechanical models or parts before they are actually manufactured. CAD/CAM related software are used in such fields, and with these software, not only can you construct the parts, but also assemble them, and observe their functionality.

3D modeling is also used in the field of Industrial Design, wherein products are 3D modeled before representing them to the clients. In Media and Event industries, 3D modeling is used in Stage/Set Design.

The OWL 2 translation of the vocabulary of X3D can be used to provide semantic descriptions for 3D models, which is suitable for indexing and retrieval of 3D models by features such as geometry, dimensions, material, texture, diffuse reflection, transmission spectra, transparency, reflectivity, opalescence, glazes, varnishes, and enamels (as opposed to unstructured textual descriptions or 2.5D virtual museums and exhibitions using Google Street View on Google Arts and Culture, for example). The RDF representation of 3D models can be used in reasoning, which enables intelligent 3D applications which, for example, can automatically compare two 3D models by volume.

Testing a 3D Solid Model

3D solid models can be tested in different ways depending on what is needed by using simulation, mechanism design, and analysis. If a motor is designed and assembled correctly (this can be done differently depending on what 3D modeling program is being used), using the mechanism tool the user should be able to tell if the motor or machine is assembled correctly by how it operates. Different design will need to be tested in different ways. For example; a pool pump would need a simulation ran of the water running through the pump to see how the water flows through the pump. These test verify if a product is developed correctly or if it needs to me modified to meet its requirements.

Box Modeling

Box modeling is a technique in 3D modeling where a primitive shape (such as a box, cylinder, sphere, etc.) is used to make the basic shape of the final model. This basic shape is then used to sculpt out the final model. The process uses a number of repetitive steps to reach the final product, which can lead to a more efficient and more controlled modelling process.

Subdivision

Subdivision modeling is derived from the idea that as a work is progressed, should the artist want to make their work appear less sharp, or "blocky", each face would be divided up into smaller, more detailed faces (usually into sets of four). However, more experienced box modelers manage to create their model without subdividing the faces of the model. Basically, box modeling is broken down into the very basic concept of polygonal management.

Quads

Quadrilateral faces, commonly named "quads", are the fundamental entity in box modeling. If an artist were to start with a cube, the artist would have six quad faces to work with before extrusion. While most applications for three-dimensional art provide abilities for faces up to any size, results are often more predictable and consistent when working with quads. This is so because if one were to draw an X connecting the corner vertices of a quad, the surface normal is nearly always the same. We say nearly because, when a quad is something other than a perfect parallelogram (such as a rhombus or trapezoid), the surface normal would be different. Also, a quad subdivides into two or four triangles cleanly, making it easier to prepare the model for software that can only handle triangles.

Advantages and Disadvantages

Box modeling is a modeling method that is quick and easy to learn. It is also appreciably faster than placing each point individually. However, it is difficult to add high amounts of detail to models created using this technique without practice.

3D Projection

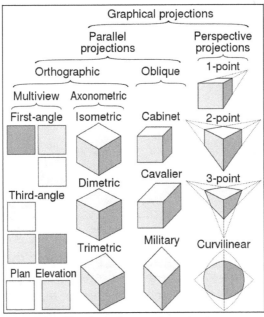

Classification of some 3D projections.

A 3D projection or graphical projection maps points in three-dimensions onto a two-dimensional plane. As graphics are usually displayed on two-dimensional media such as paper and computer monitors, these projections are widely used, especially in engineering drawing, drafting, and computer graphics. Projections may be calculated mathematically or by various geometrical or optical techniques.

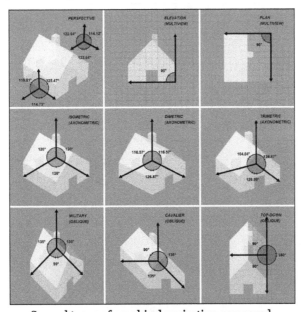

Several types of graphical projection compared.

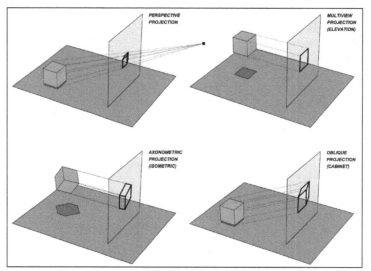

Various projections and how they are produced.

Projection is achieved by the use of imaginary "projectors"; the projected, mental image becomes the technician's vision of the desired, finished picture. Methods provide a uniform imaging procedure among people trained in technical graphics (mechanical drawing, computer aided design, etc.). By following a method, the technician may produce the envisioned picture on a planar surface such as drawing paper.

There are two graphical projection categories, each with its own method:

- Parallel projection.
- Perspective projection.

	Multiview projection (elevation)
	Axonometric projection (isometric)
	Oblique projection (military)

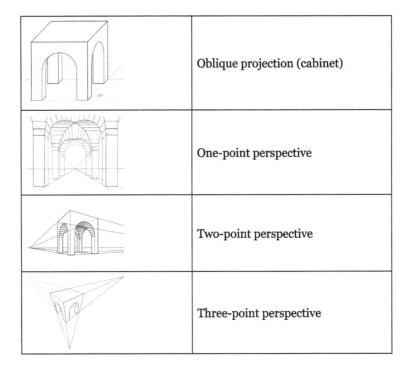

	Oblique projection (cabinet)
	One-point perspective
	Two-point perspective
	Three-point perspective

Parallel Projection

In parallel projection, the lines of sight from the object to the projection plane are parallel to each other. Thus, lines that are parallel in three-dimensional space remain parallel in the two-dimensional projected image. Parallel projection also corresponds to a perspective projection with an infinite focal length (the distance from a camera's lens and focal point), or "zoom".

Images drawn in parallel projection rely upon the technique of axonometry ("to measure along axes"), as described in Pohlke's theorem. In general, the resulting image is oblique (the rays are not perpendicular to the image plane); but in special cases the result is orthographic (the rays are perpendicular to the image plane). Axonometry should not be confused with axonometric projection, the latter usually refers only to a specific class of pictorials.

Orthographic Projection

The orthographic projection is derived from the principles of descriptive geometry and is a two-dimensional representation of a three-dimensional object. It is a parallel projection (the lines of projection are parallel both in reality and in the projection plane). It is the projection type of choice for working drawings.

If the normal of the viewing plane (the camera direction) is parallel to one of the primary axes (which is the x, y, or z axis), the mathematical transformation is as follows; To project the 3D point a_x, a_y, a_z onto the 2D point b_x, b_y using an orthographic projection parallel to the y axis (where positive y represents forward direction - profile view), the following equations can be used:

$$b_x = s_x a_x + c_x$$

$$b_y = s_z a_z + c_z$$

where the vector s is an arbitrary scale factor, and c is an arbitrary offset. These constants are optional, and can be used to properly align the viewport. Using matrix multiplication, the equations become:

$$\begin{bmatrix} b_x \\ b_y \end{bmatrix} = \begin{bmatrix} s_x & 0 & 0 \\ 0 & 0 & s_z \end{bmatrix} \begin{bmatrix} a_x \\ a_y \\ a_z \end{bmatrix} + \begin{bmatrix} c_x \\ c_z \end{bmatrix}.$$

While orthographically projected images represent the three dimensional nature of the object projected, they do not represent the object as it would be recorded photographically or perceived by a viewer observing it directly. In particular, parallel lengths at all points in an orthographically projected image are of the same scale regardless of whether they are far away or near to the virtual viewer. As a result, lengths are not foreshortened as they would be in a perspective projection.

Multiview Projection

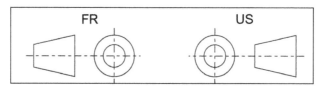

Symbols used to define whether a multiview projection is
either Third Angle (right) or First Angle (left).

With multiview projections, up to six pictures (called primary views) of an object are produced, with each projection plane parallel to one of the coordinate axes of the object. The views are positioned relative to each other according to either of two schemes: first-angle or third-angle projection. In each, the appearances of views may be thought of as being projected onto planes that form a 6-sided box around the object. Although six different sides can be drawn, usually three views of a drawing give enough information to make a 3D object. These views are known as front view, top view and end view. The terms elevation, plan and section are also used.

Axonometric Projection

Within orthographic projection there is an ancillary category known as orthographic pictorial or axonometric projection. Axonometric projections show an image of an object as viewed from a skew direction in order to reveal all three directions (axes) of space in one picture. Axonometric instrument drawings are often used to approximate graphical perspective projections, but there is attendant distortion in the approximation. Because pictorial projections innately contain this distortion, in instrument drawings of pictorials great liberties may then be taken for economy of effort and best effect.

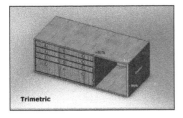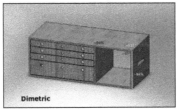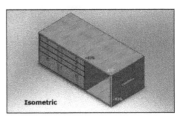

The three axonometric views.

Axonometric projection is further subdivided into three categories: isometric projection, dimetric projection and trimetric projection, depending on the exact angle at which the view deviates from the orthogonal. A typical characteristic of orthographic pictorials is that one axis of space is usually displayed as vertical.

Axonometric projections are also sometimes known as auxiliary views, as opposed to the primary views of multiview projections.

Isometric Projection

In isometric pictorials (for methods see isometric projection), the direction of viewing is such that the three axes of space appear equally foreshortened, and there is a common angle of 120° between them. As the distortion caused by foreshortening is uniform the proportionality of all sides and lengths are preserved, and the axes share a common scale. This enables measurements to be read or taken directly from the drawing.

Dimetric Projection

In dimetric pictorials (for methods see dimetric projection), the direction of viewing is such that two of the three axes of space appear equally foreshortened, of which the attendant scale and angles of presentation are determined according to the angle of viewing; the scale of the third direction (vertical) is determined separately. Approximations are common in dimetric drawings.

Trimetric Projection

In trimetric pictorials (for methods see trimetric projection), the direction of viewing is such that all of the three axes of space appear unequally foreshortened. The scale along each of the three axes and the angles among them are determined separately as dictated by the angle of viewing. Approximations in Trimetric drawings are common.

Oblique Projection

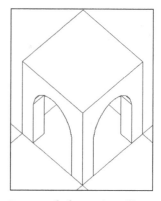

Potting bench drawn in cabinet projection
with an angle of 45° and a ratio of 2/3.

Stone arch drawn in military
perspective.

In oblique projections the parallel projection rays are not perpendicular to the viewing plane as with orthographic projection, but strike the projection plane at an angle other than ninety degrees. In both orthographic and oblique projection, parallel lines in space appear parallel on the projected image. Because of its simplicity, oblique projection is used exclusively for pictorial purposes rather than for formal, working drawings. In an oblique pictorial drawing, the displayed angles among the axes as well as the foreshortening factors (scale) are arbitrary. The distortion created thereby is usually attenuated by aligning one plane of the imaged object to be parallel with the plane of projection thereby creating a true shape, full-size image of the chosen plane. Special types of oblique projections are:

Cavalier Projection

In cavalier projection (sometimes cavalier perspective or high view point) a point of the object is represented by three coordinates, x, y and z. On the drawing, it is represented by only two coordinates, x″ and y″. On the flat drawing, two axes, x and z on the figure, are perpendicular and the length on these axes are drawn with a 1:1 scale; it is thus similar to the dimetric projections, although it is not an axonometric projection, as the third axis, here y, is drawn in diagonal, making an arbitrary angle with the x″ axis, usually 30 or 45°. The length of the third axis is not scaled.

Cabinet Projection

The term cabinet projection (sometimes cabinet perspective) stems from its use in illustrations by the furniture industry. Like cavalier perspective, one face of the projected object is parallel to the viewing plane, and the third axis is projected as going off in an angle (typically 30° or 45° or arctan(2) = 63.4°). Unlike cavalier projection, where the third axis keeps its length, with cabinet projection the length of the receding lines is cut in half.

Military Projection

A variant of oblique projection is called military projection. In this case the horizontal sections are isometrically drawn so that the floor plans are not distorted and the verticals are drawn at an angle. The military projection is given by rotation in the xy-plane and a vertical translation an amount z.

Limitations of Parallel Projection

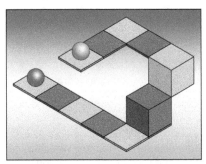

An example of the limitations of isometric projection. The height
difference between the red and blue balls cannot be determined locally.

Objects drawn with parallel projection do not appear larger or smaller as they extend closer to or away from the viewer. While advantageous for architectural drawings, where measurements must be taken directly from the image, the result is a perceived distortion, since unlike perspective projection, this is not how our eyes or photography normally work. It also can easily result in situations where depth and altitude are difficult to gauge, as is shown in the illustration to the right.

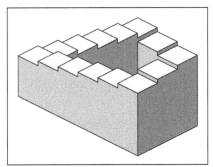

The Penrose stairs depicts a staircase which seems to ascend
(anticlockwise) or descend (clockwise) yet forms a continuous loop.

In this isometric drawing, the blue sphere is two units higher than the red one. However, this difference in elevation is not apparent if one covers the right half of the picture, as the boxes (which serve as clues suggesting height) are then obscured.

This visual ambiguity has been exploited in op art, as well as "impossible object" drawings. M. C. Escher's Waterfall, while not strictly using parallel projection, is a well-known example, in which a channel of water seems to travel unaided along a downward path, only to then paradoxically fall once again as it returns to its source. The water thus appears to disobey the law of conservation of energy. An extreme example is depicted in the film Inception, where by a forced perspective trick an immobile stairway changes its connectivity.

Perspective Projection

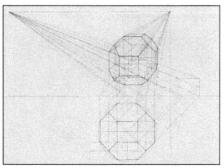

Perspective of a geometric solid using two vanishing points. In this case, the map of the solid (orthogonal projection) is drawn below the perspective, as if bending the ground plane.

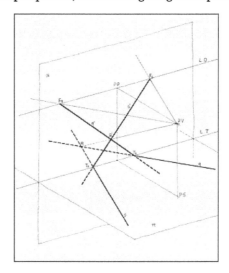

Axonometric projection of a scheme displaying the relevant elements of a vertical picture plane perspective. The standing point (P.S.) is located on the ground plane π, and the point of view (P.V.) is right above it. P.P. is its projection on the picture plane α. L.O. and L.T. are the horizon and the ground lines (linea d'orizzonte and linea di terra). The bold lines s and q lie on π, and intercept α at Ts and Tq respectively. The parallel lines through P.V. (in red) intercept L.O. in the vanishing points Fs and Fq: thus one can draw the projections s' and q', and hence also their intersection R' on R.

Perspective projection is a linear projection where three dimensional objects are projected on a picture plane. This has the effect that distant objects appear smaller than nearer objects.

It also means that lines which are parallel in nature (that is, meet at the point at infinity) appear to intersect in the projected image, for example if railways are pictured with perspective projection, they appear to converge towards a single point, called the vanishing point. Photographic lenses and the human eye work in the same way, therefore perspective projection looks most realistic. Perspective projection is usually categorized into one-point, two-point and three-point perspective, depending on the orientation of the projection plane towards the axes of the depicted object.

Graphical projection methods rely on the duality between lines and points, whereby two straight lines determine a point while two points determine a straight line. The orthogonal projection of the eye point onto the picture plane is called the principal vanishing point (P.P. in the scheme on the left, from the Italian term punto principale, coined during the renaissance).

Two relevant points of a line are:

- Its intersection with the picture plane.

- Its vanishing point, found at the intersection between the parallel line from the eye point and the picture plane.

The principal vanishing point is the vanishing point of all horizontal lines perpendicular to the picture plane. The vanishing points of all horizontal lines lie on the horizon line. If, as is often the case, the picture plane is vertical, all vertical lines are drawn vertically, and have no finite vanishing point on the picture plane. Various graphical methods can be easily envisaged for projecting geometrical scenes. For example, lines traced from the eye point at 45° to the picture plane intersect the latter along a circle whose radius is the distance of the eye point from the plane, thus tracing that circle aids the construction of all the vanishing points of 45° lines; in particular, the intersection of that circle with the horizon line consists of two distance points. They are useful for drawing chessboard floors which, in turn, serve for locating the base of objects on the scene. In the perspective of a geometric solid on the right, after choosing the principal vanishing point —which determines the horizon line— the 45° vanishing point on the left side of the drawing completes the characterization of the (equally distant) point of view. Two lines are drawn from the orthogonal projection of each vertex, one at 45° and one at 90° to the picture plane. After intersecting the ground line, those lines go toward the distance point (for 45°) or the principal point (for 90°). Their new intersection locates the projection of the map. Natural heights are measured above the ground line and then projected in the same way until they meet the vertical from the map.

While orthographic projection ignores perspective to allow accurate measurements, perspective projection shows distant objects as smaller to provide additional realism.

Mathematical Formula

The perspective projection requires a more involved definition as compared to orthographic projections. A conceptual aid to understanding the mechanics of this projection is to imagine the 2D projection as though the object(s) are being viewed through a camera viewfinder. The camera's position, orientation, and field of view control the behavior of the projection transformation. The following variables are defined to describe this transformation:

- $\mathbf{a}_{x,y,z}$: The 3D position of a point A that is to be projected.

- $\mathbf{c}_{x,y,z}$: The 3D position of a point C representing the camera.

- $\theta_{x,y,z}$: The orientation of the camera (represented by Tait–Bryan angles).

- $\mathbf{e}_{x,y,z}$: The display surface's position relative to the camera pinhole C. Most conventions use positive z values (the plane being in front of the pinhole), however negative z values are physically more correct, but the image will be inverted both horizontally and vertically.

Which results in:

- $\mathbf{b}_{x,y}$: The 2D projection of $\mathbf{a}$.

When $\mathbf{c}_{x,y,z} = \langle 0,0,0 \rangle$, and $\theta_{x,y,z} = \langle 0,0,0 \rangle$, the 3D vector $\langle 1,2,0 \rangle$ is projected to the 2D vector $\langle 1,2 \rangle$.

Otherwise, to compute $\mathbf{b}_{x,y}$ we first define a vector $\mathbf{d}_{x,y,z}$ as the position of point A with respect to a coordinate system defined by the camera, with origin in C and rotated by θ with respect to the initial coordinate system. This is achieved by subtracting $\mathbf{c}$ from $\mathbf{a}$ and then applying a rotation by $-\theta$ to the result. This transformation is often called a camera transform, and can be expressed as follows, expressing the rotation in terms of rotations about the x, y, and z axes (these calculations assume that the axes are ordered as a left-handed system of axes):

$$\begin{bmatrix} d_x \\ d_y \\ d_z \end{bmatrix} = \begin{bmatrix} 1 & 0 & 0 \\ 0 & \cos(\theta_x) & \sin(\theta_x) \\ 0 & -\sin(\theta_x) & \cos(\theta_x) \end{bmatrix} \begin{bmatrix} \cos(\theta_y) & 0 & -\sin(\theta_y) \\ 0 & 1 & 0 \\ \sin(\theta_y) & 0 & \cos(\theta_y) \end{bmatrix} \begin{bmatrix} \cos(\theta_z) & \sin(\theta_z) & 0 \\ -\sin(\theta_z) & \cos(\theta_z) & 0 \\ 0 & 0 & 1 \end{bmatrix} \left(\begin{bmatrix} a_x \\ a_y \\ a_z \end{bmatrix} - \begin{bmatrix} c_x \\ c_y \\ c_z \end{bmatrix} \right)$$

This representation corresponds to rotating by three Euler angles (more properly, Tait–Bryan angles), using the xyz convention, which can be interpreted either as "rotate about the extrinsic axes (axes of the scene) in the order z, y, x (reading right-to-left)" or "rotate about the intrinsic axes (axes of the camera) in the order x, y, z (reading left-to-right)". Note that if the camera is not rotated ($\theta_{x,y,z} = \langle 0,0,0 \rangle$), then the matrices drop out (as identities), and this reduces to simply a shift: $\mathbf{d} = \mathbf{a} - \mathbf{c}$.

Alternatively, without using matrices (let us replace $a_x - c_x$ with $\mathbf{x}$ and so on, and abbreviate $\cos(\theta_\alpha)$ to c_α and $\sin(\theta_\alpha)$ to s_α):

$$\mathbf{d}_x = c_y(s_z\mathbf{y} + c_z\mathbf{x}) - s_y\mathbf{z}$$
$$\mathbf{d}_y = s_x(c_y\mathbf{z} + s_y(s_z\mathbf{y} + c_z\mathbf{x})) + c_x(c_z\mathbf{y} - s_z\mathbf{x})$$
$$\mathbf{d}_z = c_x(c_y\mathbf{z} + s_y(s_z\mathbf{y} + c_z\mathbf{x})) - s_x(c_z\mathbf{y} - s_z\mathbf{x})$$

This transformed point can then be projected onto the 2D plane using the formula (here, x/y is used as the projection plane; literature also may use x/z):

$$\mathbf{b}_x = \frac{\mathbf{e}_z}{\mathbf{d}_z}\mathbf{d}_x + \mathbf{e}_x,$$

$$\mathbf{b}_y = \frac{\mathbf{e}_z}{\mathbf{d}_z}\mathbf{d}_y + \mathbf{e}_y.$$

Or, in matrix form using homogeneous coordinates, the system:

$$\begin{bmatrix} \mathbf{f}_x \\ \mathbf{f}_y \\ \mathbf{f}_w \end{bmatrix} = \begin{bmatrix} 1 & 0 & \dfrac{\mathbf{e}_x}{\mathbf{e}_z} \\ 0 & 1 & \dfrac{\mathbf{e}_y}{\mathbf{e}_z} \\ 0 & 0 & \dfrac{1}{\mathbf{e}_z} \end{bmatrix} \begin{bmatrix} \mathbf{d}_x \\ \mathbf{d}_y \\ \mathbf{d}_z \end{bmatrix}$$

in conjunction with an argument using similar triangles, leads to division by the homogeneous coordinate, giving:

$$\mathbf{b}_x = \mathbf{f}_x / \mathbf{f}_w$$
$$\mathbf{b}_y = \mathbf{f}_y / \mathbf{f}_w$$

The distance of the viewer from the display surface, $\mathbf{e}_z$, directly relates to the field of view, where $\alpha = 2 \cdot \arctan(1/\mathbf{e}_z)$ is the viewed angle. (This assumes that you map the points (-1,-1) and (1,1) to the corners of your viewing surface.)

The above equations can also be rewritten as:

$$\mathbf{b}_x = (\mathbf{d}_x\mathbf{s}_x)/(\mathbf{d}_z\mathbf{r}_x)\mathbf{r}_z,$$
$$\mathbf{b}_y = (\mathbf{d}_y\mathbf{s}_y)/(\mathbf{d}_z\mathbf{r}_y)\mathbf{r}_z.$$

In which $\mathbf{s}_{x,y}$ is the display size, $\mathbf{r}_{x,y}$ is the recording surface size (CCD or film), $\mathbf{r}_z$ is the distance from the recording surface to the entrance pupil (camera center), and $\mathbf{d}_z$ is the distance, from the 3D point being projected, to the entrance pupil.

Subsequent clipping and scaling operations may be necessary to map the 2D plane onto any particular display media.

Weak Perspective Projection

A "weak" perspective projection uses the same principles of an orthographic projection, but requires the scaling factor to be specified, thus ensuring that closer objects appear bigger in the projection, and vice versa. It can be seen as a hybrid between an orthographic and a perspective projection, and described either as a perspective projection with individual point depths Z_i replaced by an average constant depth Z_{ave}, or simply as an orthographic projection plus a scaling.

The weak-perspective model thus approximates perspective projection while using a simpler model, similar to the pure (unscaled) orthographic perspective. It is a reasonable approximation when the depth of the object along the line of sight is small compared to the distance from the camera, and the field of view is small. With these conditions, it can be assumed that all points on a 3D object are at the same distance Z_{ave} from the camera without significant errors in the projection (compared to the full perspective model).

Equation:

$$P_x = \frac{X}{Z_{ave}}$$

$$P_y = \frac{Y}{Z_{ave}}$$

assuming focal length $f = 1$.

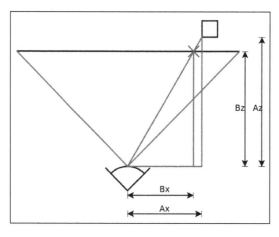

To determine which screen x-coordinate corresponds to a point at A_x, A_z multiply the point coordinates by:

$$B_x = A_x \frac{B_z}{A_z}$$

Where:

- B_x is the screen x coordinate.

- A_x is the model x coordinate.

- B_z is the focal length—the axial distance from the camera center to the image plane.

- A_z is the subject distance.

Because the camera is in 3D, the same works for the screen y-coordinate, substituting y for x in the above diagram and equation.

You can use that to do clipping techniques, replacing the variables with values of the point that's out of the FOV-angle and the point inside Camera Matrix.

This technique, also known as "Inverse Camera", is a Perspective Projection Calculu with known values to calculate the last point on visible angle, projecting from the invisible point, after all needed transformations finished.

3D Reconstruction

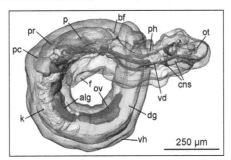

3D reconstruction of the general anatomy of the right side
view of a small marine slug Pseudunela viatoris.

In computer vision and computer graphics, 3D reconstruction is the process of capturing the shape and appearance of real objects. This process can be accomplished either by active or passive methods. If the model is allowed to change its shape in time, this is referred to as non-rigid or spatio-temporal reconstruction.

Motivation and Applications

The research of 3D reconstruction has always been a difficult goal. Using 3D reconstruction one can determine any object's 3D profile, as well as knowing the 3D coordinate of any point on the profile. The 3D reconstruction of objects is a generally scientific problem and core technology of a wide variety of fields, such as Computer

Aided Geometric Design (CAGD), computer graphics, computer animation, computer vision, medical imaging, computational science, virtual reality, digital media, etc. For instance, the lesion information of the patients can be presented in 3D on the computer, which offers a new and accurate approach in diagnosis and thus has vital clinical value. Digital elevation models can be reconstructed using methods such as airborne laser altimetry or synthetic aperture radar.

Active Methods

Active methods, i.e. range data methods, given the depth map, reconstruct the 3D profile by numerical approximation approach and build the object in scenario based on model. These methods actively interfere with the reconstructed object, either mechanically or radiometrically using rangefinders, in order to acquire the depth map, e.g. structured light, laser range finder and other active sensing techniques. A simple example of a mechanical method would use a depth gauge to measure a distance to a rotating object put on a turntable. More applicable radiometric methods emit radiance towards the object and then measure its reflected part. Examples range from moving light sources, colored visible light, time-of-flight lasers to microwaves or 3D ultrasound.

Passive Methods

Passive methods of 3D reconstruction do not interfere with the reconstructed object; they only use a sensor to measure the radiance reflected or emitted by the object's surface to infer its 3D structure through image understanding. Typically, the sensor is an image sensor in a camera sensitive to visible light and the input to the method is a set of digital images (one, two or more) or video. In this case we talk about image-based reconstruction and the output is a 3D model. By comparison to active methods, passive methods can be applied to a wider range of situations.

Monocular Cues Methods

Monocular cues methods refer to using one or more images from one viewpoint (camera) to proceed to 3D construction. It makes use of 2D characteristics(e.g. Silhouettes, shading and texture) to measure 3D shape, and that's why it is also named Shape-From-X, where X can be silhouettes, shading, texture etc. 3D reconstruction through monocular cues is simple and quick, and only one appropriate digital image is needed thus only one camera is adequate. Technically, it avoids stereo correspondence, which is fairly complex.

Shape-from-shading: Due to the analysis of the shade information in the image, by using Lambertian reflectance, the depth of normal information of the object surface is restored to reconstruct.

Photometric Stereo: This approach is more sophisticated than the shape-of-shading method. Images taken in different lighting conditions are used to solve the depth information. It is worth mentioning that more than one image is required by this approach.

Shape-from-texture: Suppose such an object with smooth surface covered by replicated texture units, and its projection from 3D to 2D causes distortion and perspective. Distortion and perspective measured in 2D images provide the hint for inversely solving depth of normal information of the object surface.

Binocular Stereo Vision

Binocular Stereo Vision obtains the 3-dimensional geometric information of an object from multiple images based on the research of human visual system. The results are presented in form of depth maps. Images of an object acquired by two cameras simultaneously in different viewing angles, or by one single camera at different time in different viewing angles, are used to restore its 3D geometric information and reconstruct its 3D profile and location. This is more direct than Monocular methods such as shape-from-shading.

Binocular stereo vision method requires two identical cameras with parallel optical axis to observe one same object, acquiring two images from different points of view. In terms of trigonometry relations, depth information can be calculated from disparity. Binocular stereo vision method is well developed and stably contributes to favorable 3D reconstruction, leading to a better performance when compared to other 3D construction. Unfortunately, it is computationally intensive, besides it performs rather poorly when baseline distance is large.

Problem Statement and Basics

The approach of using Binocular stereo vision to acquire object's 3D geometric information is on the basis of visual disparity. The following picture provides a simple schematic diagram of horizontally sighted Binocular Stereo Vision, where b is the baseline between projective centers of two cameras.

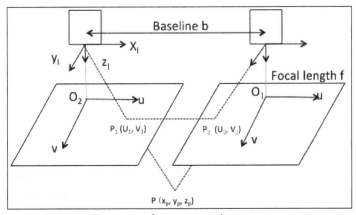

Geometry of a stereoscopic system.

The origin of the camera's coordinate system is at the optical center of the camera's lens as shown in the figure. Actually, the camera's image plane is behind the optical center of the camera's lens. However, to simplify the calculation, images are drawn in front of the optical center of the lens by f. The u-axis and v-axis of the image's coordinate system O_1uv are in the same direction with x-axis and y-axis of the camera's coordinate system respectively. The origin of the image's coordinate system is located on the intersection of imaging plane and the optical axis. Suppose such world point P whose corresponding image points are $P_1(u_1,v_1)$ and $P_2(u_2,v_2)$ respectively on the left and right image plane. Assume two cameras are in the same plane, then y-coordinates of P_1 and P_2 are identical, i.e., $v_1=v_2$. According to trigonometry relations,

$$u_1 = f\frac{x_p}{z_p}, \quad u_2 = f\frac{x_p - b}{z_p}$$

$$v_1 = v_2 = f\frac{y_p}{z_p}$$

where (x_p, y_p, z_p) are coordinates of P in the left camera's coordinate system, f is focal length of the camera. Visual disparity is defined as the difference in image point location of a certain world point acquired by two cameras,

$$d = u_1 - u_2 = f\frac{b}{z_p}$$

based on which the coordinates of P can be worked out.

Therefore, once the coordinates of image points is known, besides the parameters of two cameras, the 3D coordinate of the point can be determined.

$$x_p = \frac{bu_1}{d}$$

$$y_p = \frac{bv_1}{d}$$

$$z_p = \frac{bf}{d}$$

The 3D reconstruction consists of the following sections:

Image Acquisition

2D digital image acquisition is the information source of 3D reconstruction. Commonly used 3D reconstruction is based on two or more images, although it may employ only one image in some cases. There are various types of methods for image acquisition that depends on the occasions and purposes of the specific application. Not only the requirements of the application must be met, but also the visual disparity, illumination, performance of camera and the feature of scenario should be considered.

Camera Calibration

Camera calibration in Binocular Stereo Vision refers to the determination of the mapping relationship between the image points $P_1(u_1,v_1)$ and $P_2(u_2,v_2)$, and space coordinate $P(x_p, y_p, z_p)$ in the 3D scenario. Camera calibration is a basic and essential part in 3D reconstruction via Binocular Stereo Vision.

Feature Extraction

The aim of feature extraction is to gain the characteristics of the images, through which the stereo correspondence processes. As a result, the characteristics of the images closely link to the choice of matching methods. There is no such universally applicable theory for features extraction, leading to a great diversity of stereo correspondence in Binocular Stereo Vision research.

Stereo Correspondence

Stereo correspondence is to establish the correspondence between primitive factors in images, i.e. to match $P_1(u_1,v_1)$ and $P_2(u_2,v_2)$ from two images. Certain interference factors in the scenario should be noticed, e.g. illumination, noise, surface physical characteristic and etc.

Restoration

According to precise correspondence, combined with camera location parameters, 3D geometric information can be recovered without difficulties. Due to the fact that accuracy of 3D reconstruction depends on the precision of correspondence, error of camera location parameters and so on, the previous procedures must be done carefully to achieve relatively accurate 3D reconstruction.

3D Reconstruction of Medical Images

Clinical routine of diagnosis, patient follow-up, computer assisted surgery, surgical planning etc. are facilitated by accurate 3D models of the desired part of human anatomy. Main motivation behind 3D reconstruction includes:

- Improved accuracy due to multi view aggregation.

- Detailed surface estimates.

- Can be used to plan, simulate, guide, or otherwise assist a surgeon in performing a medical procedure.

- The precise position and orientation of the patient's anatomy can be determined.

- Helps in a number of clinical areas, such as radiotherapy planning and treatment verification, spinal surgery, hip replacement, neurointerventions and aortic stenting.

3D reconstruction has applications in many fields. They are:

- Pavement engineering.

- Medicine.

- Free-viewpoint video reconstruction.

- Robotic mapping.

- City planning.

- Tomographic reconstruction.

- Gaming.

- Virtual environments and virtual tourism.

- Earth observation.

- Archaeology.

- Augmented reality.

- Reverse engineering.

- Motion capture.

- 3D object recognition, gesture recognition and hand tracking.

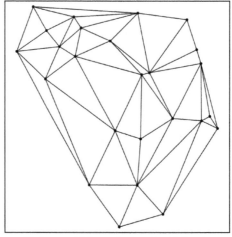

Delaunay Triangulation (25 Points).

Mostly algorithms available for 3D reconstruction are extremely slow and cannot be used in real-time. Though the algorithms presented are still in infancy but they have the potential for fast computation.

Delaunay and Alpha-shapes

- Delaunay method involves extraction of tetrahedron surfaces from initial point cloud. The idea of 'shape' for a set of points in space is given by concept of alpha-shapes. Given a finite point set S, and the real parameter alpha, the alpha-shape of S is a polytope (the generalization to any dimension of a two dimensional polygon and a three-dimensional polyhedron) which is neither convex nor necessarily connected. For a large value, the alpha-shape is identical to the convex-hull of S. The algorithm proposed by Edelsbrunner and Mucke eliminates all tetrahedrons which are delimited by a surrounding sphere smaller than α. The surface is then obtained with the external triangles from the resulting tetrahedron.

- Another algorithm called Tight Cocone labels the initial tetrahedrons as interior and exterior. The triangles found in and out generate the resulting surface.

Both methods have been recently extended for reconstructing point clouds with noise. In this method the quality of points determines the feasibility of the method. For precise triangulation since we are using the whole point cloud set, the points on the surface with the error above the threshold will be explicitly represented on reconstructed geometry.

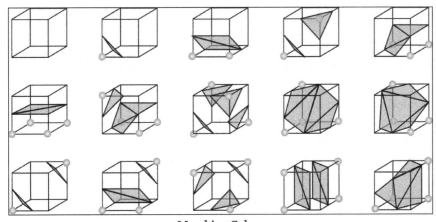

Marching Cubes.

Zero Set Methods

Reconstruction of the surface is performed using a distance function which assigns to each point in the space a signed distance to the surface S. A contour algorithm is used to extracting a zero-set which is used to obtain polygonal representation of the object. Thus, the problem of reconstructing a surface from a disorganized point cloud is reduced to the definition of the appropriate function f with a zero value for the sampled points and different to zero value for the rest. An algorithm called marching cubes established the use of such methods. There are different variants for given algorithm, some use a discrete function f, while other use a polyharmonic radial basis function is used to adjust the initial point set. Functions like Moving Least Squares, basic functions with local support, based on the Poisson equation have also been used. Loss of the geometry precision in areas with extreme curvature, i.e., corners, edges is one of the main issues encountered. Furthermore, pretreatment of information, by applying some kind of filtering technique, also affects the definition of the corners by softening them. There are several studies related to post-processing techniques used in the reconstruction for the detection and refinement of corners but these methods increase the complexity of the solution.

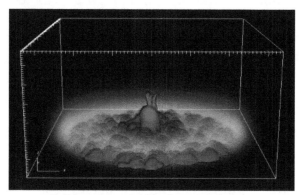

Solid geometry with volume rendering.

VR Technique

Entire volume transparence of the object is visualized using VR technique. Images will be performed by projecting rays through volume data. Along each ray, opacity and color need to be calculated at every voxel. Then information calculated along each ray will to be aggregated to a pixel on image plane. This technique helps us to see comprehensively an entire compact structure of the object. Since the technique needs enormous amount of calculations, which requires strong configuration computers is appropriate for low contrast data. Two main methods for rays projecting can be considered as follows:

- Object-order method: Projecting rays go through volume from back to front (from volume to image plane).

- Image-order or ray-casting method: Projecting rays go through volume from front to back (from image plane to volume).There exists some other methods to composite image, appropriate methods depending on the user's purposes. Some usual methods in medical image are MIP (maximum intensity projection), MinIP (minimum intensity projection), AC (alpha compositing) and NPVR (non-photorealistic volume rendering).

Tracing a ray through a voxel grid. The voxels which are traversed in addition to those selected using a standard 8-connected algorithm are shown hatched.

Voxel Grid

In this filtering technique input space is sampled using a grid of 3D voxels to reduce the number of points. For each voxel, a centroid is chosen as the representative of all points. There are two approaches, the selection of the voxel centroid or select the centroid of the points lying within the voxel. To obtain internal points average has a higher computational cost, but offers better results. Thus, a subset of the input space is obtained that roughly represents the underlying surface. The Voxel Grid method presents the same problems as other filtering techniques: impossibility of defining the final number of points that represent the surface, geometric information loss due to the reduction of the points inside a voxel and sensitivity to noisy input spaces.

VRML

VRML (Virtual Reality Modeling Language) is a standard file format for representing 3-dimensional (3D) interactive vector graphics, designed particularly with the World Wide Web in mind. It has been superseded by X3D.

WRL File Format

VRML is a text file format where, e.g., vertices and edges for a 3D polygon can be specified along with the surface color, UV-mapped textures, shininess, transparency, and so on. URLs can be associated with graphical components so that a web browser might fetch a webpage or a new VRML file from the Internet when the user clicks on the specific graphical component. Animations, sounds, lighting, and other aspects of the virtual world can interact with the user or may be triggered by external events such as timers. A special Script Node allows the addition of program code (e.g., written in Java or ECMAScript) to a VRML file.

VRML files are commonly called "worlds" and have the.wrl extension (for example, island.wrl). VRML files are in plain text and generally compress well using gzip, useful for transferring over the internet more quickly (some gzip compressed files use the.wrz extension). Many 3D modeling programs can save objects and scenes in VRML format.

Standardization

The Web3D Consortium has been formed to further the collective development of the format. VRML (and its successor, X3D), have been accepted as international standards by the International Organization for Standardization (ISO).

The first version of VRML was specified in November 1994. This version was specified from, and very closely resembled, the API and file format of the Open Inventor software component, originally developed by SGI. Version 2.0 was submitted to ISO for adoption as an international standard. A working draft was published in August 1996. The current and functionally complete version is VRML97 (ISO/IEC 14772-1:1997). VRML has now been superseded by X3D (ISO/IEC 19775-1).

Emergence, Popularity and Rival Technical Upgrade

The term VRML was coined by Dave Raggett in a paper called "Extending WWW to support Platform Independent Virtual Reality" submitted to the First World Wide Web Conference in 1994, and first discussed at the WWW94 VRML BOF established by Tim Berners-Lee, where Mark Pesce presented the Labyrinth demo he developed with Tony Parisi and Peter Kennard. In October 1995, at Internet World, Template Graphics Software (TGS) demonstrated a 3D/VRML plug-in for the beta release of Netscape 2.0 by Netscape Communications.

In 1997, a new version of the format was finalized, as VRML97 (also known as VRML2 or VRML 2.0), and became an ISO standard. VRML97 was used on the Internet on some personal homepages and sites such as "CyberTown", which offered 3D chat using Blaxxun Software. The format was championed by SGI's Cosmo Software; when SGI restructured in 1998, the division was sold to the VREAM Division of Platinum Technology, which was then taken over by Computer Associates, which did not develop or distribute the software. To fill the void a variety of proprietary Web 3D formats emerged over the next few years, including Microsoft Chrome and Adobe Atmosphere, neither of which is supported today. VRML's capabilities remained largely the same while realtime 3D graphics kept improving. The VRML Consortium changed its name to the Web3D Consortium, and began work on the successor to VRML—X3D.

SGI ran a web site at vrml.sgi.com on which was hosted a string of regular short performances of a character called "Floops" who was a VRML character in a VRML world. Floops was a creation of a company called "Protozoa".

H-Anim is a standard for animated Humanoids, which is based around VRML, and later X3D. The initial version 1.0 of the H-Anim standard was scheduled for submission at the end of March 1998.

VRML provoked much interest but has never seen much serious widespread use. One reason for this may have been the lack of available bandwidth. At the time of VRML's popularity, a majority of users, both business and personal, were using slow dial-up internet access.

VRML experimentation was primarily in education and research where an open specification is most valued. It has now been re-engineered as X3D. The MPEG-4 Interactive Profile (ISO/IEC 14496) was based on VRML (now on X3D), and X3D is largely backward-compatible with it. VRML is also widely used as a file format for interchange of 3D models, particularly from CAD systems.

A free cross-platform runtime implementation of VRML is available in OpenVRML. Its libraries can be used to add both VRML and X3D support to applications, and a GTK+ plugin is available to render VRML/X3D worlds in web browsers.

In the 2000s, many companies like Bitmanagement improved the quality level of virtual effects in VRML to the quality level of DirectX 9.0c, but at the expense of using proprietary solutions. All main features like game modeling are already complete. They include multi-pass render with low level setting for Z-buffer, BlendOp, AlphaOp, Stencil, Multi-texture, Shader with HLSL and GLSL support, realtime Render To Texture, Multi Render Target (MRT) and PostProcessing. Many demos shows that VRML already supports lightmap, normalmap, SSAO, CSM and Realtime Environment Reflection along with other virtual effects.

Wire-frame Model

A wire-frame model, also wireframe model, is a visual representation of a three-dimensional (3D) physical object used in 3D computer graphics. It is created by specifying each edge of the physical object where two mathematically continuous smooth surfaces meet, or by connecting an object's constituent vertices using (straight) lines or curves. The object is projected into screen space and rendered by drawing lines at the location of each edge. The term "wire frame" comes from designers using metal wire to represent the three-dimensional shape of solid objects. 3D wire frame computer models allow for the construction and manipulation of solids and solid surfaces. 3D solid modeling efficiently draws higher quality representations of solids than conventional line drawing.

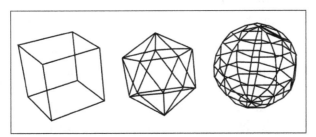

Sample rendering of a wire-frame cube, icosahedron, and approximate sphere.

Using a wire-frame model allows for the visualization of the underlying design structure of a 3D model. Traditional two-dimensional views and drawings/renderings can be created by the appropriate rotation of the object, and the selection of hidden line removal via cutting planes.

Since wire-frame renderings are relatively simple and fast to calculate, they are often used in cases where a relatively high screen frame rate is needed (for instance, when working with a particularly complex 3D model, or in real-time systems that model exterior phenomena). When greater graphical detail is desired, surface textures can be added automatically after the completion of the initial rendering of the wire frame. This allows a designer to quickly review solids, or rotate objects to different views without the long delays associated with more realistic rendering, or even the processing of faces and simple flat shading.

Perspective shown in a wire-frame representation of an architectural project.

The wire frame format is also well-suited and widely used in programming tool paths for direct numerical control (DNC) machine tools.

Hand-drawn wire-frame-like illustrations date back as far as the Italian Renaissance. Wire-frame models were also used extensively in video games to represent 3D objects during the 1980s and early 1990s, when "properly" filled 3D objects would have been too complex to calculate and draw with the computers of the time. Wire-frame models are also used as the input for computer-aided manufacturing (CAM).

There are three main types of 3D computer-aided design (CAD) models; wire frame is the most abstract and least realistic. The other types are surface and solid. The wire-frame method of modelling consists of only lines and curves that connect the points or vertices and thereby define the edges of an object.

Wireframing is one of the methods used in geometric modelling systems. A wireframe model represents the shape of a solid object with its characteristic lines and points. There are two types of wireframe modelling: Pro's and Con's. In Pro's user gives a simple input to create a shape. It is useful in developing systems. While in Con's wireframe model, it does not include information about inside and outside boundary surfaces. Today, wireframe models are used to define complex solid objects. The designer makes a wireframe model of a solid object, and then the CAD operator reconstructs the object, including detailed analysis. This technique has some advantages: generally the 3-dimensional solid objects are complex, but wireframe models can be viewed in 1 dimension, improving comprehensibility; the solid object can be modified further; the designer can ignore the geometry inside a surface while in solid modelling the designer has to give consistent geometry for all details; wireframe models require less memory space and CPU capacity.

Example of Wireframe Model

An object is specified by two tables: (1) Vertex table, and, (2) Edge table.

The vertex table consists of three-dimensional coordinate values for each vertex with reference to the origin.

Vertex	X	Y	Z
1	1	1	1
2	1	-1	1
3	-1	-1	1
4	-1	1	1
5	1	1	-1
6	1	-1	-1
7	-1	-1	-1
8	-1	1	-1

Edge table specifies the start and end vertices for each edge.

Edge	Start Vertex	End Vertex
1	1	2
2	2	3
3	3	4
4	4	1
5	5	6
6	6	7
7	7	8
8	8	5
9	1	5
10	2	6
11	3	7
12	4	8

A naive interpretation could create a wire-frame representation by simply drawing straight lines between the screen coordinates of the appropriate vertices using the edge list.

Unlike representations designed for more detailed rendering, face information is not specified (it must be calculated if required for solid rendering).

Appropriate calculations have to be performed to transform the 3D coordinates of the vertices into 2D screen coordinates.

Schlick's Approximation

In 3D computer graphics, Schlick's approximation, named after Christophe Schlick, is a formula for approximating the contribution of the Fresnel factor in the specular reflection of light from a non-conducting interface (surface) between two media.

According to Schlick's model, the specular reflection coefficient R can be approximated by:

$$R(\theta) = R_0 + (1 - R_0)(1 - \cos \theta)^5$$

$$R_0 = \left(\frac{n_1 - n_2}{n_1 + n_2} \right)^2$$

where θ is the angle between the direction from which the incident light is coming and the normal of the interface between the two media, hence $\cos \theta = (N \cdot V)$. And n_1, n_2 are the indices of refraction of the two media at the interface and R_0 is the reflection coefficient for light incoming parallel to the normal (i.e., the value of the Fresnel term when $\theta = 0$ or minimal reflection). In computer graphics, one of the interfaces is usually air, meaning that n_1 very well can be approximated as 1.

In microfacet models it is assumed that there is always a perfect reflection, but the normal changes according to a certain distribution, resulting in a non-perfect overall reflection. When using Schlicks's approximation, the normal in the above computation is replaced by the halfway vector. Either the viewing or light direction can be used as the second vector.

Sketch-based Modeling

Sketch-based modeling is a method of creating 3D models for use in 3D computer graphics applications. Sketch-based modeling is differentiated from other types of 3D modeling by its interface - instead of creating a 3D model by directly editing polygons, the user draws a 2D shape which is converted to 3D automatically by the application.

Many computer users think that traditional 3D modeling programs such as Blender or Maya have a high learning curve. Novice users often have difficulty creating models in traditional modeling programs without first completing a lengthy series of tutorials. Sketch-based modeling tools aim to solve this problem by creating a User interface which is similar to drawing, which most users are familiar with.

Uses

Sketch-based modeling is primarily designed for use by persons with artistic ability, but no experience with 3D modeling programs. Curvy3D and Teddy, below, have largely been designed for this purpose. However, sketch-based modeling is also used for other applications. One popular application is rapid modeling of low-detail objects for use in prototyping and design work.

Operation

There are two main types of sketch-based modeling. In the first, the user draws a shape in the workspace using a mouse or a tablet. The system then interprets this shape as a 3D object. Users can then alter the object by cutting off or adding sections. The process of adding sections to a model is generally referred to as overdrawing. The user is never required to interact directly with the vertices or Nurbs control points.

In the second type of sketch-based modeling, the user draws one or more images on paper, then scans in the images. The system then automatically converts the sketches to a 3D model.

A great deal of research is currently being done on sketch-based modeling. A number of papers on this topic are presented each year at the ACM SIGGRAPH conference. The European graphics Association Eurographics sponsored four special conferences on sketch-based modeling:

- Grenoble 2004.

- Dublin 2005.

- Vienna 2006.

- Riverside 2007.

Since 2007, Eurographics and ACM SIGGRAPH have co-sponsored the Sketch-Based Interfaces and Modeling Symposium which in 2011 became a part of the Expressive Graphics Symposium.

The Eurographics/SIGGRAPH Joint Symposium on Sketch-Based Interfaces and Modeling was held on:

- Annecy 2008.

- New Orleans 2009.

- Jointly with NPAR at Annecy 2010.

- At Vancouver together with NPAR and Computational Aesthetics 2011.

Depth Map

In 3D computer graphics and computer vision, a depth map is an image or image channel that contains information relating to the distance of the surfaces of scene objects from a viewpoint. The term is related to and may be analogous to depth buffer, Z-buffer, Z-buffering and Z-depth. The "Z" in these latter terms relates to a convention that the central axis of view of a camera is in the direction of the camera's Z axis, and not to the absolute Z axis of a scene.

Examples:

Cubic structure.

Depth Map: Nearer is darker.

Two different depth maps can be seen here, together with the original model from which they are derived. The first depth map shows luminance in proportion to the distance from the camera. Nearer surfaces are darker; further surfaces are lighter. The second depth map shows luminance in relation to the distances from a nominal focal plane. Surfaces closer to the focal plane are darker; surfaces further from the focal plane are lighter, both closer to and also further away from the viewpoint.

Depth Map: Nearer the focal plane is darker.

Uses

Fog effect.

Shallow depth of field effect.

Depth maps have a number of uses, including:

- Simulating the effect of uniformly dense semi-transparent media within a scene
  - such as fog, smoke or large volumes of water.

- Simulating shallow depths of field where some parts of a scene appear to be out
  of focus. Depth maps can be used to selectively blur an image to varying degrees. A shallow depth of field can be a characteristic of macro photography and
  so the technique may form a part of the process of miniature faking.

- Z-buffering and z-culling, techniques which can be used to make the rendering
  of 3D scenes more efficient. They can be used to identify objects hidden from
  view and which may therefore be ignored for some rendering purposes. This is
  particularly important in real time applications such as computer games, where
  a fast succession of completed renders must be available in time to be displayed
  at a regular and fixed rate.

- Shadow mapping, part of one process used to create shadows cast by illumination in 3D computer graphics. In this use, the depth maps are calculated from
  the perspective of the lights, not the viewer.

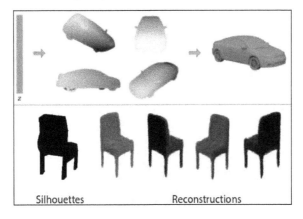

Silhouettes   Reconstructions

- To provide the distance information needed to create and generate autoster-
  eograms and in other related applications intended to create the illusion of 3D
  viewing through stereoscopy.

- Subsurface scattering can be used as part of a process for adding realism by simulating the semi-transparent properties of translucent materials such as human skin.

- In computer vision single-view or multi-view images depth maps, or other types of images, are used to model 3D shapes or reconstruct them. Depth maps can be generated by 3D scanners or reconstructed from multiple images.

- In Machine vision and computer vision, to allow 3D images to be processed by 2D image tools.

Generating and reconstructing 3D shapes from single or multi-view depth maps or silhouettes.

Limitations

- Single channel depth maps record the first surface seen, and so cannot display information about those surfaces seen or refracted through transparent objects, or reflected in mirrors. This can limit their use in accurately simulating depth of field or fog effects.

- Single channel depth maps cannot convey multiple distances where they occur within the view of a single pixel. This may occur where more than one object occupies the location of that pixel. This could be the case - for example - with models featuring hair, fur or grass. More generally, edges of objects may be ambiguously described where they partially cover a pixel.

- Depending on the intended use of a depth map, it may be useful or necessary to encode the map at higher bit depths. For example, an 8 bit depth map can only represent a range of up to 256 different distances.

- Depending on how they are generated, depth maps may represent the perpendicular distance between an object and the plane of the scene camera. For example, a scene camera pointing directly at - and perpendicular to - a flat surface may record a uniform distance for the whole surface. In this case, geometrically, the actual distances from the camera to the areas of the plane surface seen in the corners of the image are greater than the distances to the central area. For many applications, however, this discrepancy is not a significant issue.

Radiosity

In 3D computer graphics, radiosity is an application of the finite element method to solving the rendering equation for scenes with surfaces that reflect light diffusely. Unlike rendering methods that use Monte Carlo algorithms (such as path tracing), which handle all types of light paths, typical radiosity only account for paths (represented by the code "LD*E") which leave a light source and are reflected diffusely some number of times (possibly zero) before hitting the eye. Radiosity is a global illumination algorithm in the sense that the illumination arriving on a surface comes not just directly from the light sources, but also from other surfaces reflecting light. Radiosity is viewpoint independent, which increases the calculations involved, but makes them useful for all viewpoints.

Scene rendered with RRV (simple implementation of radiosity renderer based on OpenGL) 79th iteration.

Radiosity methods were first developed in about 1950 in the engineering field of heat transfer. They were later refined specifically for the problem of rendering computer graphics in 1984 by researchers at Cornell University and Hiroshima University.

Notable commercial radiosity engines are Enlighten by Geomerics (used for games including Battlefield 3 and Need for Speed: The Run); 3ds Max; form•Z; LightWave 3D and the Electric Image Animation System.

Visual Characteristics

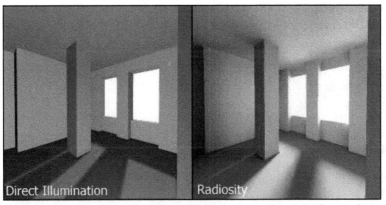

Difference between standard direct illumination without shadow umbra, and radiosity with shadow umbrella.

The inclusion of radiosity calculations in the rendering process often lends an added element of realism to the finished scene, because of the way it mimics real-world phenomena. Consider a simple room scene.

The image on the left was rendered with a typical direct illumination renderer. There are three types of lighting in this scene which have been specifically chosen and placed by the artist in an attempt to create realistic lighting: spot lighting with shadows (placed outside the window to create the light shining on the floor), ambient lighting (without which any part of the room not lit directly by a light source would be totally dark), and omnidirectional lighting without shadows (to reduce the flatness of the ambient lighting).

The image on the right was rendered using a radiosity algorithm. There is only one source of light: an image of the sky placed outside the window. The difference is marked. The room glows with light. Soft shadows are visible on the floor, and subtle lighting effects are noticeable around the room. Furthermore, the red color from the carpet has bled onto the grey walls, giving them a slightly warm appearance. None of these effects were specifically chosen or designed by the artist.

The surfaces of the scene to be rendered are each divided up into one or more smaller surfaces (patches). A view factor (also known as form factor) is computed for each pair of patches; it is a coefficient describing how well the patches can see each other. Patches that are far away from each other, or oriented at oblique angles relative to one another, will have smaller view factors. If other patches are in the way, the view factor will be reduced or zero, depending on whether the occlusion is partial or total.

The view factors are used as coefficients in a linear system of rendering equations. Solving this system yields the radiosity, or brightness, of each patch, taking into account diffuse interreflections and soft shadows.

Progressive radiosity solves the system iteratively with intermediate radiosity values for the patch, corresponding to bounce levels. That is, after each iteration, we know how the scene looks after one light bounce, after two passes, two bounces, and so forth. This is useful for getting an interactive preview of the scene. Also, the user can stop the iterations once the image looks good enough, rather than wait for the computation to numerically converge.

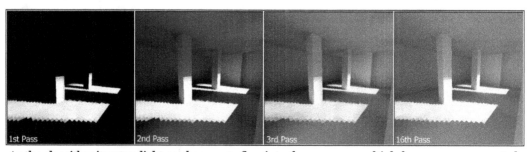

As the algorithm iterates, light can be seen to flow into the scene, as multiple bounces are computed.
Individual patches are visible as squares on the walls and floor.

Another common method for solving the radiosity equation is "shooting radiosity," which iteratively solves the radiosity equation by "shooting" light from the patch with the most energy at each step. After the first pass, only those patches which are in direct line of sight of a light-emitting patch will be illuminated. After the second pass, more patches will become illuminated as the light begins to bounce around the scene. The scene continues to grow brighter and eventually reaches a steady state.

Mathematical Formulation

The basic radiosity method has its basis in the theory of thermal radiation, since radiosity relies on computing the amount of light energy transferred among surfaces. In order to simplify computations, the method assumes that all scattering is perfectly diffuse. Surfaces are typically discretized into quadrilateral or triangular elements over which a piecewise polynomial function is defined.

After this breakdown, the amount of light energy transfer can be computed by using the known reflectivity of the reflecting patch, combined with the view factor of the two patches. This dimensionless quantity is computed from the geometric orientation of two patches, and can be thought of as the fraction of the total possible emitting area of the first patch which is covered by the second.

More correctly, radiosity B is the energy per unit area leaving the patch surface per discrete time interval and is the combination of emitted and reflected energy:

$$B(x)dA = E(x)dA + \rho(x)dA \int_S B(x')\frac{1}{\pi r^2}\cos\theta_x \cos\theta_{x'} \cdot Vis(x,x')dA'$$

where:

- $B(x)_i\, dA_i$ is the total energy leaving a small area dA_i around a point x.

- $E(x)_i\, dA_i$ is the emitted energy.

- $\rho(x)$ is the reflectivity of the point, giving reflected energy per unit area by multiplying by the incident energy per unit area (the total energy which arrives from other patches).

- S denotes that the integration variable x' runs over all the surfaces in the scene.

- r is the distance between x and x'.

- θ_x and $\theta_{x'}$ are the angles between the line joining x and x' and vectors normal to the surface at x and x' respectively.

- Vis(x,x') is a visibility function, defined to be 1 if the two points x and x' are visible from each other, and 0 if they are not.

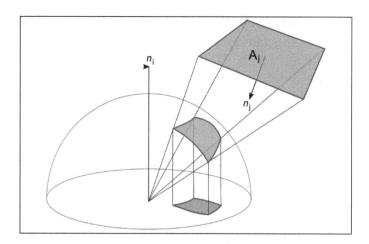

The geometrical form factor (or "projected solid angle") F_{ij}.

F_{ij} can be obtained by projecting the element A_j onto the surface of a unit hemisphere, and then projecting that in turn onto a unit circle around the point of interest in the plane of A_i. The form factor is then equal to the proportion of the unit circle covered by this projection.

Form factors obey the reciprocity relation $A_iF_{ij} = A_jF_{ji}$.

If the surfaces are approximated by a finite number of planar patches, each of which is taken to have a constant radiosity B_i and reflectivity ρ_i, the above equation gives the discrete radiosity equation,

$$B_i = E_i + \rho_i \sum_{j=1}^{n} F_{ij}B_j$$

where F_{ij} is the geometrical view factor for the radiation leaving j and hitting patch i.

This equation can then be applied to each patch. The equation is monochromatic, so color radiosity rendering requires calculation for each of the required colors.

Solution Methods

The equation can formally be solved as matrix equation, to give the vector solution:

$$B = (I - \rho F)^{-1} E$$

This gives the full "infinite bounce" solution for B directly. However the number of calculations to compute the matrix solution scales according to n^3, where n is the number of patches. This becomes prohibitive for realistically large values of n.

Instead, the equation can more readily be solved iteratively, by repeatedly applying the single-bounce update formula above. Formally, this is a solution of the matrix equation by Jacobi iteration. Because the reflectivities ρ_i are less than 1, this scheme converges quickly, typically requiring only a handful of iterations to produce a reasonable solution. Other standard iterative methods for matrix equation solutions can also be used, for example the Gauss–Seidel method, where updated values for each patch are used in the calculation as soon as they are computed, rather than all being updated synchronously at the end of each sweep. The solution can also be tweaked to iterate over each of the sending elements in turn in its main outermost loop for each update, rather than each of the receiving patches. This is known as the shooting variant of the algorithm, as opposed to the gathering variant. Using the view factor reciprocity, $A_i F_{ij} = A_j F_{ji}$, the update equation can also be re-written in terms of the view factor F_{ji} seen by each sending patch A_j:

$$A_i B_i = A_i E_i + \rho_i \sum_{j=1}^{n} A_j B_j F_{ji}$$

This is sometimes known as the "power" formulation, since it is now the total transmitted power of each element that is being updated, rather than its radiosity.

The view factor F_{ij} itself can be calculated in a number of ways. Early methods used a hemicube (an imaginary cube centered upon the first surface to which the second surface was projected, devised by Michael F. Cohen and Donald P. Greenberg). The surface of the hemicube was divided into pixel-like squares, for each of which a view factor can be readily calculated analytically. The full form factor could then be approximated by adding up the contribution from each of the pixel-like squares. The projection onto the hemicube, which could be adapted from standard methods for determining the visibility of polygons, also solved the problem of intervening patches partially obscuring those behind.

However all this was quite computationally expensive, because ideally form factors must be derived for every possible pair of patches, leading to a quadratic increase in computation as the number of patches increased. This can be reduced somewhat by using a binary space partitioning tree to reduce the amount of time spent determining which patches are completely hidden from others in complex scenes; but even so, the time spent to determine the form factor still typically scales as n log n. New methods include adaptive integration.

Sampling Approaches

The form factors F_{ij} themselves are not in fact explicitly needed in either of the update equations; neither to estimate the total intensity $\sum_j F_{ij} B_j$ gathered from the whole view, nor to estimate how the power $A_j B_j$ being radiated is distributed. Instead, these updates can be estimated by sampling methods, without ever having to calculate form factors explicitly. Since the mid 1990s such sampling approaches have been the methods most predominantly used for practical radiosity calculations.

The gathered intensity can be estimated by generating a set of samples in the unit circle, lifting these onto the hemisphere, and then seeing what was the radiosity of the element that a ray incoming in that direction would have originated on. The estimate for the total gathered intensity is then just the average of the radiosities discovered by each ray. Similarly, in the power formulation, power can be distributed by generating a set of rays from the radiating element in the same way, and spreading the power to be distributed equally between each element a ray hits.

This is essentially the same distribution that a path-tracing program would sample in tracing back one diffuse reflection step; or that a bidirectional ray tracing program would sample to achieve one forward diffuse reflection step when light source mapping forwards. The sampling approach therefore to some extent represents a convergence between the two techniques, the key difference remaining that the radiosity technique aims to build up a sufficiently accurate map of the radiance of all the surfaces in the scene, rather than just a representation of the current view.

Reducing Computation Time

Although in its basic form radiosity is assumed to have a quadratic increase in computation time with added geometry (surfaces and patches), this need not be the case. The radiosity problem can be rephrased as a problem of rendering a texture mapped scene. In this case, the computation time increases only linearly with the number of patches (ignoring complex issues like cache use).

Following the commercial enthusiasm for radiosity-enhanced imagery, but prior to the standardization of rapid radiosity calculation, many architects and graphic artists used a technique referred to loosely as false radiosity. By darkening areas of texture maps corresponding to corners, joints and recesses, and applying them via self-illumination or diffuse mapping, a radiosity-like effect of patch interaction could be created with a standard scanline renderer (cf. ambient occlusion).

Static, pre-computed radiosity may be displayed in realtime via Lightmaps on current desktop computers with standard graphics acceleration hardware.

Advantages

A modern render of the Utah teapot. Radiosity was used
for all diffuse illumination in this scene.

One of the advantages of the Radiosity algorithm is that it is relatively simple to explain and implement. This makes it a useful algorithm for teaching students about global illumination algorithms. A typical direct illumination renderer already contains nearly all of the algorithms (perspective transformations, texture mapping, hidden surface removal) required to implement radiosity. A strong grasp of mathematics is not required to understand or implement this algorithm.

Limitations

Typical radiosity methods only account for light paths of the form LD*E, i.e. paths which start at a light source and make multiple diffuse bounces before reaching the eye. Although there are several approaches to integrating other illumination effects such as specular and glossy reflections, radiosity-based methods are generally not used to solve the complete rendering equation.

Basic radiosity also has trouble resolving sudden changes in visibility (e.g. hard-edged shadows) because coarse, regular discretization into piecewise constant elements corresponds to a low-pass box filter of the spatial domain. Discontinuity meshing uses knowledge of visibility events to generate a more intelligent discretization.

Confusion about Terminology

Radiosity was perhaps the first rendering algorithm in widespread use which accounted for diffuse indirect lighting. Earlier rendering algorithms, such as Whitted-style ray tracing were capable of computing effects such as reflections, refractions, and shadows, but despite being highly global phenomena, these effects were not commonly referred to as "global illumination." As a consequence, the terms "diffuse interreflection" and "radiosity" both became confused with "global illumination" in popular parlance. However, the three are distinct concepts.

The radiosity method, in the context of computer graphics, derives from (and is fundamentally the same as) the radiosity method in heat transfer. In this context, radiosity is the total radiative flux (both reflected and re-radiated) leaving a surface; this is also sometimes known as radiant exitance. Calculation of radiosity, rather than surface temperatures, is a key aspect of the radiosity method that permits linear matrix methods to be applied to the problem.

False Radiosity

False Radiosity is a 3D computer graphics technique used to create texture mapping for objects that emulates patch interaction algorithms in radiosity rendering. Though practiced in some form since the late 90s, this term was coined only around

2002 by architect Andrew Hartness, then head of 3D and real-time design at Ateliers Jean Nouvel.

During the period of nascent commercial enthusiasm for radiosity-enhanced imagery, but prior to the democratization of powerful computational hardware, architects and graphic artists experimented with time-saving 3D rendering techniques. By darkening areas of texture maps corresponding to corners, joints and recesses, and applying maps via self-illumination or diffuse mapping in a 3D program, a radiosity-like effect of patch interaction could be created with a standard scan-line renderer. Successful emulation of radiosity required a theoretical understanding and graphic application of patch view factors, path tracing and global illumination algorithms. Texture maps were usually produced with image editing software, such as Adobe Photoshop. The advantage of this method is decreased rendering time and easily modifiable overall lighting strategies.

Another common approach similar to false radiosity is the manual placement of standard omni-type lights with limited attenuation in places in the 3D scene where the artist would expect radiosity reflections to occur. This method uses many lights and can require an advanced light-grouping system, depending on what assigned materials/objects are illuminated, how many surfaces require false radiosity treatment, and to what extent it is anticipated that lighting strategies be set up for frequent changes.

Smoothing Group

In 3D computer graphics, a smoothing group is a group of polygons in a polygon mesh which should appear to form a smooth surface. Smoothing groups are useful for describing shapes where some polygons are connected smoothly to their neighbors, and some are not. For example, in a mesh representing a cylinder, all of the polygons are smoothly connected except along the edges of the end caps. One could make a smoothing group containing all of the polygons in one end cap, another containing the polygons in the other end cap, and a last group containing the polygons in the tube shape between the end caps.

By identifying the polygons in a mesh that should appear to be smoothly connected, smoothing groups allow 3D modeling software to estimate the surface normal at any point on the mesh, by averaging the surface normals or vertex normals in the mesh data that describes the mesh. The software can use this data to determine how light interacts with the model. If each polygon lies in a plane, the software could calculate a polygon's surface normal by calculating the normal of the polygon's plane, meaning this data would not have to be stored in the mesh. Thus, early 3D modeling software like 3D Studio Max DOS used smoothing groups as a way to avoid having to store accurate vertex normals for each vertex of the mesh, as a strategy for computer representation of surfaces.

3ds Max uses Smoothing Groups to create hard/soft edges between polygons, by splitting/combining vertex normals. When neighboring polygons do not share the same Smoothing Group, this creates a hard edge between them.

Maya uses Harden Edge and Soften Edge to do the same thing.

UV Shells

To reduce shading errors with tangent-space normal maps, it is best to split the UVs everywhere there are hard edges on the model.

However, hard edges are not needed for every UV edge. There can be more UV edges than there are hard edges, in fact more UV seams are often necessary to reduce texture warping.

Hard edges need to be separated in UV space, to allow the tangent basis to twist around appropriately. This creates less extreme gradients in the normal map (which reduces shading errors when using a non-synched renderer), and reduces errors introduced by LODs.

Smoothing Tools

- turboTools for 3ds Max includes a tool to convert UV shell borders into hard edges.

- TexTools for 3ds Max includes a tool to convert hard edges into UV shell borders. The author also wrote a script to convert UV shell borders into hard edges.

- EdgeSmooth for 3ds Max is a tool to convert selected edges into hard edges, acting much like Maya's workflow. However the resulting mesh creates shading errors in some game engines.

- PolyUnwrapper ($) for 3ds Max includes a tool to convert UV shell borders into hard edges.

References

- Dey, Tamal K.; Goswami, Samrat (August 2006). "Probable surface reconstruction from noisy samples". Computational Geometry. 35 (1–2): 124–141. doi:10.1016/j.comgeo.2005.10.006

- What-is-3d-graphics: vrender.com, Retrieved 21 March, 2020

- onaitis, Jeff (2002–2004). "Box modeling Technique:". Archived from the original on 2014-03-21. Retrieved 14 April 2013

- 3d-computer-graphics, computer-graphics: tutorialspoint.com, Retrieved 19 February, 2020

- McReynolds, Tom; David Blythe (2005). Advanced graphics programming using openGL. Elsevier. p. 502. ISBN 978-1-55860-659-3

5

Applications

There are a wide-range of applications of virtual reality in different fields such as gaming, defence, sports, medical sciences, mining, education, robotics, etc. This chapter sheds light on the varied applications of virtual reality for a thorough understanding of the subject.

Virtual Reality in Gaming

Game engines of cinematic quality, broadband networking and advances in Virtual Reality (VR) technologies are setting the stage to allow players to have shared, "better-than-life" experiences in online virtual worlds.

Games, including online virtual worlds, populate the entertainment arena of the consumer market. They are engaging, mass produced, inexpensive, targeting wide audiences. Visual realism in games approaches cinematic quality. The amount of 3D content available online today exceeds what can be explored in a single person's lifetime. In contrast to gaming, VR systems require expensive hardware and customized software. They are available for limited audiences. VR systems are difficult to maintain and upgrade. Both the visual quality and the extent of virtual content are typically lower than in games. Nevertheless, VR has one feature that makes it stand out from all other platforms: the unmatched sense of presence, delivered by immersion and body tracking. The ability to make users believe that they actually "are there" has made VR a tool of choice for medical, military, and extreme condition training applications.

Games are already entering what used to be exclusively VR territory by incorporating elements of body tracking into user interface controls. The remarkable success of Nintendo's Wii underscores the value of physical interactivity in gameplay. Another example is the Sony EyeToy camera, which spawned a family of games that utilize user body motions.

VR technologies are also experiencing steady growth in both high end and inexpensive systems. Optical trackers may cost as little as a single web-camera, and cover a few feet of tracked area. High end trackers, such as PPT from WorldViz are capable of capturing user motions in a 50 x 50 x 3 meter area, with sub-millimeter precision. Head Mounted Displays (HMD) are also advancing rapidly. The model shown in Figure has 1920 x 1200 pixels per eye and 120° field of view. It weighs only 350 grams. More about wearable headsets may be found in Rolf Hainich's book.

Using an HMD and motion trackers, players will be able to literally walk into this 3D scene, with 360° viewing.

Several Examples of Augmented Reality Games

Advances in VR hardware and increased availability of VR equipment have stimulated the creation of novel gaming applications, especially in the field of Augmented Reality (AR). In AR systems, virtual content is fused with real environments. Examples are: Human Pacman game, AR Second Life Project at Georgia Tech, where 3D avatars are brought into real scenes. In AR Fac͵ade gameew Interface Devices for VR Games, players are interacting with a virtual couple in a physical apartment, using speech and natural body movements.

New Interface Devices for VR Games

In 2008, NeuroSky introduced MindSet, a wearable device which may become an icon for the integration of games and VR. MindSet has sensors that read and analyze the brain activity of players in real time. During the game, Brain Computer Interface module translates user intentions into game actions. A similar product, EPOC Neuroheadset, has been announced by Emotiv Systems.

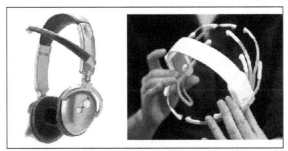

Brain Computer Interface headsets: MindSet by NeuroSky (left),
EPOC Neuroheadset by Emotiv Systems (right).

In the past decade, games and VR systems have been increasingly growing towards each other, including both hardware components and user interface techniques.

However, VR equipment still costs too much to be a gaming platform for general audiences, deterring game developers from adding support for VR components to game engines. For example, CryENGINE-2 by Crytek does not have an option for stereoscopic rendering, even for single viewport configurations used in mid-range HMDs (V8, eMagine, NVisor, etc). High-end HMDs, such as Wide5 from Fakespace Labs and pSight and xSight series from Sensics, require multipass or tiled rendering, which makes them very hard to integrate into most gaming engines. The gap between games and VR may still be too large to justify efforts to make game software VR-compatible.

Making a Virtual Reality Game

Gaming industry operates under "everyone plays" business model, which created a standard platform: a personal computer or a game console and a TV set. In order to bring VR into play, we propose to extend this model to "everyone plays on a console, advancing players continue in VR". Acknowledging that making a full title VR game for a general audience does not seem to be practical, we suggest reducing VR-playable content to short episodes and making them available to selected players.

- VR game pockets, or selected episodes of the game that can be played using VR equipment: HMD, trackers and other devices. For example, a game may have a carnival scene, where players can walk around and try different attractions. Some of these attractions might be VR-enabled, such as a traditional "Whack A Mole" game which lends itself exceptionally well to implementation in VR. This game was described in "The Irresponsible Captain Tylor" anime series in 1993.

"Whack-A-Mole" VR Game: the first person view of the field with popping targets (left),
the player, wearing an HMD and a tracked hammer (right).

Figure shows a more recent and more realistic example. This golf game is currently under development by Avatar-Reality 3, as one of the attractions on Blue Mars Virtual World. Although Blue Mars is designed for non-VR platforms, this episode provides a good illustration of what VR pockets may look like. VR Golf will require tracking of user head and both hands, for making a perfect swing. Travel on the golf course can be conveniently implemented with a virtual golf-car, using a "point-and-go" steering metaphor.

- Merit-based selection among players will balance the demand for and availability of VR resources. The game will have a specific scoring system. Progress of all users will be monitored and compared with the number and status of locally available VR stations. The number of advancing players who will be awarded the "VR-status" will depend on availability of VR equipment. The amount of time each user will be allowed to spend in VR will also be quantified by the scoring system.

Snapshot from the golf course on Blue Mars Virtual World.

- Access to VR gaming stations will be arranged according to the nature of the game and the target audience. For example, in first person shooters, players will begin the game at home. After earning a "VR status", they will continue the game at their local gaming arcades. The merit-based selection mechanism will ensure that there will be no long lines at VR booths. In educational games, developed for schools and colleges, advancing students will use VR stations installed and maintained on campus. VR stations may be also set up at conferences and conventions, especially if these events are co-located with trade shows of VR hardware manufacturers. Government agencies that have their own VR research and training facilities, such as NASA and US Army, might provide support for developing and hosting VR games for recruitment and training.

Games and VR have been increasingly adopting technological and social features of each other. However, creating a commercial VR game still remains problematic, because it challenges conventional business practices of game production. Intense competition in the gaming industry allows little room for creating applications that do not immediately improve the gameplay for intended audiences. Perhaps a mixture of funding strategies, both from government institutions and private investors, will provide the impetus for additional development of Massively Multiplayer VR Games that will combine the best features of traditional computer games and VR.

Virtual Reality in Military

Advanced Ground Vehicle Simulators

Virtual reality technologies allow soldiers to experience any type of vehicle in a far more immersive and realistic way than using your good old mouse and keyboard or even a driving simulator wheel.

Created by a team of scientists, military-type VR vehicle simulators constitute a complex platform that can recreate such things as the shape and feel of the vehicle, its maneuverability on various terrain types and behavior under different weather conditions.

Besides that, a soldier can navigate environments native to any part of the world, including the reconstructed settlements of any sort.

It is possible to simulate any vehicle type and develop virtual reality apps for any role one or several soldiers might play in that vehicle (a driver, gunner, hostage, etc.). From light reconnaissance tanks to non-line-of-sight (NLOS) mortars – anything can be modeled down to the smallest details.

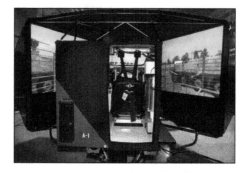

And, if you add a couple of complex games with war or small-scale conflict scenarios, a VR powered simulator like that can become an integral part of any military training. There won't be any need in special grounds and constant maintenance.

Because you can do it more frequently, it is also more efficient to conduct a sim training than spend resources like fuel and time on a field vehicle training.

VR Boot Camp Experience

The gaming industry has greatly influenced military training. As it was becoming more and more popular, the military also started to adopt gaming practice as a way to train their soldiers, many of which grew up playing video games.

Although the first military games were played on regular consoles, they allowed future soldiers to learn lots of techniques and strategies that can be applied in real-life combat scenarios.

But, virtual reality developers brought those "games" to a whole new level.

Before long, entire VR-equipped bases and training facilities have started to spring up. They use all kinds of devices and VR software including CAVE systems, motion trackers, and real-to-life equipment like vests and guns.

Setting up such a facility is not cheap, but it proves to be cost-efficient as soldiers can quickly change their training type within a relatively small area. However, the best option would be to combine virtual reality with real-life training courses.

Nobody in the military considers virtual reality as an absolute replacement. Yes, it is a great tool that in combination with traditional ways of training can help the military to increase training speed and the flexibility of their soldiers.

Medical Training

Often, military medics have to work in stressful and dangerous environments, putting their lives at risk.

Before the VR age, it was practically impossible to train medical personnel under the conditions of war-like surroundings. But now, you can recreate close-to-combat scenarios in virtual reality to simulate life-saving operations.

In the UK, a team of researchers and scientists has created such a VR simulation. It is an inflatable environment that recreates the interior of a Chinook helicopter.

Then, a trainee is put inside with a prosthetic body on the floor and a VR headset, which lets him immerse into a confined war-zone-like environment of a military evacuation scenario.

Backed by the sounds of helicopter and gunshots, this VR setup allows medical professionals to practice various skills under very stressful conditions.

Virtual reality applications can also be used to test medical personnel regularly in order to help them retain their skills.

For example, in cases of armed actions, there might be a need to reacquire medical skills within a short period. But, due to infrequent use of skills, any specialist can get "rusty."

Therefore, a group of researchers has developed a system to test medical personnel and schedule their VR training according to the results.

After going through a series of VR simulation of basic surgical tasks, they can analyze the performance of muscles (speed, distance, accuracy, etc.) and determine the level of skills decay according to the medical experience of the person.

PTSD Recovering Therapy

Also known as posttraumatic stress disorder, it is a bane of many soldiers gone through wars and conflicts.

Due to various traumatic experiences, the person can get disturbing thoughts and regular dreams about the event, which can even lead to self-harm or suicidal intentions.

There are a lot of programs that help soldiers with PTSD recover. And recently, VR applications have also come to the aid.

Now, besides the usual psychological treatment, there is another way of dealing with PTSD. Using virtual reality, you can recreate the situations that influenced the soldier's mental state in great detail.

But, in this case, it is absolutely harmless and can help them overcome their fears and anxieties by experiencing those battle scenes once more in virtual reality.

Virtual Battlefields

Unfortunately, many of the real-life military training types involve a certain degree of risk. Whether it's parachute jumping or heavy artillery exercises, fatal accidents still occur from time to time.

However, with the help of virtual reality, soldiers can be placed into a risk-free environment, which will let them safely carry out any combat drills without any harm whatsoever.

Equipped with a portable battery, a VR headset, and true-to-life guns, they can model different warfare scenarios accompanied by an AI or their real teammates.

Also, virtual reality applications are easily configurable, and you can use the same equipment for many combat missions and environments.

As a result, you can substantially reduce the training budget, and still get effective results at the same time.

VR in the Military – Pros and Cons

Training is less Costly

Using VR and AR for the training purposes reduces the expenditures related to the transportation of soldiers to specialized grounds and facilities, the maintenance of those facilities, fueling, ammunition, and other expendables.

Higher Efficiency

Just by setting up one facility or a platform, soldiers can participate in training more often. This results in more progress being made within a much shorter period.

Also, this way of "information feeding" is more effective for the younger generation.

More Possibilities

Virtual reality, combined with augmented reality, can help soldiers learn more about vehicle types and environments without any time restrictions. They can examine any vessel or weapon in detail in virtual reality without being able to get a physical object.

They can also train from anywhere because all the information can be downloaded from the cloud service.

No Risks

Shooting, driving a tank or throwing a grenade – even for training purposes – always involves danger. Virtual reality can eliminate any accidents related to those activities.

Range of Simulations and Flexibility

You can put a soldier into an armored tank, a loud helicopter or send him to an Arctic mission. Configurable environments give a lot of room for a variety of scenarios and their combinations.

Also, by recreating nausea-causing and claustrophobic conditions in virtual reality, you can help soldiers adapt better without getting them on an actual plane.

Security

There are a lot of disputes regarding the security level of VR devices used by military personnel. As a result, that hinders the implementation of virtual reality technologies in training.

This issue will be partially solved when it is decided what authentication level is enough for usage – a simple code or something more sophisticated like voice activation.

Another security issue is that there is no fool-proof method to protect a network from cyber-attacks. And if any classified information is leaked or stolen, it can have unprecedented consequences for the affected party.

Cybersickness

There are certain limitations of current VR technology that causes motion sickness if used for too long. Due to a specific frame rate, users can experience nausea because we are literally "tricking" our brain into believing that we are moving.

Software Development

Producing content also poses some challenge. It is easy to create a simulator for equipment testing (like wearing a bulletproof vest or weapon testing/assembling-disassembling), but for more complicated warfare scenarios, you need more resources.

While virtual reality is showing excellent results after being used for military training purposes, there are a lot of aspects that can be improved: graphics, battery life, haptics, etc.

But, considering the speed of VR development, all those improvements will not be long in coming.

There are quite a few VR development companies that specialize in military applications and platforms. Bringing in virtual reality is definitely the right choice if you want to optimize the training budget and boost efficiency.

Virtual Reality in Sports

The application of computer-based technology to sport is an area of intense interest. Such technologies include computerized modelling, data acquisition and analysis, mobile computers, and information technology networks. Virtual reality (VR) is another technology, and it was first applied to sport research in the 1990s, although there has been a resurgence of interest in recent years. VR refers to a computer-simulated environment that aims to induce a sense of being mentally or physically present in another place. An important feature of VR is that the individual can interact with the environment. In the context of sport, interaction might occur through an exertion interface. For example, physical effort on a machine such as an ergometer can be related to the speed of movement through a virtual race course. Motion capture video systems, infrared beams, and wearable sensors are other approaches that can be used to translate physical actions into virtual sport performance.

The key elements that define VR applications to sport are the use of computer-generated sport-relevant content and a means for the athlete to interact with the virtual environment. When defined in this way, the application of VR to sport has a number of strengths. As noted by Hoffman et al., the VR environment can be controlled and manipulated in specific and reproducible ways. Hoffman et al. used these characteristics to train participants to use a rowing race pacing strategy. VR can also be used for assessment, to gain feedback on performance, and to practice specific skills. The VR environment does not need to be limited to a single person. Other individuals may be present such as a coach, teammate, or competitor even if they are physically located in another place. The ability to connect with individuals via the Internet allows for interaction without the need for travel. Finally, the increasing availability of commercially produced software or full VR systems avoids the need for specialized technical expertise and allows VR to be used in local gyms and at home.

Also, Virtual Reality (VR) is now commonly used in many domains to train people in performing tasks in dangerous (such as aircraft pilot training) or very expensive (such as plant maintenance) environments without taking risks. In addition to the secure aspect, VR above all provides a standardized and controlled environment that allows analyses and experiments that cannot be done in real situation. For instance, it helps understanding the link between the performance of a player and the information perceived, such as on his opponent's kinematics or on a ball trajectory for instance. These experiments were previously made with videos. However, in videos, the viewpoint is fixed to the camera position during recording. This prevents interactivity, something extremely important if the player wishes to move so as to better pick up key information. Moreover, video playback depends on which actions took place at a given time. Owing to improvements in technology and processing power, virtual reality (VR) can overcome these limitations by providing numerical simulations and immersive, interactive environments.

VR when applied to sport may be defined as instances when individuals are engaged in a sport that is represented in a computer-simulated environment which aims to induce a sense of being mentally or physically present and enables interactivity with the environment. This definition highlights the computer-simulated nature and interactivity of the virtual environment, which are key element of more general definitions of VR. It also aims to highlight the application of VR to sport from the perspective of the user (athlete). Realistic responses to virtual environments are suggested to occur when the system induces a sense of presence and the perception that the events are actually occurring. In this respect, it is important that VR uses a computer-generated environment because this is a key feature that allows for interactivity and the perception of presence. In other words, the virtual environment or elements within it will move or change in response to the actions of the athlete. However, the method by which the virtual environment is presented to the athlete should not be specified in the definition because it might impose technological limitations to the application of VR to sport.

In many applications outside of sport, the virtual environment is displayed using a computer automatic virtual environment (CAVE) or head-mounted display (HMD). The CAVE is composed of a large cube made up of display screens that the user physically enters to become surrounded by the virtual environment. A HMD is a wearable device that covers the eyes and thus removes vision of the outside world. It has one or more small screens on which the virtual world is viewed in stereovision with a wide field of view. The HMD is combined with head tracking to allow the user to view areas of the virtual environment that are outside of the immediate field of view by turning their head. Being a smaller, more portable, and a more affordable system, the HMD is more popular than the CAVE, although both may be regarded as sharing the same key features of an immersive system.

However, the potential applications for using CAVE and HMD systems can be limited for some types of sports. A HMD may be impractical or potentially dangerous for some sports. For example, running a race on a treadmill using a HMD can be hazardous because vision of the moving treadmill is removed. The head movements and sweating of the athlete can also make the HMD uncomfortable to wear. Indeed, in no studies identified was a HMD system used despite researchers consistently using the term virtual reality to describe their approach. The most common approach was a two-dimensional depiction of the virtual environment using a computer screen or a projector. A computer screen or projector has the advantages of ease of use and practicality with sport but may induce less presence than a HMD or CAVE system. Further research is required to determine whether there is significant difference in presence when a computer screen or projector is used.

Several instances can be identified in which researchers used methodology that approximated the proposed definition of VR applications to sport. For example, some researchers have used a visual display that shows a video of a real environment. Feltz et al. conducted a series of studies that investigated the Ko"hler motivation gain effect with a plank exercise task. These studies showed the participant via a video (i.e. not a computer-generated avatar) and included a second individual shown on a second visual display without any interaction. Videos of real environments and people may have potential for VR applications to sport, but they must include elements of interactivity to fulfill the proposed definition of VR. Similarly, other researchers have used computer-generated environments to examine baseball batting, handball goalkeeping, and soccer goalkeeping, but these did not allow for any interactivity with the environment. In some cases, it was also found that researchers used a non-animated avatar against a blank screen, but these do not meet the proposed definition because the methods did not simulate a real environment.

Another important consideration for interactive VR applications to sport is the distinction between sport, exercise, and exergaming. Sport may be defined as an activity that requires motor skill and hand-eye coordination combined with physical exertion and includes rules and elements of competition. Exercise, used synonymously with physical exercise, is a structured activity that may include repetitive elements that is performed to maintain or improve physical fitness. Exergame/active videogame is a videogame played on commercial game console systems that combines gameplay with physical movements that are more than sedentary behavior. Exercise and exergames together represent a more general case of enhancing physical activity and may not necessarily be based on a sport.

Exercises or exergames that are not based on a sport clearly do not represent instances of VR applications to sport even if they incorporate a virtual environment. However, investigators have used sport-related computer games, particularly those that run on a games console, in research. Console games based on sports have been used to examine skill acquisition and transfer in children and adults. However, these applications lacked an appropriate exertion interface (e.g. participants ran on the spot to simulate running in the game) or essential sporting equipment (e.g. no darts were used in a dart game), and these aspects can make the task substantially different to perform the sport in real life. VR has also been applied to exercise and improving physical fitness. In several studies, researchers have used sport-related tasks such as cycling, running, and rowing. These applications have relevance to sport performance particularly because many of these studies have introduced elements of competition or pressure to meet team goals.

Virtual Reality in Mental Health

The World Health Organization has reported that one in four people in the world will be affected by mental or neurological disorders at some point in their lives. Around 450 million people currently have such conditions.

Considering that mental disorders are among the leading causes of ill-health and disability worldwide, VR is a welcome additional treatment. Studies have already shown that VR can ease certain phobias, treat PTSD, help people with psychotic disorders experience less paranoia and anxiety in public settings, and reduce social anxiety.

To date, due to cost and technology limitations, VR has not been widely available as a treatment. However, with the rise of affordable standalone and mobile VR headsets, there is increased opportunity to use VR and decentralize mental health treatment, allowing more people to benefit.

Post-traumatic Stress Disorder (PTSD)

PTSD affects 7.7 million people in the U.S., and one in three people who experience a traumatic event will have PTSD. The symptoms range from insomnia to personality changes. Exposure therapy - repeatedly exposing patients to their traumatic event in a controlled environment until triggers of the event no longer lead to anxiety - has been found to be more effective than treatments like medication and psychotherapy. VR is believed to be a particularly successful method of exposure therapy.

Research clinics have been experimenting with VR as a method since 1997. It is believed that the sensory and immersive nature of VR helps PTSD patients get better, faster than simply describing the trauma, and relapses are less frequent. It also allows clinicians to measure, document and learn from the results in order to better understand the brain and biological factors that serve to inform the prevention, assessment, and treatment of PTSD. The virtual environment means people don't need to imagine their traumatic experience - the work is done for them.

U.S. Army veteran interacts with the Bravemind VR
therapy to safely relive his deployment.

Phobias and Anxiety Disorders

For years, VR therapy has been used in clinics for the treatment of phobias and other anxiety disorders. Anxiety disorders affect at least 40 million people in the U.S (18.1%

of the population) and cost the country $42 billion per year. Specific phobias affect about 19 million individuals in the U.S.

Despite the vast number of patients afflicted by some form of anxiety disorder, only 36.9% receive treatment. This is where companies like Mimerse could make a real difference. Since 2014, this 'virtual pharmacy' has been developing therapeutic VR apps. Mimerse has been working with clinicians, scientists, healthcare and platform providers to create a scalable future of mental healthcare. The company's products include a relaxation and meditation experience for inducing calm and reducing stress, while apps to tackle phobias like the fear of public speaking and flying are coming soon. Mass-market apps like this could offer huge value for individuals globally.

Psious is a VR tool for mental health professionals. The platform is "democratizing virtual reality treatments for therapists and patients around the world" by providing mental health professionals with animated and live environments they can use in their clinical practice. The various scenarios provided within the platform comprise over 50 resources (virtual reality and augmented reality environments, 360° videos, etc.) employed for the treatment of anxiety disorders, fears and phobias, as well as for the practice of mindfulness and relaxation techniques.

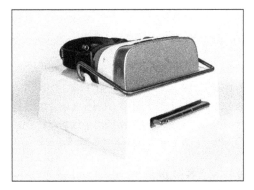

Limbix helps practitioners to treat patients with anxiety or phobias, and helps those who need pain management techniques. Real-world footage is incorporated into 360° videos designed to help patients deal with the challenges they face. Patients can face their fears, practice conversations, visit remote locations, and relax in tranquil settings while in authentic, virtual environments.

Virtual Reality in Medical Training

Virtual Anatomical Tours

Computer-generated simulations are usually divided into two categories, virtual reality and augmented reality. They are similar, but different.

Virtual reality is an entirely computer-generated view of a world — that is, purely virtual. Everything the user sees is manufactured, like the CHLA trauma bay scenario White experienced.

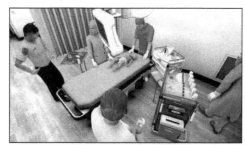

At children's hospital, residents don goggles to enter
a virtual world and practice saving a baby's life.

Augmented reality, by contrast, superimposes computer-generated images and sounds onto the real world. In medicine, this includes simulated internal organs overlaid on a real manikin. Because the AR experience isn't completely immersive, it doesn't necessarily require goggles: holding up an iPad might suffice to superimpose the image, for example.

Two years ago, faculty at Stanford University School of Medicine began using VR for training in its Neurosurgical Simulation and Virtual Reality Center. There, a platform called Surgical Theater fuses several types of brain scans from a real patient to achieve greater specificity and verisimilitude.

Seated in comfortable, theater-style chairs and wearing VR goggles, users can manipulate and view the organ from multiple perspectives. The experience feels a bit like flying through a detailed and lifelike human brain. "The beauty of this is really that you can appreciate in three dimensions what the structures look like," says Gary Steinberg, MD, PhD, chair of neurosurgery at Stanford.

After the VR experience, students step across the hall to the neurosurgical anatomy lab, where they see and touch the same anatomical structures in a cadaver. The virtual reality warmup prepares students for dissection, says Steinberg, and speeds up learning.

Steinberg raves about virtual reality in medical training. "It's obvious," he believes. "It's intuitive." In fact, Steinberg often prepares for surgery using a VR representation of a patient's imaging.

Virtual Reality in Education

Virtual reality can be used to enhance student learning and engagement. VR education can transform the way educational content is delivered; it works on the premise of creating a virtual world — real or imagined — and allows users not only see it but also interact with it. Being immersed in what you're learning motivates you to fully understand it. It'll require less cognitive load to process the information.

A few properties that makes virtual reality in education so powerful.

Better Sense of Place

When students read about something, they often want to experience it. With VR, they aren't limited to word descriptions or book illustrations; they can explore the topic and see how things are put together.

Thanks to the feeling of presence VR provides, students can learn about a subject by living it. It's easy to forget that VR experiences aren't real — a body actually believes it's in a new place. This feeling engages the mind in a way that is remarkable.

Rather than reading about Rome, VR headsets
let students be transported to Rome.

Scale Learning Experiences

Technologies such as science labs are amazing — they allow students to understand how things work based on practical experience.

But such technologies are expensive and almost impossible to scale. They are also limited in the number of things they can do.

Learn by Doing

It's a well-known fact that people learn best by doing; however, if you inspect modern education, you'll see how little learning actually happens by doing. Students are focused on reading instructions rather than using them in practice.

VR in education provides an experience anchor to the instruction. With VR education, learners are inspired to discover for themselves. Students have an opportunity to learn by doing rather than passively reading.

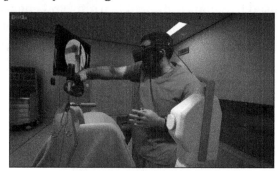

A virtual medical lab where there's no
danger of things going wrong.

Emotional Reaction

Visceral reactions to what we are experiencing are fundamental to forming memories. VR in education makes it easy to engage students the whole time, making experiences memorable.

Develop Creativity

Having virtual reality in education is useful not only for content consumption, but it's also great for content creation. By giving students powerful tools such as Tilt Brush, you help them boost their creativity.

Visual Learning

A lot of people are visual learners — VR is really helpful for this group of learners. Instead of reading about things, students actually see the things they're learning about. Being able to visualize complex functions or mechanisms makes them easier to comprehend.

Users are Ready to Embrace new Technology

The first idea that pops into anyone's mind when they think about VR technology is an entertainment experience. Many designers see VR as an extension of the gaming industry. It's true that VR has historically been dedicated to gaming, but things are changing. According to a recent survey conducted by Greenlight VR, desire for education outweighs desire for gaming content — 63.9 percent vs. 61 percent.

Categories of VR Educational Experiences

Where can we apply virtual reality in education? The answer is almost everywhere. VR creates an infinite set of possibilities that people can experience. Here are few types of experiences you can create with VR.

Virtual Fields Trips

VR technology can be used to engage students in topics related to geography, history, or literature by offering a deeply immersive senses of place and time. Simply imagine geography lessons where you can visit any place on the globe — this type of experience is much more enriching than just reading about it.

Google Expeditions is one good example of an app that's providing such an experience. Expedition is a library of field trips available for regular smartphone users. Each trip is comprised of VR panoramas, and trips vary from the Great Wall of China to Mars. People all over the world can visit places that are virtually impossible to visit in person.

Google piloted this app in hundreds of schools all over the world. The project was extremely successful, with Google taking more than 1 million students in 11 countries on expeditions.

Google Expeditions enables virtual field trips all over the world.

Of course, virtual reality will never replace real field trips and travels, nor should it. But, VR enables experiences to happen that would be otherwise impossible.

High Tech Training

VR is a good solution for highly technical training fields like the military or the medical industry. For example, the most significant challenge for medical students learning anatomy is understanding the body in three dimensions and how different systems fit together. VR education can help overcome this problem.

One good example is the VR system used by Mendel Grammar School in Opava City, Czech Republic, which helps students in biology classes learn about the anatomy of the eye. The team working on this project employed a Leap Motion controller and specially-adapted Oculus Rift headsets to provide an innovative way of learning anatomy.

Internships

Getting exposure to different careers is an essential part of the learning process. From early childhood, we dream about what we want to be when we grow up, and those dreams are usually inspired by the professionals in our lives. Often, we get this understanding through internships.

Another benefit of having virtual reality in education is its ability to help broaden students' exposure to careers. It improves people's ability to imagine themselves in others' shoes. Career expeditions show what it's like to work in a field — students can explore a day in someone's career, see what person is studying, and understand what a person likes — or doesn't like — about their job. As a result, the experience becomes familiar to students.

VR lets students explore any profession, like being an astronaut.

Group Learning

Some of the most important knowledge we gain doesn't come from what we hear from lecturers, but rather from collegiality and debate. VR education gives the opportunity to make learning experiences social by allowing students to communicate with each other. Using avatars and mapped facial expressions, people can come together to discuss, synthesize, and learn from one another.

Distance Learning

VR allows us to bridge the gap between educators and learners. With VR, distance learning tools can put educators and students together in the same room with digital representations of themselves — teachers can teleport into the VR world and guide students through their experiences.

Design Challenges for VR Education Experiences

Clearly, the future of virtual reality in education is very exciting and full of potential. We are just at the dawn of this powerful technology and designing for VR is full of challenges that we should be ready to overcome.

Creating a new Role for Teachers with VR Education

The transition from analog teaching practices to digital ones is going to change what teaching looks like. The role of a teacher will change from content delivery to content facilitation. Teachers will be focused on creating conditions for exploring, rather than providing ready-made knowledge.

Our Changing Understanding of Immersive Experiences

It's clear we're in the early stages of VR — and it's going to keep changing. However, technology will continue to push boundaries of how immersive VR can become. We're even going to see advancements in eye tracking and body tracking in coming years. What we consider an immersive experience today will be considered table stakes in the not-too-distant future.

Making VR Accessible

VR has a high price point that is a significant barrier for many users. If we analyze the success of Google Expeditions, it's clear that Google was able to reach this many students because the hardware was really accessible. To make VR education accessible to a majority of users, it's important to focus on creating VR experiences for devices users already have and repurpose them into powerful tools for education. A phone we have in our pockets and $20-100 headset devices — such as Google Cardboard or Samsung Gear VR — should be enough to give students good VR experiences.

Open New Horizons with VR Education

Virtual reality in education is on the horizon, and without a doubt, it'll change the world as we know it. Twenty-first century classrooms will be technologically advanced places of learning, with VR technology significantly increasing students' engagement and learning. VR experiences will inspire a whole new generation of young and bright students, ready to innovate and change the world.

At the same time, the next big thing in education no longer relies on technology, but rather on a teacher's decision to push forward and adopt these technologies inside the classroom. The global goal should be to make knowledge available, accessible, and affordable for everyone on the planet.

Key Benefits

Global Teleportation

An obvious place to start of course is the simple fact that VR breaks down geographical boundaries. For a school this can be priceless as it means that students can virtually visit places that are beyond their means in the real world – whether that be on the other side of the globe or even The Moon. The app that has made the biggest impact for me in this regard is probably Google Earth VR as it has allowed our students to traverse the entire planet as a part of an Explorers topic.

Time Machine Effect

Integrate it in history classrooms to allow students to travel in time and experience the past first hand. From using Timelooper to witness The Blitz and The Great Fire of London to using Discovr Egypt to explore King Tut's tomb, using virtual reality to break down the very walls of time is an incredibly powerful application of the technology in education.

Contextualised Learning

The example tend to give is that of learning about Ancient Greece and how an AR app may allow students to bring a Greek statue into the classroom but a VR app like Athenian Acropolis contextualises the learning by allowing the student to actually view the same statue in Ancient Greece.

Multi-sensory Experiences

Whilst tablets added touchscreen functionality to the multimedia experience of digital content, they don't come close to the kinaesthetic experience afforded by virtual reality. Being able to move within a virtual space and engage with elements engages learners like never before. Just look at Hold The World for example where you manipulate fossils as Sir David Attenborough helps you understand more about them.

Extraordinary Abilities

From lifting a car above your head to view it's engine to painting with fire in Tilt Brush to simply using teleportation locomotion mechanics, VR allows us to break the laws of physics and in turn opens up new learning possibilities in the classroom. It can also serve to streamline a task that would take a student much longer in the real world, thus allowing more time for repetition or additional learning experiences.

Active Autonomy

A student within a VR experience is the master of their journey, with a great deal of autonomy in how they engage with the content. This starts with the simple fact that they are able to choose where to look but expands when you offer them experiences which are not on rails and allow them to explore freely. Titanic VR, for example, lets you explore the wreckage whilst Engage includes spaces like Ancient Avebury and the surface of Mars. If a class of students are allowed to explore these virtual spaces, they don't need to "stick with the group" and thus can direct their own flow of information and learning.

Virtual Rehearsal

This concept is really gathering steam in the training industry as well as LandD depart-
ments across a variety of industries. Using VR to practice and hone skills without fear
of failure is incredibly powerful and can help students build confidence in new areas of
learning. This could mean using VirtualSpeech to practise public speaking or Victory
VR's excellent Frog Dissection app to develop skills in the Biology classroom (potentially saving a lot of money in the process).

Focused Immersion

This is somewhat of a logistical factor but does bear mentioning. The very nature of
VR being framed inside a headset means that the learner is less prone to distractions
in their physical surroundings. For some students this can be immensely beneficial as
they may be prone to distraction leading to loss of focus and ultimately loss of learning.
The immersive nature of VR means that learners are literally engulfed with learning
and this, in turn, is a key factor in the retention of information.

Remote Presence

This is what we start to see a lot more of this year I believe. Students using VR to connect with other students as well as attend lectures and lessons delivered by educators
across the globe. Multi-user, social VR platforms like Engage, AltSpace and more will
become thriving hubs for educational content as the entire concept of what a school is
and can be begins to morph into something truly new.

Virtual Reality in Pain Management

Burn Care

The use of VR for pain and anxiety attenuation during burn care procedures and reha-bilitation of burn survivors is one of the most widely researched uses of VR technology. Clearly, burn wound care causes a tremendous amount of pain, anxiety and discomfort to patients. In 2000, Hoffman et al. reported a case study examining the efficacy of VR compared with a standard video game for two adolescents (16 and 17 years old) undergoing burn wound care. VR was found to decrease pain levels, anxiety and time spent thinking about pain. Das et al. conducted a randomized control trial, compar-ing standard of care (analgesia) with analgesia plus VR for children (5–18 years old) during burn wound care. Analgesia coupled with VR was more effective in reducing pain and distress than analgesia alone. More recently, a water-friendly VR system was investigated during wound debridement for 11 patients (9–40 years), demonstrating that VR lowered pain ratings and increased fun ratings for those who reported feeling engrossed in the VR game.

Virtual reality technology has also been studied with burn patients undergoing physi-cal therapy. Hoffman et al. examined the use of pharmacologic analgesia alone versus VR in addition to analgesia during physical therapy. Patients in the VR group reported lower ratings of pain and an increased range of motion. In another study, Hoffman et al. compared the use of VR to no distraction during physical therapy. After the VR condition, patients reported decreased pain and a greater range of motion. Sharar et al. reported results across three studies and concluded that VR in addition to standard analgesia reduced pain intensity, unpleasantness and time spent thinking about pain. Carrougher et al. found similar results among burn patients undergoing physical ther-apy/rehabilitation, with nonsignificant clinical improvements in range of motion.

Patterson and colleagues were the first to use VR technology to augment hypnosis (vir-tual reality hypnosis [VRH]). This was a novel and cutting-edge approach to the in-tegration of VR with a pre-existing evidence-based treatment for reducing pain and anxiety. Procedurally, VRH is administered by providing the patient with an audio recording of hypnotic induction, suggestions for pain relief and then drifting the par-ticipant into the virtual world. Patterson et al. studied VR as a means of delivering hypnosis to patients with burns during wound care in a clinical case series of 13 pa-tients. These patients reported lower levels of pain and anxiety. Patterson used a VR distraction sequence, SnowWorld, developed by Hoffman, which allows users to glide through a 3D icy canyon while throwing snowballs at virtual snowmen, igloos, robots and penguins. Similarly, Konstantatos et al. examined the efficacy of VR relaxation in addition to morphine for pain reduction during burn wound dressing changes. Instead of using a distraction type program, such as SnowWorld, the researchers developed a VR relaxation sequence prepared by psychologists and based on hypnotherapy theory.

This provided calming visual scenery, which instructed the participant to concentrate on a moving spiral.

In general, VR has been reported to be an effective modality to decrease pain during burn care. A recent systematic review of nine studies by Morris et al. found that VR coupled with standard analgesia was effective in reducing pain during burn care in eight of the nine studies. Varying methodologies, patient characteristics and VR technology, may continue to contribute to mixed findings. Nonetheless, continued research in burn care is warranted with VR and VR enhanced interventions for managing the associated pain and anxiety.

Cancer Pain

Virtual reality technology has also been studied as a way to decrease pain, unpleasantness and anxiety associated with common painful cancer procedures and treatments, such as chemotherapy, lumbar puncture and port access. A study by Schneider and Workman examined 11 children (aged 10–17 years) receiving chemotherapy with and without VR. A total of 82% of the children stated that treatment with VR was better than previous treatments and that they would like to use VR during future treatments. Sander Wint et al. investigated VR use during lumbar puncture with a sample of 30 adolescents (aged 10–19 years). Although pain scores were lower in the VR condition, differences were not statistically significant. A study by Gershon et al., studying children and adolescents requiring port access, compared VR distraction, non-VR distraction (computer) and standard of care. Findings indicated that VR distraction was significantly better than standard of care in terms of reducing physiological arousal (i.e., pulse rate) and pain ratings. VR has also been demonstrated to decrease symptom distress and perceived time spent receiving chemotherapy, termed the time–elapse compression effect.

Routine Medical Procedures

Many routine medical procedures, such as a blood draw, intravenous placement and immunization can be painful and anxiety provoking. Gold et al. investigated the use of VR distraction during outpatient blood draw in children. The sample consisted of 100 children (8–12 years old) stratified for age and gender into four conditions: no distraction, cartoon distraction, VR via computer or VR via HMD. The children in all conditions placed their arm through a pass wall for the blood draw in order to control for visual occlusion. Children in the VR HMD group reported a lower frequency of moderate-to-severe pain intensity levels compared with the other three groups (χ^2 [15, N = 100] = 25.54, p < 0.05). No significant differences were found in average pain intensity and state anxiety between the four conditions. Gold et al. examined the use of VR with 20 children (8–12 years of age) requiring intravenous placement of contrast for an MRI CT scan. Children were randomly assigned to one of two conditions: standard of care (topical anesthetic) or VR presented via HMD plus standard of care. While children in the control condition had a fourfold increase in pain (p < 0.01), children in the VR condition reported no significant changes in pain intensity between pre- and postintravenous placement. Furthermore, children, caregivers and nurses were more satisfied with the use of VR for pain management during the procedure.

Furman et al. compared VR with watching movies as alternative forms of analgesia in 38 patients during scaling and root planning, a painful dental procedure. Pain scores were significantly lower in the VR group compared with the movie group and controls. Furman et al. modeled the study closely on a case study by Hoffman et al., which examined two patients who received scaling and root planning, and both reported lower pain ratings during the VR condition than during the movie and control conditions.

VR for Chronic Pain Management

While there is growing evidence supporting VR's effectiveness in managing acute procedural pain, little is known about the use of VR for treating patients with chronic pain and for long-term pain rehabilitation. To date, only a few studies have investigated VR for chronic pain management and the data are preliminary.

Sato et al. investigated the use of VR for treating complex regional pain syndrome in adults. In this pilot study, a VR mirror visual feedback system was created and applied to the treatment of complex regional pain syndrome in five adult patients (46–74 years old). This was a nonimmersive form of VR, as participants were not engaged in VR through an HMD. However, the game was interactive as the VR mirror visual tracking device followed the participants' hands as they completed target-oriented motor exercises such as reaching out, grasping, transferring and placing. In the study, patients participated in five to eight outpatient sessions, resulting in four of the five patients demonstrating at least 50% reduction in their pain intensity scores. This study demonstrates how VR could be applied for the treatment of chronic pain. Further investigations with larger samples and refined methodologies must be conducted to replicate these results. In addition, future studies should look at the effectiveness of immersive VR programs for the treatment of complex regional pain syndrome and other chronic pain conditions.

Sarig-Bahat et al. investigated VR's ability to treat chronic neck pain in 67 patients (22–65 years) with and without symptoms. The investigators used a VR environment, which encouraged patients to increase their range of motion by 'spraying' flies with a virtual spray canister. In theory, the more they engaged in the activity, the greater their range of motion would become. The investigators found that a single session of VR resulted in increased cervical range of motion and decreased neck pain.

Hoffman et al. explored whether immersive VR could help reduce pain during repeated physical therapy sessions for burn victims. During three sessions, seven patients (9–32 years of age) came to perform range-of-motion exercises under an occupational therapists' direction. Participants spent an equal amount of time during the session with VR distraction and without. The investigators found that pain ratings were significantly lower when patients were immersed in VR and the magnitude of pain reduction did not decrease over multiple sessions. These findings are promising as they indicate a potential for VR to be applied to long-term physical therapy.

VR has recently been studied to augment the effect of hypnosis for the treatment of chronic pain. In a case study of a 36-year old female with a 5-year history of retractable chronic neuropathic pain, investigators found that following a 6-month trial of VRH, the patient's pain ratings decreased 36% for 3.86 h and unpleasantness decreased 33% for 12.21 h on average across 33 sessions. In addition, when the first ten sessions of VRH were compared with the first ten sessions of previously completed hypnosis (non-VR) treatment, investigators found that VRH led to a reported average of 8.5 h of pain reduction and 4.3 h of being pain free, compared with an average of 1 h of pain reduction and 0 h of being pain free after hypnosis (non-VR). In conclusion, VRH was found to be more effective than hypnosis alone, by reducing pain and prolonging the treatment effects. Although the usage of VR for chronic pain management is still in its infancy, pilot findings are promising.

Experimental Pain and VR in Healthy Populations

A critical line of research is the examination of experimental pain and VR in healthy participants. This paradigm has many advantages, as investigators are attempting to isolate and deconstruct critical parameters involved in the clinical efficacy of VR. These studies allow investigators to look at the effects of VR while controlling confounding factors such as clinical pathology, exposure to pain or adjunctive medications, hospital environment, and various other patient and disease characteristics. Therefore, this type of research enables investigators to control and manipulate the effects of the unique characteristics that contribute to VR distraction or modulation.

Investigator attaches the Medoc 30 × 30 mm ATS thermal stimulator probe to administer a noxious stimulus.

Experimental pain has been delivered through a variety of mechanical and thermal modalities, including a modified tourniquet, an ischemic tourniquet, a blood pressure cuff, cold pressor and noxious warm or cold thermal pain stimulation. In general, VR has been demonstrated to be effective in increasing pain tolerance and pain threshold, and decreasing pain intensity, affective distress and pain unpleasantness.

There is scientific concern that individuals may habituate to VR and, therefore, lose its benefits over repeated exposures. Rutter et al. conducted an 8-week trial of once-weekly VR distraction during a cold pressor pain paradigm on 28 adults (18–23 years old). Results indicated that VR distraction led to significant increases in pain threshold and pain tolerance, and significant decreases in pain intensity, time spent thinking about pain and self-reported anxiety. Unique findings specific to this study demonstrated that the effects of VR remained stable across the eight sessions, indicating that repeated exposure did not alter VR's effectiveness. These findings are similar to a clinical trial of VR versus traditional physical therapy for patients following burn injuries. Hoffman et al. demonstrated that VR reduced pain across multiple physical therapy sessions and treatment effects persisted without habituation for patients with burns. Additional studies should investigate whether treatment effects continue across treatment sessions for participants with other pain conditions.

Another line of VR investigation has specifically focused on the technology and differentiating the effects of HMD versus no HMD, and high versus low HMD technology. Dahlquist et al. found that the use of an HMD resulted in an increase in pain threshold and pain tolerance for children over the age of 10 years, but had no significant differences for children under 10 years of age. Hoffman et al. compared a low- versus high-tech VR HMD for pain attenuation during an experimental thermal pain paradigm and found that the high-tech VR helmet group reported greater reductions in 'worst' pain (34%), 'pain unpleasantness' (46%) and 'time spent thinking about pain' (29%), as well as greater fun during the pain stimulus (32%) than the low-tech VR group. Only 29% of participants in the low-tech helmet group, compared with 65% of participants in the high-tech VR helmet group, showed a clinically significant reduction in pain intensity during VR. Together, these results reflect important developmental and technological considerations when evaluating the impact and efficacy of VR. The current results suggest that the use of a HMD with older children resulted in an increase in pain threshold and pain tolerance, while the use of a high-tech VR HMD was more effective at reducing pain than a low-tech VR HMD.

Patterson et al. combined posthypnotic suggestion with VR distraction versus VR alone in 103 undergraduate psychology student volunteers (18–40 years old). After receiving a thermal pain stimulus with no distracter at baseline, each participant received hypnosis or no hypnosis, followed by virtual reality distraction (VRD) or no VRD during another pain stimulus. Patterson et al. found that audio hypnosis combined with VRD reduced subjective 'worst pain' and 'pain unpleasantness' by 22 and 25%, respectively, more than VRD alone. Combination therapies, which include VR as a method for delivering hypnosis training, may be promising new therapies for managing pain.

VR and Neurobiology

Functional imaging studies of the human brain's response to painful stimuli have shown increases of activities in the anterior cingulate gyrus, the insula, the thalamus, and sometimes in other regions such as the primary somatosensory cortex and the periaqueductal gray matter. These brain regions may be considered to host a network of circuitry involved in the bottom-up, top-down and intercortical processing of painful stimuli, or even somewhere, somehow the origin of the experience of pain itself. However, these regions also respond more or less to a range of aversive to nonaversive stimuli, and a wide range of task-driven attention, distraction or affective conditions. The responses of some subsets of these regions have been related to sensation/pain intensity and pain unpleasantness by imaging with well-controlled psychophysical measures. However, difficulties in separating brain regions that process sensory information from those that mediate affective responses is presently an area of active debate. To date, functional imaging or other methods of investigation have not produced an objective, direct brain correlate of the pain experience, nor is there a clear picture of how the brain's sensory and affective mechanisms act together on the dimension of pain in response to potentially aversive stimuli.

Virtual reality has been found to attenuate pain, and this effect has been called 'VR analgesia'. The subjective ratings of pain reduction by VR has been corroborated with functional MRI (fMRI) data showing reduced brain activity increases in regions commonly strongly activated by experimental thermal pain stimulation. Hoffman's study, however, mainly focuses on whether VR game playing, as a whole, significantly reduces the increase of brain activities in the classic pain areas associated with noxious thermal stimuli. Another published study compared VR with the effects of opioids (hydromorphone injection) on brain activities related to thermal pain stimulation, and found that opioids and VR significantly reduced pain-related brain activity in the insula and thalamus, but not other regions of the pain circuitry. On the other hand, other cognitive tasks have been demonstrated to attenuate brain activity in the classic pain circuitry during experimental pain stimulation. Bantick et al. proposed a theory of pain attenuation via distraction (exemplified by an adapted Stroop task) to decrease pain perception as measured by fMRI and subjective pain ratings in eight right-handed volunteers (mean age 30 ± 9 years). The adaptive counting Stroop task required the subject to count the number of words with incongruent meanings on the display screen. Subjective reports of pain intensity were lower during the Stroop distraction condition. During the distraction task, there was an overall decrease in BOLD signal in the insula, thalamus, hippocampus and midcingulate region of the anterior cingulated cortex, which is known brain regions associated with pain perception. Inversely, an increase in BOLD signal was observed in the perigenual region of the anterior cingulated cortex and orbitofrontal cortex, demonstrating the plausibility of inter-cortical modulation or top-down inhibition of pain signaling. Valet et al. hypothesized that the cingulo–frontal cortex may exert top-down influences on the periaqueductal gray matter and posterior thalamus to modulate pain during distraction. Performing the counting Stroop task requires sustained attention plus other high-level cognitive functions. Whether the counting Stroop task's analgesic effect is explained solely by attention 'gating' or via other mechanisms cannot be determined by Bantick's or Valet's data. The increased activity in the cingulo–frontal cortex may be caused by the increased cognitive demand of the task, not simply by the mechanism of attention distraction alone. In other words, attention does not necessitate task loading, but task loading does require attention. Additional studies are required to shed light on these issues to advance our understanding of the underlying cortical processes responsible for pain attenuation.

Investigators reviewing structural brain MRI.

While known distracting cognitive tasks have demonstrated top-down modulation of pain signaling via frontal cortical processes, VR remains somewhat enigmatic with regard to its underlying neurobiological mechanisms. To date, in addition to the distraction of attention, studies have associated cognitive analgesic effects to cognitive task loading, mood, expectancy and perceived controllability. A VR environment is capable of manipulating an even more complex set of cognitive and emotional conditions than the presentation of most classic cognitive tasks. Therefore, VR's analgesic effect may originate from the interplay of these classic mechanisms or from something beyond. For example, a VR environment is well known for eliciting a 'transported' presence, over and beyond any cognitive tasks the subject is performing at the same time. Elaborate experimental designs capable of isolating the contribution of transported presence are required to illuminate the neural mechanisms underlying VR analgesia.

Current NIH Studies

The number of NIH-funded studies investigating the use of VR for pain management has doubled in the past year. Cohen is looking at the effectiveness of coaching children in deep-breathing relaxation (biofeedback) through a VR system during fracture manipulation and repair. Patterson is examining the efficacy of VR combined with hypnosis for patients who have experienced severe physical trauma and pediatric patients undergoing physical therapy postburn. In addition, Patterson will conduct an experimental study using analog electric pain to further explore the mechanisms underlying VR's analgesic effects.

Sharar will study the neurophysiologic mechanisms underlying VR as compared with other pharmacologic pain management methods. Pain will be rated through subjective measures and fMRI. Similarly, Gold will employ fMRI to explore the neurobiological mechanisms involved in VR pain attenuation in healthy adolescents (aged 14–17 years). An experimental fMRI-compatible thermal pain paradigm will be used to evaluate the hypothesis that VR will reduce brain activity in brain regions associated with pain perception (e.g., thalamus, somatosensory and motor cortices, insular cortices, cingulated cortices and basal ganglia). In addition, the reduction of brain activity observed in regions associated with pain perception during VR will concurrently be associated with increased activity in distal regions of the brain (e.g., prefrontal cortex) commonly associated with attention, emotion, cognition and response inhibition. Sharar and Gold's studies will provide important insight into VR's underlying mechanistic effects on neural activity in participants subjected to experimental pain.

Virtual Reality in Evidence-based Psychotherapy

Despite the obvious strengths and the notable progresses made by psychotherapy during the last decades, research also systematically points to a segment of patients who are nonresponsive to interventions, prompting professionals to advocate for improving the efficacy of treatments and for exploring and developing new efficient and cost-effective intervention strategies. Virtual reality (VR) has lately emerged as a promising tool in several areas of psychological intervention.

The first computer programs for CBT were developed in the 1980s in the United Kingdom and the United States. They relied on written text, checklists, and multiple-choice questions for communication with the patient. Among the benefits of using computer programs in psychotherapy and the factors motivating the continued development of computer-assisted cognitive-behavioral therapy (CCBT) are the possibility of providing unique learning experiences to clients, leading to a faster attainment of treatment goals, the reduction of therapy costs and increased access to psychological treatments for people who are unable or unwilling to attend traditional treatment.

Based on the assessment of available data, the National Institute for Health and Clinical Excellence (NICE) has included computer-based anxiety (i.e., panic, phobia,) and depression interventions among its recommended treatments.

More recently developed computer tools for CBT have incorporated virtual reality, and continuing advances in the field have led to the development of VR systems that are uniquely suited for targeting a variety of psychological conditions. Their main advantage resides in the potential of creating cost-effective, systematic assessment, training and treatment environments that allow for the precise control of complex, immersive and dynamic 3D stimulus presentations and for sophisticated interaction, behavior tracking and performance recording.

VR uses complex computer graphics and a variety of input and output devices to construct a virtual environment where the observer feels immersed. Thus, the person is no longer mere external observer of the images on the computer screen, but an active participant in the computer-generated three-dimensional world. This three-dimensional interaction is what generates presence. Presence refers to the interpretation of the virtual environment as if it were real. Although the individual is conscious of his or her experience being produced by the technology, perception to a certain extent overlooks this aspect and interprets the environment as if technology were not involved.

The main strategies used to immerse subjects into virtual environments and generate presence are head mounted displays (HMD) and computer automatic virtual environments (CAVE). HMD systems are for individual use; they are image display systems worn on the head that remain optically coupled to the user's eyes as he or she turns or moves. They are often used in combination with tracking systems, earphones, gesture-sensing gloves and haptic-feedback devices. The HMD is typically connected to a computer operated by the therapist, who guides the process. The CAVE is a multiuser, projection-based VR system. The patient and therapist are surrounded by computer generated images projected on more sides. Glasses are worn and a tracking system is attached to them, to generate a correct perspective.

VR basically brings "the outside world" into the clinician's office, and allows for a higher level of control and the appropriate tailoring of the therapeutic process to the individual needs of the client, making a valuable addition to all components of the therapeutic process.

Virtual Reality Contributions to Assessment

An accurate and comprehensive assessment is essential to a coherent conceptualization and treatment planning. A variety of combined strategies (e.g., clinical interviews, scales, observation) are typically used by clinicians to get a clear picture of the client's circumstances and problems before starting intervention. For example, in order to get an accurate image of the client's specific emotional and behavioral reactions in a given situation, the therapist can rely on psychological tests/interviews or try to gather the information by exposing the client to the situation, either imaginary or in vivo. While all these strategies can lead to valuable information, they also have their downsides.

Clinical tests are employed to measure various constructs (e.g., irrational beliefs, maladaptive schemas), and their results used to make predictions about the individual's behaviors and emotions in certain situations (e.g., speaking in front of an audience).

Thus, a particular measure – the predictor – is used to make predictions of a specific outcome – the criterion. The limitations of this method are related to two factors: (1) the reliability of the test for the particular population to which the individual belongs and (2) the fact that predictions are based on a relationship between predictor and criterion, and are limited by the validity of the predictor to the context in question. Another problem with clinical tests is their lack of ecological validity, for some situations. Interviews, on the other hand, are post-factum and often biased by memory processes. Imaginary and in vivo exposure offer direct access to the client's thoughts, emotions and behaviors in a given context. However, they are not without limitations: while imaginary exposure may be affected by the inability of the client to recall and relive relevant aspects of the situation, in vivo exposure may often prove difficult, expensive or impractical to conduct.

A discussion of these assessment-related challenges gives us a picture of where virtual reality fits in into the puzzle. VR offers the therapist the opportunity of observing and recording cognitive, behavioral, subjective and physiological patterns in environments that are very much like the real world or where the person acts as in the real world, while retaining control and eliminating potential confounded variables. This provides an understanding of human behavior and human cognition that is challenging to achieve in any other fashion. While the possibility of conducting assessment as the patient interacts with a relevant environment is important in all cases, it becomes all the more valuable in situations where exposure to real-life contexts is impossible or impractical (e.g., due to high costs). For example, VR fear of flying programs are not only useful for intervention, but also for the assessment of the cognitive, emotional, behavioral, and physiological responses of patients in a context very similar to the one they fear, and that is significantly more difficult to access.

One such VR assessment tool, called Virtual Classroom, has been developed by a group of researchers at the University of Southern California in collaboration with Digital MediaWorks Inc., Canada. The system is specifically aimed at the assessment of attentional processes. The scenario consists of a classroom environment, containing objects (desks, blackboard) and persons (teacher, children) that are normally found in this context. A window on a side wall looks out onto a playground, and at each end of opposite walls there is a door through which activity occurs. The child sits at a desk in the virtual classroom and is given a task to complete. Attention can be assessed while a series of typical classroom distracters (e.g., noise, people moving, activity on the playground and at the doors) are controlled and manipulated by the therapist.

Virtual environments have also been used to evaluate cognitive functioning in individuals with various limitations. In a recent study, Josman and colleagues employed VR to evaluate executive functioning in patients diagnosed with schizophrenia. The VR environment simulated shopping activity, and the authors found it highly suitable for the assessment of executive function deficits in schizophrenia. Although these deficits are well documented, they are generally assessed by neuropsychological tests, which provide important information, but consist of isolated, artificial tasks, with a fairly limited ability to predict the daily functioning of the patient. VR environments, on the other hand, have high ecological validity and cue habitual responses, thus giving the clinician more insight into the day-to-day behavior of the patient.

With VR technologies becoming more accessible as their price decreases, they can definitely develop into a valuable addition to the assessment process, providing the therapist information and an understanding of the client's emotions and behavior that would be otherwise difficult to access.

VR Contributions to Intervention and to the Understanding of Underlying Mechanisms of Psychological Disorders

It is interesting to note that the technical revolution in psychotherapy was anticipated by the results of a poll. A panel of 62 psychotherapy experts involved in the poll predicted trends in the field for the following decade. Among the future scenarios that they considered most likely was the expansion of evidence-based interventions, of practice guidelines and of technology in psychotherapy. These predictions have turned out to be accurate, both in which the evidence-based movement and computer-based interventions are concerned.

The nature of VR-based interventions makes them highly suitable for integration into CBT treatment programs. Over the last decade, applications have expanded as costs have dropped and hardware has improved. VR interventions have been developed for a variety of clinical conditions ranging from anxiety to eating disorders. In addition to generating presence, there are other features of VR that make it so appealing to psychotherapy: the possibility to precisely control what is presented to the client, the ability to tailor the treatment to the needs of the patient and the ability to expose the client to a wide range of conditions that would otherwise be unsafe or unpractical.

In addition, and just as important, recent research points to the potential of VR-based studies to clarify the mechanisms underlying various psychological disorders, which will eventually pay off in the development of increasingly efficient treatment packages. To give just one example, recent studies of acrophobia have pointed out that motion combined with simulated height, rather that height per se, lead to the phobic response, suggesting the need to also explore visuo-vestibular and motion mechanisms as possible diathesis factors in this disorder. Similar progresses are being anticipated in the case of substance abuse and psychotic disorders (e.g., mechanisms leading to symptom generation).

Most of the data that is currently available on VR interventions and their efficacy comes from studies of anxiety. Anxiety disorders are among the most common and frequently occurring mental disorders and they have been shown to be responsive to both medication and psychological interventions, CBT being widely employed in their management. While for the vast majority of other disorders data regarding VR interventions are based on case studies and uncontrolled studies, several randomized controlled trials have already been published for anxiety. This is not surprising considering the importance of exposure in the treatment of anxiety and the fact that VR environments provide a safe and controllable way of confronting the patient with the feared stimuli and situations. The first VR applications for psychotherapy were in fact designed to treat specific phobias. To date, virtual reality exposure therapy (VRET) applications have been developed and used for a variety of anxiety disorders including panic disorder with agoraphobia, acrophobia, spider phobia (arachnophobia), fear of flying, claustrophobia, fear of driving, social phobia and post traumatic stress disorder (PTSD).

Two recent quantitative meta-analyses summarize the results of these studies. One was conducted by Parsons and Rizzo and included 21 studies, based on the following criteria: (1) report of interval or ratio data; (2) anxiety symptom data presented before and after VRET; (3) use of at least one affect assessment instrument; (4) sufficient report of study results to allow effect size computation. Effect sizes were calculated for 6 affective domains: PTSD, social phobia, spider phobia, acrophobia, panic disorder with agoraphobia, fear of flying. An overall effect size across affective domains was also computed. Results indicated statistically significant large effects (Cohen's ds ranging between 0.87-1.79,) on all affective domains, with the largest effect sizes for fear of flying (1.59) and panic with agoraphobia (1.79). The overall effect size was also large (0.95). These are important findings in support of the potential benefits of VR exposure despite the somewhat limited number of subjects (particularly for certain affective domains) and the inclusion of uncontrolled studies in the analysis.

Similar results were reported in the meta-analysis of Powers and Emmelkamp, which included 13 studies, meeting the following criteria: (1) at least one virtual reality exposure therapy condition; (2) random assignment or matched condition; (3) either an active or inactive control group. Patients in these studies met the criteria for various types of specific phobia, social phobia, panic disorder and PTSD. Results indicated a large overall effect for VRET (assessed by domain specific measures) compared to control conditions, and medium to large effects for VRET on several other outcome categories (i.e., general subjective distress, cognitive, behavioral, psychophysiological). An interesting finding of this study was that, while both VR and in vivo exposure were more effective than no treatment, VR slightly outperformed in vivo exposure (small effect). The authors interpret these results as reflecting the higher credibility and expectancy for VRET and by the patients progressing more rapidly through the hierarchy due to a higher perception of control and safety.

The few studies combining VR treatments with cognitive techniques were excluded from this meta-analysis, due to procedural aspects that precluded the accurate evaluation of the independent effects of cognitive restructuring. One recent study, not included in this metaanalysis, compared VRET alone to VRET combined with cognitive selfstatements, and found no difference between the two conditions in patients with acrophobia. It is interesting to mention, however, that the meta-analysis indicated a very large effect size of VRET for cognitive outcome measures. This result supports the idea that behavioral techniques, such as exposure, also lead to cognitive change, affecting the patients' attributions and expectancies. We believe that studies evaluating the added value of integrating VR techniques into already established CBT treatment protocols are quite important in order to clarify the most effective ways of delivering interventions to patients.

The majority of studies addressing VR applications for psychotherapy have focused on anxiety disorders. However, VR interventions for other psychological conditions have also been proposed. It is not the scope of this chapter to offer a comprehensive review of these applications, but we mention some of them as follows.

Experiential Cognitive Therapy was developed by Giuseppe Riva and his colleagues to address obesity and eating disorders, particularly body image disturbance and the negative emotions associated with it. The VR component is integrated into a CBT approach and it consists of exposing patients to critical contexts and stimuli (e.g., kitchen, restaurant, commercials) and helping them deal with their emotional reactions and develop adaptive coping strategies. Patients' false assumptions about their own body are also confronted in the virtual environment. The authors report positive results of this strategy, particularly in which body dissatisfaction and self-efficacy are concerned.

More recently, it has been suggested that VR application could be developed not only for the assessment, but also for the treatment of patients diagnosed with psychotic disorders. Fornells-Ambrojo and colleagues used a socially relevant environment to evaluate the acceptability and safety of using VR with individuals with persecutory delusions. Their results indicate that brief experiences in VR are both safe and acceptable to people with psychosis, and that they are also relevant from the point of view of presence and of eliciting delusional thoughts. Acceptability and lack of side effects of VR exposure were also reported by Stinson and colleagues. Future studies are needed, but these data suggest the potential of VR strategies to be integrated into cognitive behavioral interventions for psychosis.

VR technologies have also been explored as potential skills training instruments for individuals with autistic spectrum disorders (ASD). A series of studies have discussed the viability and utility of VR in developing the social skills of people diagnosed with ASD. Virtual environments are considered to be fit for this task, as they can depict complex social contexts, but they are at the same time controllable and predictable, eliminating the anxiety that social interactions often elicit in people with ASD. As in the case of psychotic disorders, research on this topic is still at the beginning, but the results so far are encouraging.

Another promising line of research is related to addictions. Several studies have already looked at the potential of VR environments to elicit craving and at the possibility of using these environments as assessment and intervention tools. Saladin and colleagues evaluated the ability of a VR environment to generate craving and emotional reactivity in cocaine dependent individuals. Their results showed that scenes related to cocaine use, compared to neutral scenes, elicited craving, physiological reactivity (e.g., increased heart rate) and emotional responses (e.g., anticipatory anxiety and a reduction in positive affect). Similar results were reported by Culbertson and colleagues in a group of methamphetamine users. VR drug cueing systems have also been developed for tobacco, cannabis and heroin. These systems allow an accurate and individual assessment of factors that induce craving and drug-use behavior and provide the opportunity of designing and testing treatments for drug addiction. In which intervention is concerned, exposure to cues eliciting craving (cueexposure therapy) has already been assessed and proposed as a strategy of extinguishing the association between the substance and substance-related cues and contexts.

VR Contributions to Rehabilitation

Recent research also points to the broad usability of VR in targeting a range of physical, cognitive and behavioral rehabilitation issues. Beginning with the early 1990, there has been an increased interest in the study and promotion of these strategies. According to Rizzo and Kim ecological validity, stimulus control and repetitive delivery, real-time feedback, self-guided exploration, the safe environment and the opportunity to tailor the interface to the individual's impairment are just some of the factors that make VR a feasible intervention tool in rehabilitation.

Several research teams have already integrated VR in the assessment and rehabilitation protocols of cognitive processes in patients suffering from developmental disorders, neurological conditions (e.g., traumatic brain injury) and psychiatric conditions (e.g., schizophrenia). VR applications have been developed and tested for attention processes, spatial abilities, memory and executive functions. VR scenarios have also been designed to teach patients daily activities such as meal preparation, use of public transportation, street crossing and shopping.

The focus of CBT on promoting adjustment, well being and personal health among individuals with disabling conditions has led to it becoming one of the most widely accepted treatments in rehabilitation psychology. Although clinical data on VR rehabilitation strategies is still insufficient (particularly in which controlled studies are concerned), their integration into CBT packages holds significant promise, considering the documented adequate match between the two. Moreover, CBT rehabilitation protocols are usually complex interventions that, depending on the patient's condition, not only address issues of cognitive and behavioral skills retraining and development, but also aspects of coping with the disorder, treatment adherence, vocational reintegration, lifestyle change, patient and family education.

VR and the Therapeutic Alliance

While there are some studies that have looked at the limits (e.g., side effects, costs) and acceptability of VR strategies by various categories of patients, little attention has been given to their effects on the therapeutic alliance. A typical VR-related concern regarding alliance has to do with the reduction of face to face interaction between therapist and client. Future research must address this issue in a systematic manner and reconcile the apparently conflicting data on the importance of the therapeutic alliance on the one hand, and the effectiveness of treatments that involve limited therapist input on the other hand. According to Chu et al., technological developments and their inclusion in therapy challenge the traditional conceptualization of the clinician's role, and the study of alliance must be extended to take into account a variety of new therapeutic relationship forms.

However, a difference must be made here between entirely computer-based psychotherapy interventions, where the process takes place without a therapist being involved, and the integration of VR strategies into traditional CBT protocols. In this latter situation, the four basic components of the therapeutic process (i.e., assessment, conceptualization, intervention, alliance) are not altered. In other words, VR strategies are a valuable addition to the therapy process, which retains and strengthens all its other active ingredients. This assumption seems to be confirmed by studies that have found high levels of acceptability, involvement and preference of patients for VR technologies.

Virtual Reality Cognitive-behavioral Environment and Treatment Protocol for ADHD

Attention-deficit and hyperactivity disorder (ADHD) is among the most prevalent psychiatric childhood disorders, affecting 8% to 10% of children. Although it persists into adolescence in up to 80% of cases, it is considered a childhood disorder, and largely diagnosed during childhood. The accurate diagnosis and treatment of ADHD is of significant importance, considering that, when left untreated, it can lead to school underachievement, affect professional prospects and cause relational problems. Adolescents with ADHD are more likely to display risk-taking behaviors such as reckless driving, risky sexual activities, substance abuse and criminal behavior.

Over the past few years, clinical research and consensus guidelines have established the most effective treatment approaches for ADHD. A recent review of evidence-based psychosocial treatments for children and adolescents with ADHD identifies behavioral parent training and behavioral school interventions as empirically validated interventions. Both approaches involve teaching parents and educators to use behavior modification strategies such as praise, positive attention and rewards to increase positive behavior, and ignoring, time-out and response-cost to decrease unwanted behavior. Overall, medication and behavioral approaches have been shown to be effective in the clinical management of ADHD, but they do have limitations that advocate for the need of developing additional intervention strategies. To some extent, the limitations of behavioral approaches overlap with those of medication as: (1) effects appear to be short-term; (2) not all children respond to treatment; and (3) data do not support the long-term benefits of these interventions. Multimodal programs, such as the one proposed by Dopfner and colleagues are considered to be the best alternative. Multilevel programs involve work on the cognitions and behaviors of the child, using a combination of parent training and childfocused cognitive behavioral intervention. The CBT component of multimodal programs includes: (1) reinforcement techniques (e.g., positive reinforcement, guidance, shaping) (2) techniques for eliminating maladaptive behavior (e.g., extinction, response-cost) and (3) cognitive restructuring techniques (e.g., disputation, hypothesis testing).

Development of a VR Treatment Tool for ADHD

The goal was to develop a VR intervention tool that could be integrated into a traditional CBT approach for ADHD. Our intention was to create a high ecological validity instrument that would allow us to conduct intervention in a context simulating the everyday environment of the child. This instrument is being developed, in collaboration, by the members of the Department of Clinical Psychology and Psychotherapy, Babeş-Bolyai University, Cluj-Napoca Romania, Dr. Albert "Skip" Rizzo from the Institute for Creative Technologies, University of Southern California, San Diego and Digital Media Works Canada. The team at Babeş-Bolyai University is led by Dr. Daniel David and its members are Raluca Anton, Anca Dobrean, David Opris, and Aurora Szentagotai.

Our starting point was the Virtual Classroom program, developed by Rizzo and colleagues. The Virtual Classroom was intended and tested as a study and assessment tool, but its creators had envisioned the possibility of the system being used for treatment. It is a head mounted display (HMD) system, and the scenario consists of a classroom environment, containing objects (desks, blackboard) and persons (teacher, children) that are normally found in this context. A window on a side wall looks out onto a playground, and at each end of opposite walls there is a door through which activity occurs. The child sits at a desk in the virtual classroom and is given a task to complete. Attention can be assessed through tasks of various difficulties, while a series of typical classroom distracters are controlled and manipulated by the therapist.

This objective and reliable evaluation strategy addresses and eliminates some of the problems of traditional assessment techniques in ADHD (e.g., issues related to low ecological validity). An initial clinical trial comparing 6-12 years old children diagnosed with ADHD (n=8) and non-diagnosed children (n=10) has shown significant differences between the two groups on a number of variables such as reaction times under distracting conditions, number of omission and commission errors and levels of motor activity. No negative side-effects were reported by the participants. Our aim was to transfer the advantages of using VR with children diagnosed with ADHD from the assessment to the intervention level. Based on the literature showing that multimodal interventions are the most efficient in the clinical management of the disorder, we decided to build on this approach by implementing some of its components into a virtual environment. In other words, the program relies on established behavioral and cognitive techniques, but they are used in a virtual school context.

Focus on school behavior is an important aspect of the program, as it allows clinical work to be conducted in an environment that normally raises multiple challenges to children with ADHD. Given the ecological nature of the intervention, our expectation was that skills acquired during therapy would be easier transferred into the real classroom, improving the child's functioning in this important area of everyday life. While most parents support the implementation of newly learned skills at home, this is often not the case at school. Our intervention was designed to address this problem and give children the opportunity of practicing new behaviors in the (virtual) classroom as well.

ClinicaVRtm classroom adapted for intervention.

It is important to mention that we do not propose a new therapeutic paradigm. We instead "relocate" the intervention from the clinician's office into the virtual classroom. As far as we know, this is the first VR program that allows the clinician to use relevant CBT techniques in the treatment of ADHD. A number of features were introduced in the program to support the CBT intervention:

- Graphic display of child performance.
- Pause button.
- Self-talk event recording.
- Distracters/environment control.
- Reward/punishment system.
- Feedback component.

- Tasks difficulty grading component.

- Head movement tracking.

These features are designed to serve several purposes, such as: (1) give the therapist control of the virtual environment (pause button; distracters control); (2) offer the therapist information regarding the child's performance and behavior (graphic display of child performance; head movement tracking); (3) support the application of cognitive (self-talk event recording; feedback component) and behavioral (reward/punishment system; task difficulty grading) techniques.

From a technical point of view, the system consists of two computers connected through a wired or wireless network. One computer (the patient's computer) is running the ClinicaVRtm Classroom, while the other one (the therapist's computer) is running the School Master. An eMagin Z800 head mounted display is used for presenting the virtual environment to the patient. Using a graphical control interface, the therapist controls the ClinicaVRtm Classroom and gets real-time feedback on the patient's performance.

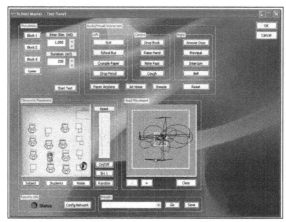

ClinicaVRtm Classroom adapted for intervention.

Intervention Protocol

The protocol designed to include this modified version of the ClinicaVRtm Classroom is based on the program proposed by Dopfner, Shurmann and Frolich. This is a flexible, family-based program and the strategy varies from family to family and from child to child. Flexibility does not refer, however, to modifying cognitive or behavioral techniques but, for example, to skipping certain phases if they are not considered useful for the client.

A number of studies have shown that family-based interventions are quite efficient for managing children with defiant behavior and that combining family intervention with self–education techniques significantly improves the child's behavior. However, one problem during therapy is related to the difficulties of exposing children and their families to real environments where they can practice newly acquired skills. We expect the learning and practice process to be much easier in a virtual environment that simulates real-life situations.

Neurorehabilitation

Spinal cord injury (SCI) is the second-leading cause of paralysis in the United States. Each year, approximately 17,000 new cases of SCI occur in the United States, with the average age of injury being 42 years. While rehabilitation lengths of stay in the acute care unit after an SCI have been on the decline since the 1970s, patients still remain under care an average of 35 days. Less than one percent of patients with SCI have acquired complete recovery of neurological function at the time of discharge.

Within a matter of hours of initial SCI, inflammatory markers are released into the body, causing decreased likelihood of regeneration due to severe astroglial-fibrous scarring around coalesced cystic cavities. The short time span before scarring and limits in treatment options contribute to the increasing number of patients with chronic SCI. As rates of incidence, survival rates, and life expectancy increase, the goals of care have largely shifted to focus on improvement of quality of life after injury. Unfortunately, lifetime care costs after an SCI can range anywhere from $1.1 to 4.6 million per patient, bringing an overwhelming burden upon the patient physically, psychosocially, and financially.

Virtual reality (VR) is the use of technology, such as a head-mounted display (HMD), tracking system, and sound device, to create an interactive three-dimensional (3D) experience. HMDs typically consist of a wearable display with two screens to project stereoscopic images of a three-dimensional computer modeled environment to the viewer. Each turn of the head or change in position relates to a synonymous translation of movement in the virtual setting. Other methods of creating an immersive environment in addition to the use of HMD include the use of large computer screens attached to the walls of the room, covering each facet of the user's periphery to provide an encompassing virtual backdrop. The tracking system uses body-mounted accelerometers that connect the user's movement in real life to the displayed movement in the virtual environment. Additional equipment to enhance the life-like experience play on other human sensations, such as sound and tactile response. Frequently, sound is connected to the user through earphones, while tactile responses are coupled to devices such as haptic-feedback gloves or wearable sleeves. Ultimately, the goal of the equipment is to create the most immersive experience possible.

Three categories of VR systems based on levels of immersion include nonimmersive, semi-immersive, and immersive. Levels of immersion are categorized by the quantity of senses stimulated by the system to construct a sense of reality established by a computer-generated environment. Nonimmersive systems are the most rudimentary, consisting solely of a monitor, keyboard, and mouse; semi-immersive systems include a larger monitor-to-body ratio to depict a virtual scenario; and immersive systems are the most advanced, using an HMD to project a comprehensive visual scene that covers all aspects of a person's visual fields.

Previously, the cost of these VR systems limited their accessibility by the general public. However, VR technology is more affordable now with the improvement in technology. In addition, the functionality of VR has expanded from entertainment into healthcare. The ever-increasing capabilities for VR technology portend an innovative approach to treatment possibilities within the medical field, including management of psychiatric disorders (e.g., exposure therapy) and central nervous system (CNS) disorders (e.g., rehabilitation for phantom limb pain or following traumatic brain injury). While further research into long-term effects of VR rehabilitation are limited, creating a representative safe environment to practice mental and physical strategies mirrored in reality with the ease in interchangeability of environments generated by a computer system has vast implications in the future of medicine.

Games used to Facilitate Mobility

GestureTek's GX-VR system was used to compare participants with SCI to those who were nondisabled in three programs. Users took part in three games—1) Birds and Balls (users attempt to touch approaching balls to turn them into birds before the balls burst); 2) Soccer (users simulate playing in a soccer game); and 3) Snowboarding (users simulate snowboarding down a mountainside while avoiding obstacles)—to measure changes in mobility. Success was measured in the Birds and Balls, Soccer, and Snowboarding games based on percentage of balls touched, balls prevented from crossing the goal line, and obstacles avoided, respectively. In addition, researchers measured outcomes through the SFQ, FRT, and Functional Independence Measure. Both the control and experimental groups reported a positive experience and high level of immersion in the different environments, but no significant difference was found regarding changes in the SFQ, FRT, or Functional Independence Measure. Some side effects after use of VR therapy included discomfort due to fatigue and pain from injury site. However, the discomfort was experienced by these participant at the same body site and level of intensity they experienced while undergoing conventional therapies.

Researchers compared relationships between FRT and success in the VR programs. Groups who scored above the median in FRT performed significantly better in some of the games than those who scored below the median. In Level 3 of Birds and Balls, the above the median FRT group average response time was faster than the below the median FRT group average response time ($z=-2.42$, $p=0.014$). In Level 2 of Soccer, the above the median FRT group average success percentage was higher than below the median FRT group average success percentage ($z=-2.22$, $p=0.022$). No other significant differences were found between these groups in the rest of the levels or games. When performance of nondisabled subjects was compared to that of SCI groups, the nondisabled group outperformed the SCI group.

Similar to Kizony et al, An and Park used soccer and volleyball programs, but also used other games—Conveyor (users move virtual boxes between conveyor belts), Formula racer (users race in a virtual Formula 1 racing car), and Airborne (users steer a parachute through different obstacles in order to land)—in a semi-immersive VR experience to measure changes in mobility in patients with SCI. Patients used the Interactive Rehabilitation Exercise (IREX) VR system, which included a television screen, camera, gloves, computer monitor, and mat to play six programs. Researchers used the LOS and BBS tests to measure standing balance ability. They measured upright mobility function with the TUG test, ABC scale, and WISCI II scale. Participants improved significantly from pre- to post-intervention after six weeks in overall LOS (OLOS) scores (32.00–46.40, $p<0.01$), BBS scores (35.70–40.10, $p<0.01$), TUG test times (19.35–17.14, $p<0.05$), ABC scores (67.90–76.85, $p<0.05$), and WISCI-II scores ($p<0.05$). No one dropped out of the study or reported adverse effects from the study.

Six participants with chronic iSCI longer than one year used the Nintendo Wii Fit as nonimmersive VR therapy. Researchers chose 10 VR programs of various games that dealt with a mix of balance, endurance, speed, and reaction time. Researchers measured gait speed using the Flying Start method of the 10 Meter Walk Test, TUG, Forward Functional Reach Test (FFRT), Lateral Functional Reach Test (LFRT), and the RAND SF-36 health measure survey. Researchers found significant increases, pre- to postintervention, in gait speed ($p=0.001$, $d=0.35$), FFRT ($p<0.001$, $d=1.12$), and LFRT ($p=0.001$, $d=0.88$). No significant differences were found in pre-to post-test in TUG ($p=0.25$, $d=-0.04$) and SF-36 ($p=0.09$, $d=0.45$). In the follow-up at four weeks, patients continued to maintain gait speed and forward and lateral functional reach.

Khurana et al randomized 30 patients into two groups to assess the benefit of real-world, task-specific rehabilitation versus VR game-based training. Real-world, task-specific training was accomplished by performing specifically designed exercises that moved the upper body outside the base of support, with progressively increasing movement to intensify the difficulty over time. VR game-based training was accomplished by playing games that also moved the upper body outside the base of support, with increasing levels of difficulty as the games went on. Outcomes were assessed by the modified Functional Reach Test (mFRT), the T-Shirt Test, and the Spinal Cord Independence measure (SCIMIII) one day prior to starting treatment and one day after training completion. Under the mFRT assessment, both groups demonstrated improvement with respect to time ($p=0.001$) and time x group ($p=0.001$), but not with respect to group ($p=0.057$). By T-Shirt Test analysis, the VR game-based training group improved more quickly than the real-world task-specific training group with respect to group (10 second improvement vs. 2.4-second improvement; $p=0.05$), but not with respect to time ($p=0.14$) or time x group ($p=0.99$). Under SCIM-III analysis, there was a significant pooled improvement for time ($p=0.001$), but not for Group ($p=0.07$) or time x group ($p=0.16$).

Lower Limb Mobility

In an attempt to focus solely on lower limb movement, Villiger et al studied the neurorehabilitation effect of VR augmented leg movement training in 14 patients with iSCI. The VR system used was a prototype of the subsequently commercialized You-Grabber, which was modified by adding two accelerometer sensor nodes for a total of four. The nodes were placed on the back of the ankle and the lower calf of each leg of participants. Patients interacted with the VR through a game interface through which the user could choose from a variety of activities, such as juggling a ball between their feet with ankle flexion to kicking a ball into the stars with knee extension. This study was subsequently followed up by Villiger et al using a similar VR system with nodes that were placed in different locations. In this newer study, a mobile prototype of the YouKicker system relayed information from accelerometer nodes attached to the dorsum of the foot and the distal tibia of each participant to a virtual projection of the feet and legs from a first-person view. Clinically relevant exercises represented through VR games were then played by 11 subjects with chronic iSCI who were able to achieve higher scores than their initial scores based on faster ankle flexion, knee extension, or leg abduction.

The training session consisted of approximately 300 repetitions of ankle movements or 75 repetitions of knee movements. For all 13 patients with chronic iSCI who were able to walk, their 10-meter walk test speed reached minimal clinically important difference (MCID), and 8 of 13 met or exceeded minimal detectable change (MDC) for an average increase of 11.9 percent. At 3- to 4-month post-assessment, 11 of 13 reached MCID, and 7 of 13 reached MDC. Significant increases in BBS scores (16.5% improvement, p=0.001), muscle strength as defined on a scale from 0 to 50 (7.3% improvement, p=0.001), and mobility as measured by both SCIM (8.5% improvement, p=0.001) and WISCI II (12% improvement, p=0.004) were observed in all 13 subjects at both completion of the training program and 12 to 16 weeks after treatment follow-up assessments.

In patients with chronic iSCI, each VR session consisted of around 500 ankle-based movements or 100 knee-based movements. Progress was measured by lower extremity motor score (LEMS), BBS, and TUG. At post-series assessment, significant muscle strength (LEMS, p=0.008), balance (BBS, P=0.008), and functional mobility were noted (TUG, p=0.005). Additionally, 7 of 11 subjects improved at least one grade in ankle dorsiflexion. Finally, at the 2- to 3-month follow-up, all subjects showed lasting benefits with respect to functional mobility (TUG, p=0.005). All 11 patients reported some improvement at conclusion of treatment series, seven of them reporting marked improvement.

Bodyweight Gait Protocol for Walking

Using a different methodology to improve mobility, Donati et al assessed a long-term VR training approach (12 months) in eight patients who had chronic SCI, with the goal to improve walking ability. The intensive six-part protocol included 1) VR combined with EEG-driven visuo-tactile feedback, 2) both seated and upright, 3) a robotic exoskeleton style bodyweight support gait system used to walk on both a treadmill, 4) and an over-ground track, 5) an EEG-controlled robotic exoskeleton on a treadmill, and 6) gait training with an EEG-controlled sensitized robotic exoskeleton. In Parts 1, 2, 5, and 6, the patients received continuous, real-time tactile feedback. The complexity was increased as the patients progressed and learned each step sufficiently. Altogether, the eight participants had nearly 2,000 hours of neurorehabilitation over 2,052 sessions. Sensation to monofilament and pinprick improved across all patients, and Present Pain Intensity scores decreased. Improvement in motor function was noted for all patients through EMG recordings.

Additionally, 7 of 8 patients recovered some function to two or more muscles below their SCI, determined by ASIA protocol assessment, and all eight patients recovered consistent motor function to at least one muscle below their SCI per EMG recordings. Half of the patients had changed ASIA classification by the completion of the study, three of them moving from ASIA A to ASIA C. Per WISCI scores, all patients experienced a 3-to-6-point gain. Some patients went from not being able to ambulate to being able to ambulate with walker, braces, and the assistance of one person.

Fine Hand Movements

With hopes of improving fine hand movements, Dimbwadyo-Terrer et al used the VR system CyberGlove, a glove placed around the user's hand to provide tactile feedback sensation and record up to 22 joint angle measurements. The user's hand movements translated to a virtual hand displayed on a liquid crystal display (LCD) screen. Users took part in three tasks involving reach and release of objects. In a similar study, Dimbwadyo-Terrer et al evaluated 31 tetraplegic patients with SCI using the Toyra VR therapy, which captures and records real-time motions using sensors attached to the person's body.

Similarly, the tasks involved VR sessions in the form of interactive environments geared toward improving autonomy during ADLs, through display of an object and requirement of the subject to perform the motor action necessary to work said object. In both studies, the control group underwent only conventional therapy, which included ADL training, upper limb functional exercises, and physiotherapy sessions, while the experimental group underwent conventional therapy plus VR therapy.

In the Dimbwadyo-Terrer et al study, researchers used the Muscle Balance Scale to obtain muscle force measurements, Barthel Index (BI) to obtain functional capacity measurements, and Nine Hole Peg Test and Jebsen Taylor Hand Function to obtain fine finger movement measurements. SCIM-III self-care scale, FIM, BI and Motricity Index were also assessed. No significant differences were found in either group included in both of Dimbwadyo-Terrer et al's studies. However, in the CyberGlove study, the time to completion of tasks decreased in a majority of the users, and in the Toyra study.

Virtual Reality to Simulate Visual Tasks for Robotic Systems

Virtual reality (VR) can be used as a tool to analyze the interactions between the visual system of a robotic agent and the environment, with the aim of designing the algorithms to solve the visual tasks necessary to properly behave into the 3D world. The novelty of our approach lies in the use of the VR as a tool to simulate the behavior of vision systems. The visual system of a robot (e.g., an autonomous vehicle, an active vision system, or a driving assistance system) and its interplay with the environment can be modeled through the geometrical relationships between the virtual stereo cameras and the virtual 3D world. Differently from conventional applications, where VR is used for the perceptual rendering of the visual information to a human observer, in the proposed approach, a virtual world is rendered to simulate the actual projections on the cameras of a robotic system. In this way, machine vision algorithms can be quantitatively validated by using the ground truth data provided by the knowledge of both the structure of the environment and the vision system.

In computer vision, in particular for motion analysis and depth reconstruction, it is important to quantitatively assess the progress in the field, but too often the researchers reported only qualitative results on the performance of their algorithms due to the lack of calibrated image database. To overcome this problem, recent works in the literature describe test beds for a quantitative evaluation of the vision algorithms by providing both sequences of images and ground truth disparity and optic flow maps. A different approach is to generate image sequences and stereo pairs by using a database of range images collected by a laser range-finder.

In general, the major drawback of the calibrated data sets is the lack of interactivity: it is not possible to change the scene and the camera point of view. In order to face the limits of these approaches, several authors proposed robot simulators equipped with visual sensors and capable to act in virtual environments. Nevertheless, such software tools are capable of accurately simulating the physics of robots, rather than their visual systems. In many works, the stereo vision is intended for future developments, whereas other robot simulators in the literature have a binocular vision system, but they work on stereo image pairs where parallel axis cameras are used. More recently, a commercial application and an open source project for cognitive robotics research have been developed both capable to fixate a target, nevertheless the ground truth data are not provided.

Visual System Simulator

Figure shows the real-world images gathered by a binocular robotic head, for different stereo configurations: the visual axes of the cameras are kept parallel and convergent for fixating an object in the scene. It is worth noting that both horizontal and vertical disparities have quite large values in the periphery, while disparities are zero in the fixation point. Analogously, if we look at the motion field generated by an agent moving in the environment, where both still and moving objects are present the resulting optic flow is composed both by ego-motion components, due to motion of the observer, and by the independent movements of the objects in the scene.

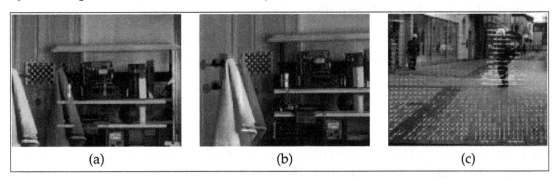

(a)   (b)   (c)

Binocular snapshots obtained by real-world vision systems. (a)-(b): The stereo image pairs are acquired by a binocular active vision systemfor different stereo configurations: the visual axes of the cameras are (a) kept parallel, (b) convergent for fixating an object in the scene (the small tin). The anaglyphs are obtained with the left image on the red channel and the right image on the green and blue channels. The interocular distance is 30 cm and the camera resolution is 1392 × 1236 pixels with a focal length of 7.3 mm. The distance between the cameras and the objects is between 4 m and 6 m. It is worth noting that both horizontal and vertical disparities are present. (c): Optic flow superimposed on a snapshot of the relative image sequence, obtained by a car, equipped with a pair of stereo cameras with parallel visual axes, moving in a complex real environment. The resolution of the cameras is 1392 × 1040 pixels with a focal length of 6.5 mm, and the baseline is 33 cm. Different situations are represented: ego-motion (due to the motion of the car) and a translating independent movement of a pedestrian (only the left frame is shown).

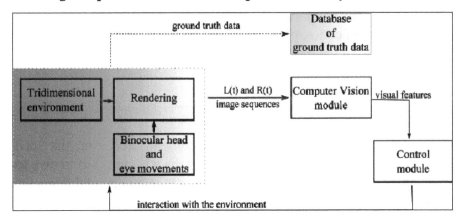

The proposed active vision system simulator. Mutual interactions between a robot and the environment can be emulated to validate the visual processing modules in a closed perception-action loop and to obtain calibrated ground truth data.

The aim is to simulate the active vision system of a robot acting and moving in an environment rather than the mechanical movements of the robot itself. In particular, we aim to precisely simulate the movements (e.g. vergence and version) of the two cameras and of the robot in order to provide the binocular views and the related ground truth data (horizontal and vertical disparities and binocular motion field). Thus, our VR tool can be used for two different purposes:

- To obtain binocular image sequences with related ground truth, to quantitatively assess the performances of computer vision algorithms.

- To simulate the closed loop interaction between visual perception and action of the robot.

The binocular image sequences provided by the VR engine could be processed by computer vision algorithms in order to obtain the visual features necessary to the control strategy of the robot movements. These control signals act as an input to the VR engine, thus simulating the robot movements in the virtual environment, then the updated binocular views are obtained.

Tridimensional Environment

The 3D scene is described by using the VRML format. Together with its successor X3D, VRML has been accepted as an international standard for specifying vertices and edges for 3D polygons, along with the surface color, UV mapped textures, shininess and transparency. Though a large number of VRML models are available, e.g. on the web, they usually have not photorealistic textures and they are often characterized by simple 3D structures. To overcome this problem, a dataset of 3D scenes, acquired in controlled but cluttered laboratory conditions, has been created by using a scanner laser.

It is worth noting that the complex 3D VRML models can be easily replaced by simple geometric figures (cubes, cones, planes) with or without textures at any time, in order to use the simulator as an agile testing platform for the development of complex computer vision algorithms.

Rendering

The scene is rendered in an on-screen OpenGL context. Moreover, the SoOffScreen-Renderer class is used for rendering scenes in off-screen buffers and to save to disk the sequence of stereo pairs. The renderer can produce stereo images of different resolution and acquired by cameras with different field of views. In particular, one can set the following parameters:

- Resolution of the cameras (the maximum possible resolution depends on the resolution of the textures and on the number of points of the 3D model).

- Horizontal and vertical field of view (HFOV and VFOV, respectively).

- Distance from camera position to the near clipping plane in the camera's view volume, also referred to as a viewing frustum, (nearDistance).

- Distance from camera position to the far clipping plane in the camera's view volume (farDistance).

- Distance from camera position to the point of focus (focalDistance).

Binocular Head and Eye Movements

The visual system, presented in this Topic, is able to generate the sequence of stereo image pairs of a binocular head moving in the 3D space and fixating a 3D point (X^F, Y^F, Z^F). The geometry of the system and the parameters that can be set are shown in figure.

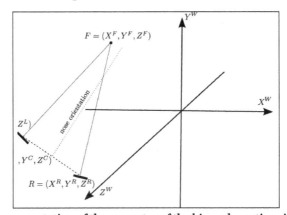

Schematic representation of the geometry of the binocular active vision system.

The head is characterized by the following parameters (each expressed with respect to the world reference frame $\left(X^W, Y^W, Z^W\right)$):

- Cyclopic position $\mathbf{C} = \left(X^C, Y^C, Z^C\right)$.

- Nose orientation.

- Fixation point $\mathbf{F} = \left(X^F, Y^F, Z^F\right)$.

Once the initial position of the head is fixed, then different behaviours are possible:

- To move the eyes by keeping the head (position and orientation) fixed.

- To change the orientation of the head, thus mimicking the movements of the neck.

- To change both the orientation and the position of the head, thus generating more complex motion patterns.

These situations imply the study of different perceptual problems, from scene exploration to navigation with ego-motion. Thus, in the following, we will present the results obtained in different situations.

For the sake of clarity and simplicity, in the following we will consider the position $C = (X^c, Y^c, Z^c)$ and the orientation of the head fixed, thus only the ocular movements will be considered. Different stereo systems will be described (e.g. pan-tilt, tilt-pan, etc.), the simulator can switch through all these different behaviours. The results presented in the following consider a situation in which the eyes can rotate around an arbitrary axis, chosen in order to obtain the minimum rotation to make the ocular axis rotate from the initial position to the target position.

Database of Ground Truth Data

In the literature several database of ground truth data can be found, to quantitatively assess optic flow and disparity measures. One of the best known and widely used is the Yosemite sequence, that has been used extensively for experimentation and quantitative evaluation of the performances of optical flow computation techniques, camera motion estimation, and structure from motion algorithms. The data was originally generated by Lynn Quam at SRI and David Heeger was the first to use it for optical flow experimentation. The sequence is generated by taking an aerial image of Yosemite valley and texture mapping it onto a depth map of the valley. A synthetic sequence is generated by flying through the valley.

Other simple, but widely used, image sequences with associated ground truth data are the Tran sla ting tree and the Diverging tree by. Moreover, it is possible to find the Marbled-Block sequence, recorded and first evaluated by, a polyhedral scene with a moving marbled block and moving camera.

A large number of algorithms for the estimation of optic flow have been benchmarked, by using these sequences. Unfortunately, it is difficult to know how relevant these results are to real 3D imagery, with all its associated complexities (for example motion discontinuities, complex 3D surfaces, camera noise, specular highlights, shadows, atmospherics, transparency). To this aim have used two methods to generate more complex sequences with ground-truth data: a ray-tracer which generates optical flow, and a Tcl/Tk tool which allows them to generate ground truth optical flow from simple (i.e. polygonal) real sequences with a little help from the user.

Nevertheless, these sequences are too simple and the needs of providing more complex situation leads to the creation of databases that include much more complex real and synthetic scenes, with non-rigid motions. The authors rather than collecting a single benchmark dataset (with its inherent limitations), they collect four different sets, each satisfying a different subset of desirable properties. A proper combination of these datasets could be sufficient to allow a rigorous evaluation of optical flow algorithms.

Analogously, for the estimation of binocular disparity, synthetic images have been used extensively for quantitative comparisons of stereo methods, but they are often restricted to simple geometries and textures (e.g., random-dot stereograms). Furthermore, problems arising with real cameras are seldom modeled, e.g., aliasing, slight misalignment, noise, lens aberrations, and fluctuations in gain and bias. Some well known stereo pairs, with ground truth, are used by researcher to benchmark their algorithms: the Tsukuba stereo pair, and Sawtooth and Venus created by. Though these sequence are widely used also in recent papers, in the last years the progress in the performances of stereo algorithms is quickly outfacing the ability of these stereo data sets to discriminate among the best-performing algorithms, thus motivating the need for more challenging scenes with accurate ground truth information. To this end, describe a method for acquiring high-complexity stereo image pairs with pixel-accurate correspondence information using structured light.

Nevertheless, databases for the evaluation of the performances of active stereo systems are still missing. The stereo geometry of the existing database is fixed, and characterized by parallel axis cameras. By using the software environment we developed, it is possible to collect a large number of data in different situations: e.g. vergent stereo cameras with different fixation points and orientation of the eyes, optic flow maps obtained for different ego-motion velocities, or different gaze orientation. The true disparity and optic flow maps can be stored together with the 3D data from which they have been generated and the corresponding image sequences. These data can be used for future algorithm benchmarking also by other researchers in the Computer Vision community. A tool capable of continuously generating ground truth data can be used online together with the visual processing algorithms to have a continuous assessment of their reliability. Moreover, the use of textured 3D models, acquired in real-world conditions, can solve the lack of realism that affects many datasets.

Computer Vision Module

Visual features (e.g. edges, disparity, optic flow) are extracted by the sequence of binocular images by the Computer Vision module. It can implement any kind of computer vision algorithm. The faithful detection of the motion and of the distance of the objects in the visual scene is a desirable feature of any artificial vision system designed to operate in unknown environments characterized by conditions variable in time in an often unpredictable way. In the context of an ongoing research project we aimed to investigate the potential role of motor information in the early stages of human binocular vision, the computation of disparity and optic flow has been implemented in the simulator by a distributed neuromorphic architecture, described in. In such distributed representations, or population codes, the information is encoded by the activity pattern of a network of simple and complex neurons, that are selective for elemental vision attributes: oriented edges, direction of motion, color, texture, and binocular disparity. In this way, it is possible to use the simulator to study adaptation mechanisms of the responses of the neural units on the basis of the relative orientation of the eyes.

Control Module

This module generates the control signal that is responsible for the camera/eye movements, in particular for version and vergence, and for the movement of the neck (rotation and position). By considering the neck fixed, and thus focusing on eye movements only, the simulator has been exploited to study a model of vergence control based on a dual-mode paradigm. The goal of the vergence control module is to produce the control signals for the eyes to bring and keep the fixation point on the surface of the object of interest without changing the gaze direction. Since the task is to nullify the disparity in fovea, the vergence control module receives inputs from the same disparity detector population response and converts it into the speed rotation of each eye. Other control models can be easily adopted to replace the existing one, in order to achieve different behaviours or to compare different algorithms and approaches.

Geometry of the Stereo Vision

The most frequently used methods to render stereo image pairs are: (1) the off-axis technique, usually used to create a perception of depth for a human observer and (2) the toe-in technique that can simulate the actual intensity patterns impinging on the cameras of a robotic head.

Off-axis Technique

In the off-axis technique, the stereo images are generated by projecting the objects in the scene onto the display plane for each camera; such projection plane has the same position and orientation for both camera projections. The model of the virtual setup is shown in figure: F represents the location of the virtual point perceived when looking at the stereo pair composed by F^L and F^R.

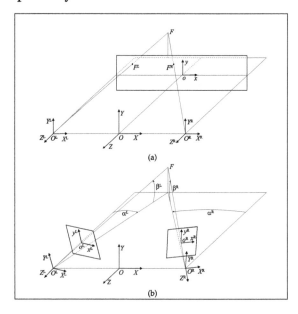

(a) Geometrical sketch of the off-axis technique. The left and right camera frames: (X^L, Y^L, Z^L) and (X^R, Y^R, Z^R). The image plane (x, o, y) and the focal length Oo. The image points F^L and F^R are the stereo projection of the virtual point F. The baseline b is denoted by $O^L O^R$. (b) Geometrical sketch of the toe-in technique. The left and right camera frames: (X^L, Y^L, Z^L) and (X^R, Y^R, Z^R). The left and right image planes: (x^L, o^L, y^L) and (x^R, o^R, y^R). The left and right focal lengths: $O^L o^L = O^R o^R$, named f_o. The camera optical axes $O^L F$ and $O^R F$ are adjusted to fixation point F. The baseline b is denoted by $O^L O^R$, the pan angles by α^L and α^R, and the tilt angles by β^L and β^R.

To produce a perception of depth for a human observer, it is necessary to pay attention to some specific geometrical parameters of the stereo acquisition setup (both actual and virtual):

- The image planes have to be parallel.

- The optical points should be offset relative to the center of the image.

- The distance between the two optical centers have to be equal to the interpupillary distance.

- The field of view of the cameras must be equal to the angle subtended by the display screen.

- The ratio between the focal length of the cameras and the viewing distance of the screen should be equal to the ratio between the width of the screen and of the image plane.

This is the correct way to create stereo pairs that are displayed on stereoscopic devices for human observers. This technique introduces no vertical disparity, thus it does not cause discomfort for the users. However, it is difficult to perceptually render a large interval of 3D space without a visual stress, since the eye of the observer have to maintain accommodation on the display screen (at a fixed distance), thus lacking the natural relationship between accommodation and vergence eye movements, and the distance of the objects. Moreover, the visual discomfort is also due to spatial imperfections of the stereo image pair. The main factors yielding visual discomfort are: vertical disparity; crosstalk, that is a transparent overlay of the left image over the right image and vice versa; blur, that is different resolutions of the stereo image pair.

Toe-in Technique

Since our aim is to simulate the actual images acquired by the vergent pan-tilt cameras of a robotic head, the correct way to create the stereo pairs is the toe-in method: each camera is pointed at a single target point (the fixation point) through a proper rotation. The geometrical sketch of the optical setup of an active stereo system and of the related toe-in model.

It is worth noting that, for specific application fields, the toe-in technique is also used for the perceptual rendering of the stereo image pair to a human observer. In the field of the telerobotic applications, it is important to perceive veridical distances in the remote environment, and the toe-in technique allows choosing where the stereo images are properly fused and the optimal remote working area. However, the parallel axes configuration is again effective when a large workspace is necessary, e.g. for exploration vehicles. The toe-in method is also helpful in the field of stereoscopic television, since the perception of the 3D scene is more easily manipulated, and the objects can be seen between the observer and the display screen, i.e. it is possible to render the crossed, zero, and uncrossed disparity.

The disparity patterns produced by the off-axis and toe-in techniques are shown in figures, respectively.

Mathematics of the Toe-in Technique

Our aim is to formally describe the toe-in technique in order to generate stereo image pairs like in a pan-tilt robotic head. To this purpose, the skewed frustum (necessary to obtain the off-axis stereo technique) is no longer necessary. Accordingly, we introduced the possibility of pointing the left and the right optical axes at a single 3D target point, byrotating two symmetric frustums, in order to obtain the left and the right views both fixating a point F.

In general, the two camera frames X^L and X^R are related by a rigid-body transformation in the following way:

$$X^R = \mathcal{R}X^L + \tau$$

where $\mathcal{R}$ and $\mathcal{T}$ denote the rotation matrix and the translation, respectively. The coordinate transformation described by above equation can be converted to a linear transformation by using homogeneous coordinates. In the following, we use the homogeneous coordinates to describe the coordinate transformation that brings the cameras from a parallel axes configuration to a convergent one.

$$\mathbf{T}^{L/R} = \begin{bmatrix} 1 & 0 & 0 & \pm\dfrac{b}{2} \\ 0 & 1 & 0 & 0 \\ 0 & 0 & 1 & 0 \\ 0 & 0 & 0 & 1 \end{bmatrix}$$

Then the azimuthal rotation (α^L and α^R) and the elevation (β^L and β^R) are obtained with the following rotation matrices:

$$\mathbf{R}_\alpha^{L/R} = \begin{bmatrix} \cos_\alpha^{L/R} & 0 & \sin_\alpha^{L/R} & 0 \\ 0 & 1 & 0 & 0 \\ \sin_\alpha^{L/R} & 0 & \cos_\alpha^{L/R} & 0 \\ 0 & 0 & 0 & 1 \end{bmatrix}$$

$$
\mathbf{R}_\beta^{L/R} = \begin{bmatrix} 1 & 0 & 0 & 0 \\ 0 & \cos\beta^{L/R} & \sin\beta^{L/R} & 0 \\ 0 & \sin\beta^{L/R} & \cos\beta^{L/R} & 0 \\ 0 & 0 & 0 & 1 \end{bmatrix}
$$

The complete roto-translation of the view-volumes is:

$$
\begin{bmatrix} \mathbf{O}^{L/R} \\ 1 \end{bmatrix} = \mathbf{R}_\beta^{L/R}\mathbf{R}_\alpha^{L/R}\mathbf{T}^{L/R} \begin{bmatrix} \mathbf{O} \\ 1 \end{bmatrix}
$$

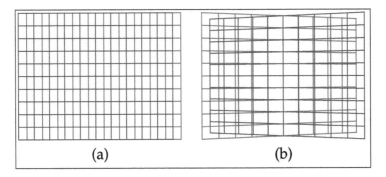

(a)   (b)

The projections of a fronto-parallel square onto the image planes, drawn in red for the left image and blue for the right. The texture applied to the square is a regular grid. (a) The projection obtained with the off-axis technique: only horizontal disparity is introduced. (b) The projection obtained with the toe-in technique: both vertical and horizontal disparities are introduced.

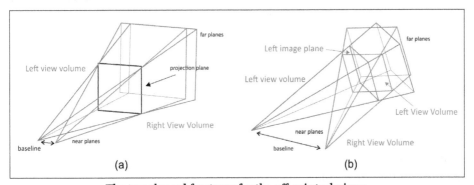

(a)   (b)

The two skewed frustums for the off-axis technique.
(b) The two view volumes of the stereo cameras for the toe-in technique.

Thus, the projection direction is set to the target point F, then the left and the right views project onto two different planes, as it can be seen in figure.

In this way, it is possible to insert a camera in the scene (e.g. a perspective camera), to obtain a stereoscopic representation with convergent axes and to decide the location of the fixation point. This emulates the behavior of a couple of verging pan-tilt cameras.

Camera Rotations

In general, the frame transformation can be described by consecutive rotations (and translations), the specific rotation described by equation $\begin{bmatrix} \mathbf{O}^{L/R} \\ 1 \end{bmatrix} = \mathbf{R}_{\beta}^{L/R} \mathbf{R}_{\alpha}^{L/R} \mathbf{T}^{L/R} \begin{bmatrix} \mathbf{O} \\ 1 \end{bmatrix}$ is the Helmholtz sequence (neglecting the torsion of the camera, i.e. the rotation around the visual axis). This rotation sequence is related to the gimbal system of the actual camera (we are simulating). In particular, the horizontal axis is fixed to the robotic head, and the vertical axis rotates gimbal fashion around the horizontal axis. That is, first we rotate through $\beta^{L/R}$ around the horizontal axis, and then we rotate through $\alpha^{L/R}$ around the new updated vertical axis.

We can simulate a different gimbal system by using the Fick sequence (i.e., the vertical axis is fixed to the robotic head), described by:

$$\begin{bmatrix} \mathbf{O}^{L/R} \\ 1 \end{bmatrix} = \mathbf{R}_{\alpha}^{L/R} \mathbf{R}_{\beta}^{L/R} \mathbf{T}^{L/R} \begin{bmatrix} \mathbf{O} \\ 1 \end{bmatrix}$$

It is worth noting that the fixation point is described by different values of the angles. For non conventional cameras, it is also possible to describe the camera rotation movements from the initial position to the final one through a single rotation by a given angle $_\gamma$ around a fixed axis a_γ:

$$\begin{bmatrix} \mathbf{O}^{L/R} \\ 1 \end{bmatrix} = \mathbf{R}_{\alpha}^{L/R} \left(\gamma, \mathbf{a}_{\gamma} \right) \mathbf{T}^{L/R} \begin{bmatrix} \mathbf{O} \\ 1 \end{bmatrix}$$

In this way, we can study how the additive degrees of freedom of non conventional (e.g. bio-inspired) systems may have effects on the computational processing of visual features.

General Camera Model

A simple and widely used model for the cameras is characterized by the following assumptions: the vertical and horizontal axes of rotation are orthogonal, through the nodal points, and aligned with the image planes. However, the commercial cameras without a careful engineering can violate the previous assumptions, and also the cameras equipped with a zoom, since the position of the nodal point changes with respect to the position of the image plane as a function of focal length. A general camera model takes into account that the pan and tilt can have arbitrary axes, and the image plane are rigid objects that rotate around such axes. The actual camera geometry is described by:

$$\begin{bmatrix} \mathbf{O}^{L/R} \\ 1 \end{bmatrix} = \mathbf{R}_{pan} \mathbf{R}_{pan} \mathbf{T}_{pan}^{-1} \mathbf{T}_{tilt} \mathbf{R}_{tilt} \mathbf{T}_{tilt}^{-1} \begin{bmatrix} \mathbf{O} \\ 1 \end{bmatrix}$$

where R denotes a rotation around the tilt/pan axis, and T denotes a translation from the origin to each axis. In particular, the following steps are performed: first a translation

T to the center of rotation, then a rotation R around the respective axis, and eventually a back translation for allowing the projection.

The horizontal and vertical disparity maps for the different gimbal systems and for the general camera model. The stereo virtual cameras are fixating nine targets on a fronto-parallel plane, the central target is straight ahead and the other eight targets are symmetrically displaced at ±14°. The baseline of the cameras is 6.5 cm with a field of view of 21°, and the plane is at 65 cm from the cameras. For the general camera model, we simulated a displacement of the nodal points of 0.6 cm, and a misalignment of the tilt and pan axes with respect to the image plane of 3°.

Geometry of the Motion Flow

In many robotic applications it is important to know how the coordinates of a point and its velocity change as the camera moves. The camera frame is the reference frame and we describe both the camera motion and the objects in the environment relative to it. The coordinates of a point X_0 (at time t = 0) are described as a function of time t by the following relationship:

$$X(t) = \mathcal{R}(t)X_0 + \mathcal{T}(t)$$

where $\mathcal{R}(t)$ and $\mathcal{T}(t)$ denote a trajectory that describes a continuous rotational and translational motion.

From the transformation of coordinates described by the equation $X(t) = \mathcal{R}(t)X_0 + \mathcal{T}(t)$, the velocity of the point of coordinates X(t) relative to the camera frame can be derived:

$$\dot{\mathbf{X}}(t) = \omega(t) \times \mathbf{X}(t) + \mathbf{v}(t)$$

where × denotes the cross product, $\omega(t)$ and $\mathbf{v}(t)$ denote the angular velocity and the translational velocity of the camera, respectively.

The motion fields for different kinds of camera movements. For the sake of simplicity, the visual axes are kept parallel and only the left frame is shown. The virtual set-up is the same of figures.

Software Implementation

The virtual reality tool we propose is based on a C++/OpenGL architecture and on the Coin3D graphic toolkit. Coin3D is a high level 3D graphic toolkit for developing cross-platform real time 3D visualization and visual simulation software. It is portable over a wide range of platforms, it is built on OpenGL and uses scene graph data structures to render 3D graphics in real time. Coin3D is fully compatible with SGI Open Inventor 2.1, the de-facto standard for 3D visualization in the scientific and engineering communities. Both OpenGL and Coin3D code co-exist in our application.

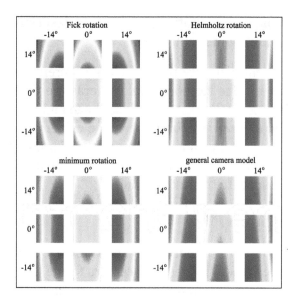

Horizontal disparity patterns for different kinds of rotations and camera models. For each panel nine different gaze directions are shown. The disparity values are coded from red (uncrossed disparity) to blue (crossed disparity).

In order to obtain a stereoscopic visualization of the scene useful to mimic an active stereo system, rather than to make a human perceive stereoscopy, we have not used the stereo rendering of the SoCamera node in the library, since it adopts the off-axis geometry. We have created our own Cameras class, that contains a pointer to a SoPerspectiveCamera, which can be moved in the left, right and cyclopic position. The class stores the status of the head:

- 3D position of the neck.

- projection direction of the cyclopic view.

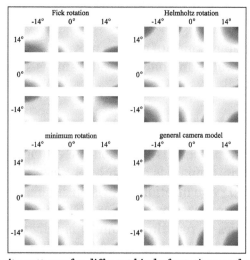

Vertical disparity patterns for different kind of rotations and camera model.

- Direction of the baseline, computed as the cross product between the projection direction and the up vector.

And the status of each view:

- 3D position and rotation (R R and R L) computed with respect to the (0, 0,−1) axis.

- Values of the depth buffer with respect to the actual position of the camera.

The left and the right views are continuously updated after having computed the rotation R^R and R^L necessary to fixate the target. Also the position of the neck, the projection direction, and the direction of the baseline can be updated if the neck is moving.

The scene from the point of view of the two stereo cameras is then rendered both in the on-screen OpenGL context and in the off-screen buffer. At the same time the depth buffer is read and stored. It is worth noting that, since Coin3D library does not easily allow the users to access and store the depth buffer, the SoOffscreenRender class has been modified in order to add this feature. After such a modification it is possible to access both the color buffer and the depth buffer.

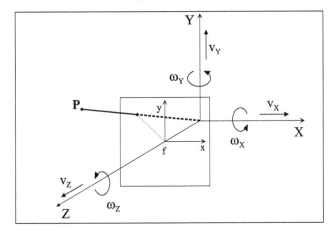

iewer-centered coordinate frame. The relative motion between an observer and the scene can be described at each instant t as a rigid-body motion, by means of two vectors (i.e., kinetic characteristics): the translational velocity $v = (v_x, v_y, v_z)^T$, and the angular velocity $\omega = (\omega_x, \omega_y, \omega_z)^T$.

The ground truth maps can be then generated and stored.

Ground Truth Data Generation

To compute the ground truth data it is necessary to exploit the resources available from the graphics engine by combining them through the computer vision relationships that describe a 3D moving scene and the geometry of two views, typically used to obtain a 3D reconstruction.

Stereo Cameras

Formally, by considering two static views, the two camera reference frames are related by a rigid body transformation described by the rotation matrix R and the translation T, thus the two projections (left and right) are related in the following way:

$$\lambda^R \mathbf{x}^R = \mathcal{R}\lambda^L \mathbf{x}^L + \mathcal{T}$$

where x^L and x^R are the homogeneous coordinates in the two image planes, and λ^L and λ^R are the depth values.

In order to define the disparity, we explicitly write the projection equations for equation $\begin{bmatrix} \mathbf{O}^{L/R} \\ 1 \end{bmatrix} = \mathbf{R}_\beta^{L/R} \mathbf{R}_\alpha^{L/R} \mathbf{T}^{L/R} \begin{bmatrix} \mathbf{O} \\ 1 \end{bmatrix}$ (Helmholtz sequence). The relation between the 3D world coordinates X =(X, Y, Z) and the homogeneous image coordinates x^L =(x^L, y^L, 1) and x R =(x^R, y^R, 1) for the toe-in technique is described by a general perspective projection model. A generic point X in the world coordinates is mapped onto image plane points x^L and x^R on the left and right cameras, respectively. It is worth noting that the fixation point F in figure is projected onto the origins of the left and right image planes, since the vergence movement makes the optical axes of the two cameras to intersect in F. For identical left and right focal lengths fo,theleft image coordinates are:

$$x^L = f_0 \frac{X + \cos_\alpha^L + Z \sin_\alpha^L}{X + \sin_\alpha^L \cos\beta^L - \gamma \sin\beta^L - Z \cos\alpha^L \cos\beta^L}$$

$$y^L = f_0 \frac{X + \sin_\alpha^L \cos\beta^L - \gamma \sin\beta^L - Z \cos\alpha^L \cos\beta^L}{X + \sin_\alpha^L \cos\beta^L - \gamma \sin\beta^L - Z \cos\alpha^L \cos\beta^L}$$

where $X_+ = X + b/2$. Similarly, the right image coordinates are obtained by replacing α^L, β^L and X_+ in the previous equations with α^R, β^R and $X = X - b/2$, respectively. We can define the horizontal disparity dx = $x^R - x^L$ and the vertical disparity dy = $y^R - y^L$, that establish the relationship between a world point X and its associated disparity vector d.

Moving Camera

Considering the similarities between the stereo and motion problems, as they both look for correspondences between different frames or between left and right views, the generalizations of the two static views approach to a moving camera is in principle straightforward. Though, the description of the stereoscopically displaced cameras and of the moving camera are equivalent only if the spatial and temporal differences between frame are small enough, since the motion field is a differential concept, but not the stereo disparity. In particular, the following conditions must be satisfied: small rotations, small field of view, and v_z small with respect to the distance of the objects from the camera. These assumptions are related to the analysis of video streams, where the camera motion is slow with respect to the frame rate (sampling frequency) of the acquisition device. Thus, we can treat the motion of the camera as continuous.

The relationship that relates the image velocity (motion field) $\dot{}x$ of the image point x to the angular (ω) and the linear (v) velocities of the camera and to the depth values is described by the following equation:

$$\dot{\mathbf{x}} = \omega \times \mathbf{x} + \frac{1}{\lambda}\mathbf{v} - \frac{\dot{\lambda}}{\lambda}\mathbf{x}$$

where λ and $\dot{\lambda}$ are the depth and its temporal derivative, respectively.

For planar perspective projection, i.e. $\lambda = Z$, we have that the image motion field $\dot{}x$ is expressible as a function of image position x =(x,y) and surface depth Z = Z(x,y) (i.e., the depth of the object projecting in (x,y) at current time):

$$\begin{bmatrix} \dot{x} \\ \dot{y} \end{bmatrix} = \frac{1}{z}\begin{bmatrix} f_o & 0 & -x \\ 0 & f_o & -y \end{bmatrix}\mathbf{v} + \begin{bmatrix} -xy/f_o & \left(f_o + x^2/f_o\right) & -y \\ -\left(f_o + y^2/f_o\right) & xy/f_o & x \end{bmatrix}\omega$$

To apply the relationship described by equations $\lambda^R \mathbf{x}^R = \mathcal{R}\lambda^L \mathbf{x}^L + T$ and $\dot{\mathbf{x}} = \omega \times \mathbf{x} + \frac{1}{\lambda}\mathbf{v} - \frac{\dot{\lambda}}{\lambda}\mathbf{x}$ we first read the z-buffer (w)ofthe camera through the method added in the SoOffScreenRenderer class, then we obtain the depth values with respect to the reference frame of the camera in the following way:

$$\lambda = \frac{f_n}{w(f-n)-f}$$

where f and n represent the values of the far and the near planes of the virtual camera, respectively.

Finally, from equation $\lambda^R \mathbf{x}^R = \mathcal{R}\lambda^L \mathbf{x}^L + T$ it is possible to compute the ground truth disparity maps d,andfrom equation $\dot{\mathbf{x}} = \omega \times \mathbf{x} + \frac{1}{\lambda}\mathbf{v} - \frac{\dot{\lambda}}{\lambda}\mathbf{x}$ it is possible to obtain the ground truth motion field $\dot{\mathbf{x}}$.

References

- Vr-military-training-the-next-step-of-combat-evolution: jasoren.com, Retrieved 25 April, 2020

- Application-of-Virtual-Reality-Technology-in-Sport-Skill-330076278: researchgate.net, Retrieved 08 March, 2020

- Virtual-reality-will-change-learn-teach: theblog.adobe.com, Retrieved 13 January, 2020

- How-virtual-reality-can-help-the-global-mental-health-crisis, solrogers: forbes.com, Retrieved 17 May, 2020

- Future-or-fad-virtual-reality-medical-education, news-insights: aamc.org, Retrieved 16 June, 2020

6

Issues Related to Virtual Reality

There are many issues that persist with the use of virtual reality including health related issues like headaches, eyestrain, dizziness, and nausea, cyber sickness and other security risks. This chapter closely examines these issues related to virtual reality.

Human Sensory Limitations

For a virtual environment systems to be compatible with their users, it is vital for designers to understand design constraints imposed by human sensory and motor physiology. The physiological and perceptual issues that directly impact the design of virtual environment systems are visual perception, auditory perception, and haptic and kinesthetic perception. The human visual system is very sensitive to any anomalies in perceived imagery and becomes prominent when motion is introduced into a virtual reality. In auditory perception, there is challenge for audio localization to obtain realistic auditory environment. Localization is helps differentiating sound sources and their direction. In VR, localization is determined by intensity differences and temporal or phase differences between signals at the ears.

The mechanical contact with the skin is called a haptic sensation (touch). The sensations of the skin adapts with the exposure to a stimuli. The sensation decreases in sensitivity to a continued stimulus and may disappear completely in long run. It also varies on receptor type, whether to rapidly adapt and relate to pressure, touch and smell or not. Therefore, it is very important to incorporate haptic feedback in virtual environments. Whereas, Kinesthesia is an awareness of the movements and relative position of body parts and is determined by the rate and direction of movement of the limbs. The challenge of kinesthesia in VR include the fact that a small rate of movement of a joint can be too small for perception and certain kinesthetic effects are not well understood.

Cyber Sickness

Cybersickness is a condition that may occur during or after exposure to a virtual environment and it can induce symptoms like headache, eye strain, nausea or in extreme cases vomiting. It is estimated that around 30% to 80% of population experiences some degree of cybersickness.

Cybersickness is sometimes referred as visually induced motion sickness because it has a close relationship with motion sickness and simulator sickness. Unlike in motion sickness or simulator sickness, cybersickness can occur without stimulation to vestibular system and in contrast motion sickness and simulator sickness symptoms can occur without stimulation to visual system which shows the distinction between these condition. The term simulator sickness was coined by Barrett and Thornton as they wanted to point out that illness in military simulators could not be caused by motion sickness as it was totally excluded, hence the term simulator sickness. Stanney et al. has pointed out also that cybersickness has a different sickness profile from simulator sickness as in cybersickness disorientation symptoms tend to be highest and oculomotor symptoms lowest, but in simulator sickness oculomotor symptoms tend to be highest and disorientation symptoms lowest. Stanney et al. found also that cybersickness is three times more severe than simulator sickness.

In a recent study Davis et al. concluded that cybersickness, simulator sickness and motion sickness have similar symptoms while they are induced in different types of exposure and the theories behind the symptoms are still argued. The term cybersickness has been expanding and used with smartphones and movies so the term VR sickness can also be used for virtual reality exclusively.

Cybersickness is often studied from biological point of view where the symptoms studied are more often bodily functions like nausea and eyestrain, rather than emotions or state of mind like stress or anxiety. There are few theories about origin of motion and simulator sickness that have also been used to explain cybersickness. These theories have been proposed to why cybersickness occurs but there is no consensus which theory is right. Most common theories are sensory mismatch theory and postural instability theories.

Sensory mismatch theory (sometimes referred as sensory conflict theory or cue conflict theory) is most popular and relevant theory in cybersickness studies. Sensory mismatch theory argues that sickness develops either because human brain is receiving incoherent stimuli in visual and vestibular systems or some sensory system is not receiving the stimuli and causing the conflict. Virtual environments can cause incoherent stimuli from the real world as the resolution, colors, lighting or latency for example might not correspond with the real world. The vestibular system that communicates motion, and is responsible for balance, might not receive any inputs even when the visual system is receiving information about motion, can also cause sickness. Strongly related to this mismatch, there can be an illusion of self-movement where the user feels as if he or she is moving without any motion. This phenomenon is called vection and has been argued as root source for cybersickness. In simulator and motion sickness the sensory mismatch works the other way around as one might feel motion but not see it.

Naturally, sensory mismatch theory has been argued as root source of sickness in motion and simulator studies as well. Before the actual theory was formed, Barrett and Thornton were one of the first to use the term simulator sickness as they noticed similar symptoms to motion sickness in subjects that were testing fixed-base simulators where motion was absent. In their study they thought sickness might occur because of deep involvement. They had noticed sickness was induced only in simulators where subjects were watching the scene from inside-outside perspective, similar to driving a car, instead of outside-inside perspective, similar to driving a radio-controlled car. Theyalso noticed car passengers get motion sickness, but the driver does not, which indicated again low involvement causes more sickness. To cure simulator sickness Barrett and Thornton proposed simulators should move accordingly to the scene so the cue conflict would not occur. However, Casali and Kolasinski did not found that added motion, vestibular stimuli, decreased sickness in subjects but in a recent study by D'Amour, Bos and Keshavarz added seat vibrations did not reduce the symptoms but vibrations to head reduced symptoms slightly. McCauley and Sharkey argued again that a lack in feedback to the vestibular system is causing sickness in simulators and any improved visual display would not solve this problem as the lag causes the conflict. Sensory mismatch theory is popular because it has lot of data to back it up and wide exposure.

Sensory mismatch theory has been criticized because it cannot predict when cybersickness occurs or how severe the symptoms will be and the theory only states sickness is preceded by a sensory conflict. It also does not explain individual differences or why conflict causes sickness.

Riccio and Stoffregen have proposed another theory of postural instability for motion sickness, where instabilities in posture causes the sickness. They argue that interference of different senses does not cause sickness and that such conflict is easy to withstand. Postural instability theory suggests there are patterns of interactions between the user and environment that can predict the sickness unlike in sensory mismatch theory. Stoffregen and Smart found at their tests that motion sickness was indeed preceded by instability in subject's posture. As they measured postural sway they found out that increases in range, velocity and variance of postural sway increased motion sickness. Other studies have found out similar results where motion sickness is preceded by increased postural sway. Cobbhas criticized the theory because it lacks standardized methods to effectively measure the instability as she found out that postural instability was produced only when using posturographic techniques instead of subjective measures. Akiduki et al. also found out that there was a time lag in between the symptoms and instability which implies that instability is an outcome of cybersickness.

Similar to postural instability theory, rest frame theory argues that mismatch in sensed gravitation and perceived up-direction causes cybersickness. Chang et al. compared two virtual rollercoasters where one condition had two vertical and two horizontal lines as a rest frame providing sense of direction and other did not. They found out that rest frame condition caused less cybersickness. In a similar study Duh, Parker and Furness also found out a superimposed grid on a visual scene caused less sickness than no-grid condition when comparing different levels of grid brightness and oscillation frequency.

Poison theory is often mentioned as one theory of onset of cybersickness. Treisman argues that symptoms in motion sickness are a reaction that has been learned through evolution as possibly dangerous ingested toxins have caused similar disturbances in visual and vestibular systems. He argues that strong reaction like vomiting should have some meaning in survival as the reaction is widespread among animals even when it is highly uncomfortable sensation. Poison theory has been criticized and LaViola Jr. argues that the theory lacks predictive power in why some individuals experience in motion sickness and other do not, or why vomiting does not occur always with cybersickness. Vomiting is also occurring sparsely and sometimes not even considered in cybersickness measurements.

Measuring Cyber Sickness

There are many ways to observe and measure cybersickness like questionnaires, interviews, observing and physiological measures. Questionnaires are undoubtedly most popular measure because they are easy and cheap to use and develop but they yield highly subjective information about the symptoms. McCauley and Sharkey note that it is hard to measure cybersickness objectively because there are lot of different symptoms and they are usually subjective and non-observable with varying effects on individuals and development time. Also, symptoms might appear instantly or hours after the exposure. Postural sway can produce objective data if done by a computer but the swaying itself is not providing much information about the state of the subject and symptoms. Some symptoms like sweating, raised heart rate, EEG and blood pressure can be observed objectively but need specific equipment.

Simulator Sickness Questionnaire by Kennedy et al. is the most used questionnaire in cybersickness. The questionnaire is based on Penascola Motion Sickness Questionnaire which was originally developed for assessing motion sickness but had some irrelevant and misleading symptoms that have been removed. In Simulator Sickness Questionnaire there are 16 symptoms that have been categorized in to nausea, oculomotor and disorientation and some symptoms belong to several categories like general discomfort or difficult concentrating. The questionnaire has each symptom rated in a 4- point scale from none to severe which can be calculated in to nausea, oculomotor, disorientation and total scores for further analysis. Stanney, Kingdon, Graeber and

Kennedy have stated that total scores under 7,48 are healthy and Kennedy, Drexler, Compton, Lanham and Harm think total score under 10 is not significant and over 20 is problematic.

There are few similar questionnaires that have been developed for motion sickness or sickness in virtual reality. Muth, Stern, Thayer and Koch have developed a nausea profile questionnaire exclusively for measuring nausea and they categorized their symptoms to somatic distress, gastrointestinal distress and emotional distress. Gianaros et al. have made a similar questionnaire, Motion Sickness Assessment Questionnaire, which has almost identical symptoms that have been categorized into sopite, gastrointestinal, central and peripheral symptoms. Ames, Wolffsohn and McBrien have categorized their symptoms in Virtual Reality Symptom Questionnaire roughly to general body symptoms and eye-related symptoms. Unlike aforementioned questionnaires, Keshavarz and Hecht have used a simple approach with Fast Motion Sickness score where the sickness is measured during the experience by asking generally how the subject is feeling and scoring the sickness from zero to 20. To study the effects of motion sickness history to current tendencies to experience motion sickness, Golding published a simplified form of Motion Sickness Susceptibility Questionnaire that has also been used in simulator sickness and cybersickness studies.

As questionnaires are very subjective measures that rely on the user's skill and habit to report their experiences, the results can vary quite much. Postural sway has been argued as a contributing factor to cybersickness by Riccio and Stoffregen and they have also used the swaying as measure to predict sickness. Swaying can be measured by amplitude, magnitude and frequency of swaying where larger swaying has been seen to cause more sickness. Stoffregen and Smart observed postural sway on both lateral and anterior-posterior axes and measured variability, range and gain, and found significant differences between the sick and well groups in their study.

Physiological measures can unveil how cybersickness is experienced inside our bodies in an objective manner without subjects reporting. Kim, Kim, Kim, Ko and Kim have conducted an excessive study on several physiological measures like EEG, heart rate, eyeblink rate, skin conductance and temperature and fingertip pulse. The study has revealed some connection of the central and autonomic nervous systems connection to cybersickness. Ohyama et al. measured heart rate variability from microvascular blood flow and electrocardiogram during virtual reality exposure and noticed increases in sympathetic nervous activity.

Difficulties in measuring and evaluating cybersickness are probably the reason why there are no straight answers to why cybersickness is still emerging and why the root cause is still hidden. Davis et al. have evaluated that questionnaires are popular because they are easy and cheap to do and therefore have long history and validation while physiological measures usually require some costly hardware and are harder to analyze. While better methods are developed, and tested questionnaires and interviews can provide a lot of information about what causes cybersickness and what does not.

Causes and Symptoms

Cybersickness has a lot of different symptoms like eye strain, headache, disorientation and even vomiting. These symptoms can arise during or after exposure to virtual realities which can disturb the experience but also affect life outside the virtual environment for example when driving a car after the exposure. To add on that, LaViola Jr. has also stated that there are no foolproof methods to erase cybersickness. Safety standards are also absent as Rebenitsch and Owen has pointed out. The symptoms have been quite often caused by poor hardware or devices but as technology has improved human factors have been emphasized more. In this thesis the causes to cybersickness have been categorized into issues in devices and technology, individual differences and design in applications.

Permissions

All chapters in this book are published with permission under the Creative Commons Attribution Share Alike License or equivalent. Every chapter published in this book has been scrutinized by our experts. Their significance has been extensively debated. The topics covered herein carry significant information for a comprehensive understanding. They may even be implemented as practical applications or may be referred to as a beginning point for further studies.

We would like to thank the editorial team for lending their expertise to make the book truly unique. They have played a crucial role in the development of this book. Without their invaluable contributions this book wouldn't have been possible. They have made vital efforts to compile up to date information on the varied aspects of this subject to make this book a valuable addition to the collection of many professionals and students.

This book was conceptualized with the vision of imparting up-to-date and integrated information in this field. To ensure the same, a matchless editorial board was set up. Every individual on the board went through rigorous rounds of assessment to prove their worth. After which they invested a large part of their time researching and compiling the most relevant data for our readers.

The editorial board has been involved in producing this book since its inception. They have spent rigorous hours researching and exploring the diverse topics which have resulted in the successful publishing of this book. They have passed on their knowledge of decades through this book. To expedite this challenging task, the publisher supported the team at every step. A small team of assistant editors was also appointed to further simplify the editing procedure and attain best results for the readers.

Apart from the editorial board, the designing team has also invested a significant amount of their time in understanding the subject and creating the most relevant covers. They scrutinized every image to scout for the most suitable representation of the subject and create an appropriate cover for the book.

The publishing team has been an ardent support to the editorial, designing and production team. Their endless efforts to recruit the best for this project, has resulted in the accomplishment of this book. They are a veteran in the field of academics and their pool of knowledge is as vast as their experience in printing. Their expertise and guidance has proved useful at every step. Their uncompromising quality standards have made this book an exceptional effort. Their encouragement from time to time has been an inspiration for everyone.

The publisher and the editorial board hope that this book will prove to be a valuable piece of knowledge for students, practitioners and scholars across the globe.

Index

Printed in the USA
CPSIA information can be obtained
at www.ICGtesting.com
JSHW051408221024
72173JS00006B/1320

9 781639 895601